FERDINAND AND ISABELLA

Ferdinand
and
Isabella

∽❧∽

FELIPE FERNÁNDEZ-ARMESTO

TAPLINGER PUBLISHING COMPANY
NEW YORK

First published in the United States in 1975 by
TAPLINGER PUBLISHING CO. INC.
New York, New York

Library of Congress Catalog Card Number: 73-14366

NOV. 15, 1976

ISBN 0-8008-2621

Contents

Illustrations

The author and publisher would like to thank the following for their kind permission to reproduce the illustrations for this book: Her Majesty the Queen; Biblioteca Nacional, Madrid; the Mansell Collection, London; the Mary Evans Picture Library, London; MAS, Barcelona and Oronoz, Madrid

Maps

Preface

'Although they are monarchs, they are human beings.' That enchanting judgement on Ferdinand and Isabella was included by their own chronicler, Hernán de Pulgar, in a letter he wrote early in their reign. It was no mere truism, for contemporaries were apt to dwell more on the divine than the human connotations of kingship, while a monarch's private life had to be subordinated to the exigencies of statecraft. Isabella revealed a similar state of mind several years later, when an assassination attempt on her husband made her realize 'that kings may die suddenly, the same as other men'. The degree to which kings were 'the same as other men' was a matter for surprise. And, as I try to suggest in the pages which follow, Isabella's private tragedy was her vulnerability to the personal disappointments she encountered as a wife and mother, whereas the best hope of a monarch's felicity lay in strictly political rewards.

The aim of this book is to portray Ferdinand and Isabella both as monarchs and human beings. Whenever an historian tries to write a biography, he faces the problem of finding the right blend of historical and biographical material – in this case between the story of the private lives and unfolding characters of the monarchs and the description of the realms and society they ruled. The sources which survive for the history of their times are so extensive that they could not fairly be managed by a single author even after a lifetime's study, while the available clues to their private life are insufficient for a completely satisfying and deeply intimate biography. I have tried to give a convincing personal account in human terms of their childhoods and married life, against the background of the main themes of Castilian political, social and intellectual history. The results of the marriage of Ferdinand of Aragon to Isabella of Castile are often described as 'the union of two crowns': in fact the two realms were embraced by no common institutions, outside the persons of the monarchs, except the Inquisition which they established in Castile and extended to Aragon. Like any other marriage theirs was rather in the first instance the union of two bodies and spirits, and it has been my aim to recapture as much as possible of that aspect of my subject, as well as the political consequences in the events of their reign of the vicissitudes of their mutual relationship and family life. Although in this book I reject the idea that Ferdinand and Isabella 'unified' Spain or created a single or a 'modern' state, I do concede them one work of more than merely conjugal unification: they helped significantly to extend what was in effect a single predominant hegemony – though it was never absolute or exclusive – over both the Atlantic and the Western Mediterranean. In partial consequence, the interpenetration of those two areas of trade and cultural exchange was perhaps the most striking feature of the following century.

Most of the existing books on Ferdinand and Isabella have failed to present them convincingly, because the subject overlaps with so many areas of polemics: whether the evils of the Inquisition outweighed its virtues; whether the expulsion of the Jews benefited or disadvantaged Spain; whether the discovery of America and greatness of Spain were good for mankind. Because of the controversy these questions inspire, the monarchs have found eulogists and detractors, but few impartial biographers. Recently, two issues have clouded historians' work. The past efforts of the present Spanish regime to identify its policies with those of the Catholic Monarchs have distorted the historiography of Ferdinand and Isabella in Spain. The regime has used the names and even the emblems of its presumed predecessors to justify its work of centralization and discouragement of minority cultures. The monarchs' symbol of the yoke-and-arrows has become the scutcheon of the Falange. Typical of the historical products of this propaganda exercise are César Silió Cortés' biography, *Isabel la Católica fundadora de España* (Valladolid, 1938) and Manuel Ballesteros Gaibrois' *La obra de Isabel la Católica* (Segovia, 1953). The first work was seen by its author as an act of resistance against the 'reds', whose armies were closing about him as he wrote; the second, though supported by more extensive historical knowledge than Silió Cortés possessed, was justificatory in tone and laudatory in appraisal of its subject – and, ominously enough, received a prize from the Falange in 1951. Over the same period, partly because of the association of the figures of Ferdinand and Isabella with the Nationalist government and the regime's long policy of entente with the Church, efforts have been mounted in Spain to have Isabella canonized. Among the more blatant contributions to this campaign have been the works of R. García y García (*Virtudes de la Reina Católica*, Madrid, 1951) and V. Rodríguez Valencia *Isabel la Católica en la opinion de españoles y extranjeros*, Valladolid, 1970). In writing this book I have assumed that history should not be written *à parti pris*.

The wish to sanctify Isabella – with the reaction against the excesses of her eulogists by more objective historians – has diverted much recent work on the monarchs into the sterile byways of juridical argument over the lawfulness of their marriage and the legitimacy of Isabella's succession. In dealing with these questions, I have tried to see them as they appeared to contemporaries without adducing arguments which have only come to light in the works of recent historians and jurists. The book by Father Tarisicio de Azcona (*Isabel la Católica*, Madrid, 1964) offers a curious point of reference in this connexion. Although it appeared in the 'Biography and Hagiography' section of the Biblioteca de Autores Cristianos, and is broadly favourable to Isabella, the author made an uncompromising effort to state the facts truly, even where these redounded to the queen's discredit, in the belief that her merits were sufficient to withstand a little adverse criticism. When Father Azcona discussed the vexed question of the disputed paternity of Isabella's rival for the throne, the Princess Juana, he called her 'Juana de Castilla' – the proper title for the legitimate heiress apparent – rather than by her contemporary names of *'la Beltraneja'* (used by her enemies in token of the supposed

A*

parentage of her mother's lover) or *'la Excelente Señora'* (used by her supporters and neutrally by both sides after her withdrawal from the contest for the crown). Father Azcona proudly drew special attention to his use of this new designation for the princess – but he seems here to have pressed historical objectivity to the point of anachronism. It is to avoid anachronisms that I have tried to confine myself to the terms of the contemporary debate and generally throughout this book to present the reader with the ways of understanding of the men of the late fifteenth century, rather than impose the alien standpoint and prejudices of the present on the problems of the past. This particularly affects the views I suggest of events like the persecution of heretics or the expulsion of the Jews, which would be outrageous today, but had their special justification in the world of Ferdinand and Isabella.

No book on a subject as large as this can be written without an immense debt to all the scholars in the field. I must mention at once three books, written recently in Spain to the immeasurable benefit of the study of Ferdinand and Isabella, despite all the obstacles over which other attempts to write about the monarchs have collapsed. Firstly, *Fernando el Católico en Baltasar Gracián* (Madrid, 1945) by Angel Ferrari Nuñez revolutionized our understanding of the reign by exposing the origins of some of the recurrent myths and false suppositions in the murky recesses of historiographical tradition : in particular Ferrari showed how the idea that the Catholic Monarchs 'created the modern Spanish state' originated with the great seventeenth-century Jesuit antiquarian, Baltasar Gracián, and how the preference of some historians for Ferdinand and of others for Isabella often owed more to the authors' prejudices than to objective appraisal. Secondly, Jaime Vicéns Vives, whose memory is held in honour by historians of Spain for his research, written work and direct inspiration of younger scholars, left at his death an unfinished account of Ferdinand, *Historia crítica de la vida y reinado de Fernando* II *de Aragón* (Zaragoza, 1962). In his earlier work, *Fernando el Católico, rey de Sicilia* (Madrid, 1952), Vicéns Vives was perhaps overindulgent in his assessment of Ferdinand and stressed too much the 'modernity' of his government; but by the time of the *Historia crítica* he had achieved a balance of judgement which remains a model of historical scholarship. For the period it covers (down to 1481) I am much indebted to that book. Finally, Father Azcona's biography of Isabella, despite its shortcomings, constituted a giant's leap forward in Isabeline studies, and I have drawn on the author's researches at several points.

I have tried to take all the recent work on the reign into account and to name in the text or bibliography all the scholars whose researches have contributed something to this book. To have given exact critical references would have doubled the book's size. I have relied on the sources which modern investigation has made available and, except in stated cases, have drawn my own conclusions. This book has been written as a leisure-time occupation from the duties of doctoral research and is intended to be read for pleasure as well as instruction. I have had in mind the requirements of readers to whom the subject is unfamiliar, rather than professional historians or specialists in the period.

Certain criteria of selection have had to be applied, and these must be declared. I have concentrated on the history of Castile and refer to Aragon mainly for the sake of comparison. I am concerned with the monarchs' life together and therefore refer only briefly to the years after Isabella's death. It has seemed wise not to burden the book with a hypertrophy of facts and dates: I have not aimed at a definitive history – that must await many more years of research; nor an encyclopaedic compilation – that is available elsewhere. But I have tried to suggest ideas about the monarchs and ways of looking at their reign; these may stimulate the reader to disagree. My account, for instance, of the personalities of Ferdinand and Isabella is bound to be subjective and may not convince those who support the campaign for Isabella's canonization, particularly where I have tried to say something about the queen's sexual comportment. Generally, the interpretations and views in this book are intended to be without prejudice to any revisions the reader may make or future research necessitate. I have tried to include enough facts to provide an adequate basis of information for the reader and of support for the argument. Deliberately, I have not repeated the story of Columbus's relations with the monarchs, which I have written about elsewhere, but take the opportunity to discuss the little-known subject of the monarchs' attitude to the native peoples of the newly-discovered lands. With that exception, I attempt to present a panorama of the various aspects of Castilian history under Ferdinand and Isabella.

It is a pleasure to thank Mr Christopher Falkus, who first suggested that I write about the Catholic Monarchs, the President and Scholars of Magdalen College, who have allowed me to depart from the normal line of duty, Professor P. E. L. Russell, Dr J. R. L. Highfield and Dr G. L. Harriss, who have helpfully perused the manuscript or portions of it and suggested corrections, the Marquess and Marchioness of Goubea, who have been generous with hospitality, and my mother, Betty Millán de Fernández Armesto, whose editorial work was frankly invaluable.

OXFORD
20 March 1974

I

The War of Succession

1474-9

(i) The *Dramatis Personae*

On the ninth day after his death, 20 December, 1474, the body of King Henry IV of Castile was sealed in a temporary grave. His demise had occurred against a background of rebellion, conspiracies and daily crimes of violence. Uncertainty over the succession provoked disorder within the kingdom and invited invasion from without.

The death of a king was always a perilous event for the whole country: the working of justice and such few central institutions as there were depended so much upon the person of the monarch that a vacant throne, or even a moment's hesitation in which the succession remained undetermined, was enough to provoke anarchy. Normally, the danger was averted by means of the device of heredity: whenever a king died, his nearest heir would be ready to take on his duties; but the situation at the end of Henry's reign was confused by the conflicting pretensions of three rival claimants to the throne. Moreover, the previous dozen years had been marked by weak kingship, civil war and resultant chaos, so that now the collapse of law and order had a cumulative quality that made it devastatingly complete. Finally, the magnates of the realm had for long – sometimes latently, sometimes openly – been the enemies of order, given to violence by their education and economic circumstances, and the rivals of the King for local lands, revenues, jurisdictions and strongholds. The realm was a loose grouping of heterogeneous lordships and superiorities, saved from disintegration by the unifying presence of the king. On a monarch's passing, the nobles habitually helped themselves; it was like seizing coals from a dying fire before they turned cold or were reduced to ashes.

Spain at that time was the common name for the five states which occupied the Iberian peninsula. The Moors, who had conquered most of the land seven hundred years before, had been driven back at intervals during the Middle Ages, until the area they ruled was now caged by the Southern Sierras, and confined to the mountains of Granada and a stretch of coast east of Gibraltar. Of the Christian kingdoms, Castile had grown largest during the Reconquest and now stretched from the Atlantic north-west to Seville and the mouth of the Guadalquivir. The crown of Castile over-arched the lesser crowns of many nominal kingdoms and lordships, which the monarchs had added to their realms as the Reconquest stole southwards. Most of these – the kingdoms of Toledo, Jaén, Córdoba, Murcia, Seville – were mere names and traditions, but the kingdom of León, in the north-west and, more especially, the Lordship of Biscay in the Basque Provinces had peculiar institutions and an independent dignity of their own. The kingdom of Galicia, though subsumed in that of León, had separate administrative significance and was marked off by its peculiar language and customs. To the east and west of the Castilian kingdoms, lay the realms of Aragon and Portugal, both quite distinct, but both sharing with Castile some sense of a shared culture, compared with the alien Moors, and the awareness of belonging to *Hispania*. In all these Christian states a tradition was preserved of kinship with the Visigothic rulers of all Spain, whom the Moors had overthrown so long ago: kings and their jurists traced their regality back to Gothic times, while noblemen vaunted their claims to Gothic blood and even humble folk recalled the names of the old Gothic kings and the legends transmitted by medieval epics. The influence of Italian humanists, who despised the Goths and looked to a remoter *bon tempo antico*, had not yet been felt in this respect, even among the best-educated Spaniards; under Ferdinand and Isabella, only the humanist Alonso de Palencia criticized the Goths, and it is interesting that he likened their decadence to that of the ancient Romans. Despite the common Gothic tradition, and despite a measure of bilinguism or even trilinguism among educated men in Portugal, Castile and Aragon, Portuguese and Castilians generally hated each other and were mutually pejorative in their writings, while Aragonese and Castilians were reciprocally jealous and fearful: it seems that the polyglot powers of composition of some authors depended on the provenance of their patrons. On the other hand, Aragon and Castile were linked by the dynastic ties of their royal houses and a comparable exchange of blood between their nobilities. Thus there was some prospect of these two states drawing closer together as time went on, though the Portuguese would certainly not wish to adhere to any common future. Within the Crown of Aragon itself there were pronounced cultural divisions, conflicts of interest between the mountains, seaports and coastal plain, which were ominously complemented by political and institutional differences. Finally in the north the independent kingdom of Navarre clung to the slopes of the Pyrenees, playing little part in the life of *Hispania* but often coveted and interfered with by the Aragonese kings.

Castile already had a history of dynastic war and internal disorder. On the death of Henry IV, the weakest of the pretenders to the doubtful crown was a fragile and obscure girl of thirteen years, the Princess Juana, presumed the daughter of the late King but widely impugned as the illicit offspring of an amorous adventure of the Queen's. Her childhood had been ruled by uncertainty not only of her pre-natal past but also of her future, as the magnates – and the King himself – successively adopted and abandoned her cause, at times swearing to uphold her right to the succession, at others alternately cancelling and renewing their vows. At the time of Henry's death she was without a following, a nobleman's prisoner in the fortress of Madrid; yet though she had no immediate prospect of power, her cause was bound to make headway as time went on: the fact that she was of marriageable age was a powerful temptation to a foreign prince to espouse both her party and her person – a temptation which the King of Portugal shortly proved unable to resist. Furthermore her powerful captor, the

Marquess of Villena, was aware of the advantages she represented and was likely to join her side; and she could count on the favour of all the malcontents whose ambitions and demands her rivals were unable to satisfy.

While Juana languished in Madrid, a second claimant was weighing his chances beyond the borders of Castile in Zaragoza: Ferdinand, the King of Sicily and prince of Aragon, the late King's cousin and brother-in-law, had claims to make in his own right and that of his father, King John. They might have been tempted to use the power of their own realms to seize the throne of Castile by force; but the Crown of Aragon was at that moment, when its own civil wars were barely in the past, absorbed in conflict with France. Ferdinand could therefore count on no help from that quarter as he spurred along the road from Zaragoza across Castile with only a few companions, wrapped in anonymity, cloaked against the cold, to stake his claim before the great magnates and prelates, and try to win with words what he could not wrest by war.

The last of the rivals was Ferdinand's wife, Isabella, the younger sister of the departed King. She enjoyed two immense advantages: her claim was generally believed to be the strongest in law, for Juana's legitimacy had only a diminishing number of defenders, and Ferdinand's involved pretensions were based more upon the laws of Aragon than of Castile; moreover, Isabella was ideally placed to receive the news of the King's death, which occurred in Madrid, for she resided at that time not far to the north in the city of Segovia, where the royal treasure was also conveniently deposited. Within a few hours of Henry's last breath, Isabella inhaled for the first time the air of regality. She immediately had her own succession proclaimed – probably jointly in her name and that of her husband and rival, Ferdinand; she next secured the treasure and within a few days donned the crown. She thus rapidly acquired three further advantages.

It was around her girlish figure, twenty-three years old, short and slight but probably already cast in a rotundity that would soon grow into plumpness, that the great men of the realm now began to congregate, ostensibly to tender their allegiance but more urgently to make demands and trade support for honours and concessions. Contemporary descriptions of the Queen are vitiated by their strong tendency to flatter her, but we know

4

that her face was round and sanguine, its roundness emphasized by the current fashion of covering hair and neck with a circular headress. It was a plain face, endearing only because of its youthful freshness. Pale eyebrows were set high in it; the nose was irregular, the mouth slightly pouting. First among the magnates to present themselves at her inchoate court and look upon that face with the reverence reserved for monarchy were the Cardinal-Archbishop of Seville and the Count of Benavente, both of whom, like almost all the nobles of Castile, had changed sides twice during the civil wars of Henry's reign. The Cardinal was remarkable as a prelate and great secular potentate who managed with some success to combine his two roles : for contemporaries both respected his churchmanship and feared his power and political skill. He had toyed with the idea of supporting Juana, especially when she was in the control of his family, the Mendozas, but, confided by Henry with high office and deep trust, he pursued a policy of peace in the last years of the old king's reign, apparently with a broadly consistent advocacy of Isabella's succession. In the last phase, the Count of Benavente, who had gained a great deal in the course of the wars and now seemed more anxious to defend rather than increase his bloated patrimony, was associated with him, having previously sided first with the King and then with the party of magnates : henceforth he was among Isabella's most constant supporters.

The other leading member of the Mendoza clan, Diego Hurtado de Mendoza, Marquess of Santillana, was also present to support his brother's demand for the chancellorship of Castile and his own for a dukedom. So was the Mendozas' enemy, the aquiline Archbishop Carrillo of Toledo, Primate of Spain and erstwhile rival of Archbishop Mendoza for the cardinalate. Carrillo had been the unifying spirit of the opposition to Henry IV. Not of great family himself, his ambitions were aroused and pride fed by the heady progress of his ecclesiastical career : as Archbishop of Toledo he held large secular honours and jurisdictions that amounted to one of the greatest sources of material power in the land; a chronicle he himself commissioned extolled in him the same warlike qualities which his detractors condemned : as primate of Spain he enjoyed jurisdiction over the Church and a dignity second only to the king's. But his two dearest aims, it seems, remained outstanding: he wanted to be cardinal – and became vindictive when he failed to do so; finally he wished to be able to dictate to the monarch. His particular desire was a share in the patronage of offices in the royal gift, and he plainly intended his support of Isabella to be conditional on her accepting his own nominees. There is no evidence to support the rumours that he was already involved in a conspiracy against Isabella when he presented himself in Segovia to render her homage; but his jealousy of the Mendozas was probably beginning to draw him away from Isabella towards the party of Juana. Kingmaking certainly flattered his vanity and may have been becoming a habit; Pulgar's chronicle said that he treated the kingdom like a cheap hat, quitting it at will, and giving it to whoever would pay him well. In the moment at which he kissed Isabella's hand, he may indeed have been contemplating treachery in his heart.

Also present at these tenderings of allegiance was Don Beltran de la Cueva, whom Henry IV had elevated to be Duke of Alburquerque and whom Henry's foes had alleged to be the real father of Princess Juana. Present too, it seems likely, was the Constable of Castile, Pedro Fernández de Velasco. The Velasco, Counts of Haro, though closely related to some of Isabella's most unremitting opponents, probably joined her in order to secure the Constableship of Castile, an office their family had recently obtained. The increasingly powerful Manrique clan, who had been among Isabella's loyalest supporters since her marriage, was represented by Don Pedro, Count of Treviño, and Don Juan, Count of Castañeda. The loyalty was tendered of the houses richest in royal blood, of Enríquez de Castilla, hereditary Admirals of Castile; de la Cerda, Counts of Medina Celi; and Fernández Alvarez de Toledo, Dukes of Alba. And the loyal professions of the college of bishops were ample in extent if unreliable in depth.

Last among the important figures clustered clamorously around the new queen in Segovia was the administrator of that city for the late King, Andrés de Cabrera. The magnates thought him insignificant. They despised him for his Jewish blood and inferior status as a royal dependant who lacked great inherited honours of his own. The people of the city hated him as an upstart and a king's servant who encroached on their civic privileges. But what Cabrera lacked in breeding and popularity he made up in crude ability and influence, both with the late King and – what counted for more after December, 1474 – with the new Queen, Isabella. He had mediated between them in the conflicts of the previous reign and almost achieved peace before Henry's death: it was probably his influence – as we shall soon suggest – that dissuaded Isabella from attempting to depose Henry when she first had the chance in 1468. Thus Cabrera had lived out the last reign on a tightrope, preserving the favour of both parties, as though the devil were his protector and never suffered his foot to fall. His hold over Isabella was exercised through his wife, Beatriz de Bobadilla, Isabella's childhood companion and lifelong confidante. When Henry IV died, Cabrera possessed an even more cogent advocate of his own merits – the royal treasure, which was in his keeping in Segovia; the ceremony before the gates of the city, in which he acknowledged Isabella as queen and handed her the keys, was as important a symbol of her accession as the coronation itself. Isabella never forgot her debt to Cabrera; she protected and promoted him when Segovia later rebelled against his rule; she made him Marquess of Moya and, contrary to her usual practice and the very laws of Castile, bestowed royal property upon him. When she came to make her will thirty years later she acknowledged that his support had been vital to the success of her bid for the throne, commending 'the loyalty with which he served us that we might have and take the succession to our kingdoms'.

Of the nobles who did not gather at Segovia, or who attended only vicariously in the persons of representatives, some were detained by the exigencies of their own feuds, others by motives of disloyalty. Thus though the loyalty of the house of Manrique was attested by the presence of Don Pedro and Don Juan (and assured by their confirmation in their offices and the gift to Don Juan of the custody of one of the royal seals) yet the head of the family, Don Rodrigo, was unable to be in attendance because he was battling for what all contemporaries acknowledged as one of the loftiest dignities in the realm – and perhaps the highest of all after that of the king: the Mastership of the Order of Santiago was a position of enviable – and therefore hotly disputed – military and economic power. The Order's immense lands, widely dispersed but especially dense in New Castile, pastorally farmed at great profit, were a source of patronage and direct wealth for the Master, who not only could cull the rents of many of them for himself, but also had the right to bestow *encomiendas* – the administration, that is, in perpetuity, of part of the Order's holdings – on new members, in whose election he played a commanding role. On the death of the last Master, Don Rodrigo Manrique had been the choice of part of the Order to succeed him, while Alfonso de Cárdenas, who held the *encomienda mayor* of León (the headship of the largest province of the order), was the choice of most of the rest. Neither was rightfully Master; both were technically allies in the larger division of the kingdom between rival pretenders, for both were partisans of Isabella. Yet each was laying waste the lands of the other, reducing the strongholds of the Order's lands to his own obedience and generally attempting to control as much of the Order's members and resources as possible before the election should be more clearly resolved.

Meanwhile, the coastal south of Andalucia was rent by another feud between parties nominally loyal to the new queen, the Duke of Medina Sidonia on the one hand and the Marquess of Cadiz on the other. Pulgar's account makes it seem that Cadiz was personally persuaded by Isabella to espouse her cause; more probably he favoured her anyway but was disgruntled at the favour shown to Medina Sidonia, whom the monarchs appointed to supreme command in Andalucia. At the same time further inland, on the upper reaches of the Guadalquivir a similar private war was being waged on a smaller scale between the houses of Aguilar and Fernández de Córdoba, the latter quick to declare for Isabella, the former hesitant but eventually opting for the same cause. Their links in Isabella's interest barely interrupted these private hostilities, which confused and overlapped with the ensuing warfare between followers of Isabella and Juana. When the town of Alcaraz, for instance, shortly revolted against the rule of the Marquess of Villena, and therefore in favour of Isabella, men of the Marquess of Cadiz fought alongside those of Villena out of private enmity for the house of Medina Sidonia, which succoured the insurgents.

Across the whole breadth of Castile, as far as the near-lawless kingdom of Galicia, which was satiated with the dissensions of its own local nobility, the opposition to Isabella was led by the great families which refused her homage: those of Zúñiga,

Dukes of Arévalo; and two stems of a single family tree – Pacheco, Marquesses of Villena, and Girón, who at that time held the Mastership of the Order of Calatrava and the County of Urueña. While Isabella was making sure of her supporters in Segovia, Villena sat sullenly in Madrid, composing ultimata. His attitude was determined by two factors: he had custody of the Princess Juana, whom his family had wrested from the Mendozas, and he coveted the Mastership of Santiago, which his father's death had only recently vacated. Although he had little support in the Order, which was divided between Rodrigo Manrique and Alfonso de Cárdenas, he hoped his own candidacy would profit from the prevailing discord; he had a further – and even remoter – hope that the Pope would intervene in his favour. Meanwhile he would use Juana, and the threat of supporting her, to coerce Ferdinand and Isabella into endorsing his pretensions.

The motives of the different nobles who took particular sides in the struggle for the crown were mixed, varied and much affected by local factors. But as far as one can generalize at all, it does appear that many of those who took Isabella's part in 1474 had already done exceedingly well out of the civil discord of the previous reign and in particular had gained much in the way of concessions of lands or offices from the crown. Families like the Mendoza and Manrique, Velasco and Fernández Alvarez de Toledo had extensive holdings in what had formerly been royal land, inalienable in law, if not in practice, from the monarchs' patrimony: such possessions could easily be vulnerable to revocation by a strong or unsympathetic sovereign, and it may be that their holders espoused Isabella's cause in order to safeguard them by putting the future monarch in their debt or by obliging her to confirm the illegal grants. Similar considerations operated to attract office-holders or royal pensioners to her cause. By contrast, the supporters of Princess Juana may have formed – to consider them from one point of view – a coalition of the disaffected. They were the nobles who had not prospered so well in the recent troubles and who, rather than defend their gains, as Isabella's friends desired, wished to expand them in a new conflict. This division gave the future Catholic Monarchs a great advantage: it meant that the forces of stability were on their side and also that they represented in contemporary eyes the best hope of future security; it was no

doubt partly abhorrence of the acquisitiveness of Juana's supporters that drew so many of the urban oligarchies and
colonies of foreign merchants to her rival's side.

If the nobility was divided in its loyalties, the crown fiefs,
fortresses and towns were almost entirely with Isabella and her
husband. Throughout December and January the monarchs
were ringingly proclaimed in the cities of the kingdom with the
traditional formula 'Castile! Castile! For the King *Don
Fernando* and the Queen *Doña Isabel*!' But the apparent solid-
ity of the towns was fragile in reality. The corporations were
jealous of their privileges and independence and quick to take
offence. Rumours of the imminent revocation of amnesties were
straining loyalties in Toledo. The monarchs responded with
letters of reconciliation. The political disorders in the kingdom
were exacerbated by the state of alienation into which much of
the royal patrimony had fallen and which both the people and
the monarchs remembered with fear for the rest of the reign.
To political turbulence was added an unprecedented outbreak
of violent crime, not exaggerated by later chroniclers to em-
phasize Ferdinand's and Isabella's work of pacification, but
confirmed in contemporary letters. Finally on the borders of
Castile, the secular enemy, the Moors of the kingdom of
Granada, were stirring menacingly, hoping to profit from the
conflict among the Christians by increasing their frontier raids or
possibly withholding their traditional tribute; and the Kings of
France and Portugal were seeking an advantage in the troubles of
Castile.

(ii) Ferdinand and Isabella in 1475

In this context it was clearly necessary for Ferdinand and
Isabella to settle their differences over the succession. An
attempt had been made to write an agreement on this problem
into their marriage contract five years previously, when a
measure of joint rule, within the recognition of Isabella's exclusive hereditary right, had been envisaged; but this arrangement
was defective in making no provision for the succession after
Isabella's death and in taking insufficient account of
Ferdinand's pretensions in his own right and that of his father.
It was, however, a serviceable basis on which a definitive
accord could be worked out. The marriage contract had begun
by affirming that Isabella alone was the 'rightful heir to these
kingdoms of Castile and León'; Ferdinand had promised to

educate the children of the marriage in Castile and not to prefer non-Castilians in the offices and ecclesiastical positions of that realm, or make any appointments without Isabella's approval. All instruments of government were to be issued jointly in the names of Ferdinand and Isabella not only in Castile but also in the Crown of Aragon, which Ferdinand expected to inherit in his own right; on the other hand, this was apparently to be only a formality, and Isabella was not to have any special powers in the Crown of Aragon, except the superiorities traditionally assigned to the Queen of those dominions over six of its fiefs. Most important of all, the oaths of allegiance in Castile and tenderings of homage customarily exacted from all the nobles, and any other subjects who held honours directly from the crown, were to be paid exclusively to Isabella; the contract made particular mention of the oaths of the governors of royal fortresses, which in times of civil war were of paramount importance.

Although it was implicit in this contract that Ferdinand was to be at least titular king in Castile, this was not a concession commensurate with his own aspirations. He felt that the succession belonged to him or, strictly speaking, to his father, John of Aragon, as the nearest male heir, and further or alternatively to him, Ferdinand, as Isabella's husband: both these points had some foundation in Aragonese law, and, though the traditions and convictions alike of the Castilians were against them, Ferdinand was not likely readily to abandon them. Moreover, the articles agreed at the time of the marriage had made no provision for the descent of the crown should Isabella pre-decease Ferdinand. Probably Isabella's supporters in Castile assumed that the crown would pass to any child the marriage might produce; but even after a daughter was born to the monarchs the following year Ferdinand seems to have persuaded Isabella otherwise: in a memoir she circulated to the towns of Castile in 1471, Isabella had declared that among her reasons for marrying Ferdinand had been 'that he is so closely linked by birth to these kingdoms that, should God ordain anything untoward for me, to him the right of succession to these kingdoms shall belong'. Isabella had also said that this was the import of advice she had received from the magnates and prelates of Castile – but this seems too unlikely to be true: a powerful, foreign prince was the last type of pretender the magnates were disposed to acknowledge. And it was precisely over this issue of the descent of the crown after the Queen's death that the arguments at Segovia between Ferdinand and the Castilians would rage most hotly.

Not only did their marriage contract therefore leave unsettled outstanding differences between Isabella and Ferdinand; it also was rapidly outmoded by the progress of personal relations between husband and wife. When she looked back over her married life thirty years later, it seemed to Isabella, who had grown old by then and missed the romance of youth, that she and Ferdinand had always lived in 'deep love and conformity'. This conventional political formula, habitually used by the monarchs to describe their relationship, was at best an idealization. Ferdinand was by nature a philanderer, of a disposition little given to love. Isabella, as I hope we shall see, was always vexed by his peccadilloes and missed in her husband the dedication she felt for him. The early years of their marriage, before their accession in Castile, must, one suspects, have been the most difficult from an amorous point of view, particularly as Isabella failed in that period to bear Ferdinand a son – which from both a psychological and political point of view was the best, indeed the only, service she could render him. For the first decade of married life – almost exactly coinciding with the times of the civil wars – all Isabella could produce were miscarriages and an infant girl. Alongside the war of arms they were waging in the kingdom at large, one can imagine how Ferdinand and Isabella fought out a war of nerves in their private chambers. Perhaps because she was already trying (as we know she tried later) to part him from his paramours and hedge his pleasures, Ferdinand seems subconsciously to have seen his wife as something hostile. And it was above all on the arrangements for the succession to the throne of Castile that he concentrated his mistrust. His anxiety may also have been increased by a fear that the marriage contract insulted his manhood, for by assuring to Isabella sovereign authority in her realms, it seemed to encroach on what he felt were his superior rights as husband.

When news of Henry IV's death reached him in Zaragoza, it chanced that the notice came not from Isabella, but from Cardinal Mendoza, for the Queen's courier was still on the road. Ferdinand's immediate reaction was to suspect his wife of treachery. As we have seen, he had apparently persuaded her to agree that the succession should pass to him on her death, but this was an insecurely documented concession which the Castilians opposed, and which Ferdinand must have felt was in danger; what was more, he suspected, apparently without foundation, that Isabella might have had herself proclaimed in her own name to the exclusion of his own and in contradiction of the marriage agreement. He rode headlong for Segovia.

The demands he issued on arrival went beyond anything he had hitherto proposed, as far as we know, to Isabella. He argued that he or his father was Henry IV's true heir and that anyway his wife's rights should be deferred to him. In Aragon there was some foundation for these claims, where the laws of succession were ambiguous about women's rights; but the Castilians regarded them as an alien intrusion. The xenophobia of contemporary Castilians stands out in countless documents; the danger that a foreign king would dispense offices to persons 'not native to these realms' preoccupied them. In 1469, in addition to the numerous assurances already given in the marriage contract, Ferdinand had been obliged to sign a public document promising never to make any grants of Castilian lands or offices without his wife's consent: it was, therefore, naturally with alarm that the magnates in Segovia received his new demands, which made so light of the existing agreements and implied new threats for the future. The decisive argument against Ferdinand's pretensions, which the chronicle of Pulgar puts into Isabella's mouth, linked the Queen's own rights with those of their daughter, Isabel, who, born four years previously, was heir presumptive to her mother in default of a male prince. The Queen is said to have argued, addressing Ferdinand,

My lord, there is no reason why you should raise these matters. Where there is that conformity which, by God's grace exists between you and me, there can be no differences. Wherefore, whatever is decided here, you as my husband are still king of Castile, and what you command shall be done in the realm. . . . And as for the governing of these kingdoms we must remember that, if God's will so pleases, the Princess, our daughter, must marry . . . a foreign prince, who would appropriate for himself the government of these kingdoms and would wish to place the fortresses and royal patrimony in the power of other foreigners of his nation who would not be Castilians, or it could happen that the kingdom would fall into the hands of a race of strangers, which would be a grave charge upon our consciences, a disservice to God and the utter ruin of our successors and our native subjects.

Ferdinand perhaps decided that it would be easier to come to a private agreement with his wife than to argue with and – what was more dangerous – possibly alienate her Castilian supporters. He accepted a document of 'Concord', drawn up, it seems, by Archbishops Carrillo and Mendoza, which actually confined him more straitly than the marriage contract and even ascribed to Isabella in Aragon some of the rights Ferdinand was to enjoy in Castile, since the royal dues of Aragon and Sicily, as well as of Isabella's realm, were, according to this concord, to be disposed of jointly by both monarchs. Within Castile, Ferdinand was to be excluded from any say in appointments to the Church or to offices in which the crown's income was handled: though these preferments were still to be made in the joint names of Ferdinand and Isabella, they were to be 'at the Queen's will alone'. The marriage contract had imposed no such strict conditions upon Ferdinand.

The reasons why Ferdinand was willing to accept such an unfavourable arrangement with the magnates in January become clearer when one takes into account the private agreement he reached with Isabella the following April. She gave him power of attorney, attested before a public notary, 'to provide, command, create and ordain' just as she herself could in Castile: the effect of this might have been to establish two sovereigns – two persons, that is, invested with legislative power – in the realm rather than the customary one; in theory, the Queen's 'consent', which the marriage contract had insisted upon for all Ferdinand's acts as king inside Castile, was henceforth implicit in anything Ferdinand might do in his wife's name. In fact, however, the King never acted without the Queen's active participation in any way that might cause opposition in the realm. We shall see shortly just how their joint rule worked in practice. For the time being, despite the political reverse he had suffered in Segovia, Ferdinand's dominance over his wife appeared to assure him of dominance in the kingdom. The heraldic lion of León and Castile would be confined, it seemed, behind the or and gule bars of the Crown of Aragon.

For the next four years, however, a more dangerous rival disputed Ferdinand's and Isabella's throne. Afonso v of Portugal took his decision to plight his troth to Princess Juana and intervene in Castile early in 1475. Portuguese writers were reticent about this betrothal – for in the course of the ensuing war it proved to be a blunder – and it is hard to know precisely how it came about. Henry iv had actively canvassed the possibility in the years before his death. The counsel of the disaffected magnates of Castile must have influenced Afonso; but his aims were probably short-term territorial and commercial gains rather than any grand dynastic design. For no pretender to the crown could prevail without an heir to succeed him, and Afonso had only six years to live when he took Juana as his betrothed. Moreover, even if the marriage were to prove fertile, the Portuguese succession had already been separately assured through Afonso's previous marriage, and there was no prospect of a union of the Portuguese and Castilian crowns. Nevertheless, the seriousness of Afonso's intentions was demonstrated symbolically in the coins he issued, depicting himself as king of Castile; for the right of coinage was a jealously guarded perquisite of royalty, and the diffusion of his portrait throughout the land in the form of coins was an expression of the wide currency of his power. With Juana's already powerful party augmented by the strength of Portugal, and with the defection to her side of Archbishop Carillo, Ferdinand and Isabella were now in the most dangerous and critical situation to have befallen them since their marriage.

(iii) The Course of the War

War became a juridical necessity: a trial of the rival causes of Juana and Isabella before the highest court there was – that of the God of Battles. It is in this sense that the ironic words of Enríquez del Castillo have to be taken: 'the magnates of the realm resorted to arms, as is the custom among princes, for whom right is might. And it is a common saying that in the Court of Rome they give crowns to the victors and excommunicate the vanquished'. The Pope's secretary lent a certain verisimilitude to this last comment when Ferdinand and

Isabella protested at pontifical vacillation between the two parties in Spain; he wrote, 'as soon as His Holiness sees the party of the lord Ferdinand and the lady Isabella prosper, he will help and favour them with all the honour and justice he can'. But this was not hypocrisy. The Pope was merely deferring to the judgement of an even loftier authority. When Ferdinand beat Afonso in battle in 1476, the 'Bachiller Palma' hailed it as a divine judgement: 'Oh, victory most marvellous, where God, Who is a true judge, passed sentence and declared the truth by way of arms!'

The royal chancery combined functions analogous to those of a modern war cabinet and propaganda machine. Ferdinand and Isabella circulated the kingdom with writs which often included substantial justifications of the orders they contained. The war was represented as an uncomplicated conflict between right and wrong. Afonso was repeatedly depicted in images proper to the devil; he, who before the war had always been for the monarchs' correspondence 'our very dear and much-beloved cousin' became now 'the enemy and sower of tares'. In 1478, when he invaded Portugal, Ferdinand reasoned with his subjects in these terms, including a characteristically nostalgic reference to time past which the monarchs aimed to re-establish:

> Now when we were intending to take in hand the good government and justice of these our kingdoms, so that they should be relieved of past travails and fatigues and all should live preserved in justice as in the good days gone by, we were informed that the adversary aforesaid in his evil and harmful purpose, is trying to create all ill and hurt in these our said kingdoms and sow all darnel and discord therein.

The first issue of new coins by Ferdinand and Isabella bore the old legend *'Despiciam inimicos meos'* which now had an obvious application to Afonso.

It was to be a war without fronts, with rebellions and counter rebellions spread across Castile like pinheads in a map, but there were to be three main theatres of conflict: one in the north, where Afonso was poised to invade and where the Duke of Arévalo was stirring up insurgency; another in the centre where the Marquess of Villena was most active; and a last in the South, where the Count of Urueña sought to exploit the divisions among the monarchs' supporters. Throughout the first six months of 1475, Ferdinand and Isabella made hurried preparations, imposing what order and unity they could on the land, and devising economies and expedients to salvage the shipwrecked resources of the crown, which in time of war could only founder in a sea of expenses. Among their first acts was to dispossess the rebels of their offices and nominally, within a short space of time, sequester their lands and rents: the monarchs' writs against the Zúñigas and Giróns are interesting, since as well as reproaching them in familiar feudal terms as rebels 'against their natural lords', they also denounced them as 'foes of the fatherland'. The appeal of that phrase seems to have been to a sense of the national differences between Portugal and Castile rather than of the vassalic duty owed to a lord.

They established commissioners to represent them and to help co-ordinate resistance in all the chief towns and fortresses. But so as not to alienate particularist sentiment, the monarchs ordered their representatives to respect local privileges, except in frontier strongholds: this process was rather like a multiple *coup d'état*, since in each successive town and garrison the royal representative would symbolically take over the source of power from those who traditionally exercised it: he would show the royal writs in his favour to the local authorities, who would kiss them and place them on top of their heads, as was the custom with letters that bore royal commands, and say that they acknowledged them as the words of the King and Queen and were disposed to comply with whatever orders they contained. The royal nominees would then take the insignia of government – 'the rods of justice' as they said – into their hands; they sat upon – or replaced – the municipal councils and could make or vote any local ordinance at will. In practice, of course, the monarchs were as yet in no position to aggrieve local liberties, and for the duration of the war their representatives tended to act well within their powers and to co-operate with the local men rather than override them. On balance, although a civil war was an unpromising beginning to a reign, and although the cost to Ferdinand and Isabella was great and enduring, the war helped on the other hand to spread royal institutions throughout the country and to make easier the acceptance of royal servants in localities which might not have tolerated them in time of peace.

Ferdinand and Isabella replied to Afonso's pretensions by laying formal claim to the Portuguese Crown. They continued by ordering the fortification of ports and stongholds, allocating the costs to supporters who would have to be repaid later, or stipulating that they had to be met from local resources. A fleet to defend the western ports, those most exposed to Portuguese attacks, and to interrupt the Portuguese shipping lanes to Africa, was formed in Biscay. The Castilian rear was secured by means of a truce with the Moors of Granada. Truck with Portugal was outlawed, while efforts were made to disturb the enemy's trade with his African colonies; piratical raids were mounted from the Castilian outposts in the Canary Islands, and commercial voyaging to the mainland, which successive treaties with Portugal had banned, was reopened.

Meanwhile, Ferdinand and Isabella sought to improve economic conditions within the country by fixing anew the value of the coinage and banning the export of money and precious metals. Finally they attempted to conjoin their realms in their support: they confirmed all existing privileges, save the rebels', including those of the most important minorities, the Genoese merchants and the Jews; they declared that subjects of the Crown of Aragon were to be treated 'as natives of this realm (Castile)'. And they summoned the *Cortes* – the representatives of the seventeen corporate towns, the nobility and the clergy – to present their grievances and render advice.

Afonso v was making equally active preparations on the far side of the border. Early that summer he struck into Castilian territory along the valley of the river Duero on the northern limit of the tableland. His object was to seize the city of Burgos, universally acknowledged as the chief town of the realm, cutting off Galicia and fomenting rebellion elsewhere. Penetrating deep into Castile, and masking the strongholds that resisted him, Afonso proclaimed himself king in Plasencia on 25 May. Isabella, meanwhile, was in the midst of a fretful pregnancy. On the 28th, in Toledo, shortly after receiving news of Afonso's cavalcade, she headed north to be nearer the centre of events. On the 31st a miscarriage in Cebreros near Avila put a temporary end to her hopes of a manchild, who might in turn have raised the hope of an end to the war.

Ferdinand made the dramatic but purely formal gesture of challenging Afonso to a duel. Theoretically this might have been a way of avoiding war, but in reality there was no prospect of the rivals meeting in single combat. Unrealized challenges continued to be a commonplace among kings well into the next century. Ferdinand was in the prime of youth, whereas Afonso was passing middle age. Moreover, a duel was contrary to Afonso's interests while his efforts were still attended with their initial success; by the time Ferdinand marched to meet him in the late summer of 1475, the castle, but not the city, of Burgos was in the hands of the Portuguese King's supporters; Zamora, the frontier city, was besieged and partly his; and Toro, the strategically placed town between the two, wholly in his power.

The campaign which now ensued, called by Pulgar's chronicle a 'drama', really more closely resembled a ballet, as the two small and ill-disciplined armies pirouetted about the strongholds of Zamora, Toro and Burgos, in an uncompleted *pas de deux*, neither enjoying means for a long campaign, yet neither daring to come to a rapid conclusion. The crucial problem was finance. With the consent only of the secular magnates, Ferdinand and Isabella sequestered half the plate of all the churches in the kingdom, because, as Pulgar noticed, no revenue was yet forthcoming from the royal patrimony, still half-disordered and half-usurped from the time of the civil wars. The Duke of Alba lent them his tableware. The Admiral of Castile financed the refortification of Seville from his private fortune. But no expedient sufficed and the monarchs remained unable to pay their soldiers' wages. They had to contract an embarrassing burden of debt and put themselves under obligation to the nobles on whose support they depended.

The exigencies of his financial position prompted Ferdinand to offer battle repeatedly to Afonso and to be willing to risk an encounter even at hazardous odds. Afonso could scarcely afford to waste time either, as from year to year the possibility recurred that Isabella would bear a son : the presence of a male heir among their party would be a powerful argument in Ferdinand's and Isabella's favour. On the other hand, Isabella's miscarriage in 1475 allowed Afonso a little leisure : the following year's campaigning was characterized by Ferdinand's inability to bring his foe to battle. The Portuguese siege of

Zamora was quickly raised, though the castle remained in the power of Afonso's partisans.

A decisive encounter was delayed until March 1476. In January Castilian troops had recaptured Burgos castle in Isabella's presence: that was a significant advance. But Afonso's garrison in Zamora still held out against Ferdinand's besieging forces. The King of Portugal felt obliged to try to raise the siege of Zamora's citadel and soon the Castilian forces were themselves enclosed in an outer ring of encircling Portuguese. Afonso, however, lacked the means, financial and logistic, to sustain his siege of the besiegers and at the end of February broke camp to retreat to his stronghold at Toro, deeper within Castilian territory. Ferdinand pursued. The chance had to be seized of winning a battle before lack of finance should compel him to leave the field. By his own account, his fears of the enemy's small numerical advantage were dispersed by his faith in the justice of his own cause.

Toro is sited on a threatening eminence where the mountains of León stoop suddenly to touch the surface of the Duero, which separates them from the Castilian plain. The weather had been wet and the river, which dries to a trickle in summer, was swollen with rain. Even as they faced each other, the hostile armies hesitated to attack, but when they closed and parted, the advantage clearly lay with Ferdinand. The Portuguese fled the field to take refuge in the town, accusing their Castilian friends – Carrillo and his associates – of treachery; according to one account they might have been abandoned to capture by Ferdinand's men, had not the Prince of Portugal, Don John, intervened to protect them. The Battle of Toro by no means saw Afonso crushed; but the victory was sufficiently convincing to draw new strength to Ferdinand's banner and to prevent any further Portuguese attacks upon the heartland of Castile. Moreover, Ferdinand could resume the reduction of Zamora until on 19 March, within three weeks of the Battle of Toro, the citadel was his.

The gravest hour of the crisis had passed. Henceforth Ferdinand and Isabella clearly held the upper hand for the remainder of the war and were therefore no longer in such immediate danger of losing the crown. But circumstances remained grave. Some of Juana's supporters in Castile remained in arms; though their numbers diminished as the Zúñiga came to terms and the Pacheco lands were gradually conquered, there was a continuing focus of disaffection and revolt. The abiding insecurity bred further disaffection, especially in the towns, and to insurgencies in Juana's favour were added rebellions on behalf of local or municipal liberties which the monarchs were powerless to extinguish. While Juana remained betrothed to the Portuguese King, there could be no peace with Afonso, nor could the monarchs devote themselves to the reconstruction of their own finances or the re-ordering of their own realms. Nor could they turn to deal with the Moors of Granada, with whom they were annually compelled to extend their truce. Moreover, though Afonso's invasion had been driven back and Ferdinand was able to carry the war into his enemy's territory by 1478, the Portuguese forces remained a threat, particularly at sea, and menaced the highly-valued outposts of Castilian expansion in the Canary Islands.

Isabella and Ferdinand knew that a dynastic conflict must be resolved by a dynastic remedy. They realized that if they could produce a male heir, or if they could show that adhesion to their line would ensure a peaceful succession in the future, that would be a decisive argument in their favour. But the relative infertility of their marriage so far, which had produced a single surviving daughter, was a dangerously cogent argument in the contrary sense. Throughout the war they attempted to negotiate a promising marriage for their daughter and in May 1476 informed the town of Seville that 'We have agreed matrimony and marriage of the Princess *Donna Isabel* our very dear and very beloved daughter with *Don Fernando*, Prince of Capua, grandson of the Most Serene King of Naples'. But any hope that Isabel, who was only five years old, would supply the longed-for heir, was long-term in the extreme, and in fact nothing came of the negotiations with Naples.

Finally, however, God showed his favour – as it seemed to contemporaries – for Isabella's cause by giving her a son of her own. The decisive event of the war of succession occurred not on the battlefield but in the Queen's bedchamber in Segovia, where, in June 1476, Isabella was confined awaiting the birth. On the last day of the month between ten and eleven in the morning a prince was born and ten days later was christened John after both his grandfathers. The prince's birth was the signal for three days' festivities and many more occasions for

B

pageantry. On 9 August he was presented to the people for the first time, when the curate Bernáldez described the scene:

> The King went ahead very jovially upon a white hackney, dressed in a surplice braided and fringed in gold, and a hat on his head fringed with gold thread, and his horse's harness was gilded of black velvet. The Queen went capering on a white palfrey in a very richly gilt saddle and a very rich harness of gold and silver and she wore for her dress a very rich brial of brocade with many pearls of different kinds.

But above all Don John's birth signalled the end of the war. The child was strong and hale. There could be no doubt that the best hope of future security lay with Ferdinand's and Isabella's line. Their foes were disheartened, their friends and all waverers encouraged. Opposition, already enfeebled, collapsed in the succeeding months, for the monarchs were generous even now with pardons for those who changed timely to their side, and merciless with any who continued resistance. In the lands of the rebel-magnates commissions were set up to dispose of their property to the monarchs' supporters and to penalize the vassals who had followed their insurgent lords.

Afonso of Portugal now became ready to come to terms. He had probably been discouraged by his failure to involve in the war the French, who had not participated save by way of sea-raids on the Basque country. An attempt to involve England on his behalf had proved equally fruitless. At the beginning of 1479 John of Aragon died and Ferdinand mounted the Aragonese throne, thus further greatly increasing his and Isabella's advantage. In the Treaty of Alcaçovas-Toledo, which, after many diplomatic exchanges, finally brought the war to a close in September 1479, Ferdinand and Isabella obtained their main objective: the catalyst of discord, their niece, Juana, was to be put away in a nunnery and her betrothal to the King of Portugal dissolved. She outlived both Ferdinand and Isabella in her relative obscurity, but never ceased to afflict them with anxiety; yet it seems that there was never any substance in their fears of Juana, or their successors', while Portugal valued Castilian friendship. Even now, Ferdinand and Isabella could not obtain so important a concession as the cloistering of Juana except at a great price: despite defeat in the war the Portuguese gained some of their principal war aims; in particular,

Castile recognized as a Portuguese monopoly the exploration, trade and conquest of the whole southern extension of Africa, and future Castilian navigation in the Atlantic was to be limited to the latitudes of the Canaries. Yet despite the chaos they had inherited from Henry IV and the destruction wrought in the war years, Ferdinand and Isabella were now for the first time secure in their royal dignity and at last had a chance to put their power to work in the pursuit of their further ambitions and policies. Before turning to the elaboration of their aims, we must look back over the formation of their personalities and relationship, and see what their lives up to that time had contributed to their characters.

2

Infancy and Adolescence
1451–74

Isabella the Catholic, though she came to wear many crowns
and style herself monarch a score of times over, was not one of
those sovereigns of whom it can be said that they were born to
rule. She was the daughter of a king; but it was a rare thing
then for a king's daughter ever to rule in her own right. Had
the laws which normally governed the succession prevailed,
either the natural laws of longevity or the positive laws of the
kingdom of Castile, Isabella would never have been queen
there. Thus, when she was born, no one even suspected the
greatness that would be thrown upon her. Not only was her
birth unattended by the portents that so often marked the
nativity of medieval princes, but it was also barely noticed by
contemporaries: it is a remarkable fact, indicative of the slight
importance that men at the time attached to Isabella's advent,
that no contemporary note was made of the date of her
birth – though we can be fairly certain that it fell on 22 April,
Maundy Thursday, 1451: that is the testimony of a later entry
in the *Cronicón de Valladolid* and is consistent with the dates
of the documents in which news of the birth was circulated in
the kingdom. A still more telling detail is that when the royal
messenger who bore the announcement of her birth reached
the city of Burgos, the municipal authorities, while expressing
their pleasure in conventional terms, tipped the harbinger a

mere five hundred *maravedis*, whereas when Isabella's younger brother, Alfonso, was born, his messenger got three times that amount even though Alfonso was the cadet prince of the line and therefore also unlikely to succeed to the throne. The explanations of this lack of regard or enthusiasm for Isabella in the earliest days of her life are not far to seek : she was a girl, and women everywhere made unwelcome monarchs at least until the seventeenth century; furthermore she was unlikely to come to power. The consequence was that she was marked out from the first and educated to be not a sovereign but a diplomatic chess-piece of only secondary importance – not a pawn but certainly not a queen in her own right either : the qualities expected of her were wifely and dynastic, so that she should make a diplomatic marriage in the interests of her house and then, free of monarchical responsibilities, be at liberty to pursue her own happiness.

The stamp of this upbringing remained with her all her life until at last it made her the victim of personal tragedy and the prey of early death. For, as I hope we shall see, although she was remarkably swift to tell the importance of interests of state – of the crown, as men said then, – although she actually realized how those interests sometimes conflicted with her desires for herself, and although she had a great deal of native political talent, yet she could never fully make the adjustment which the change in her fate demanded. It is dangerous even for the humblest man to make personal happiness the aim of his life, for happiness is elusive and disappointment rife. For a monarch, who must attend first to his realm and only second to himself, the pursuit of happiness is fatal. Isabella sought happiness in the satisfaction of her husband and the contentment of her children. But her husband's infidelities and the brief lives or ill fortunes of her offspring scorched and slowly consumed her heart. Not all the greatness with which her dominions were blessed could make up for the malignant luck with which her family was cursed.

At no time in her childhood was Isabella educated for empire; yet in another respect it was not long before fate intervened to alter the planned course of her life. Before she had time to store away any childish memories of what court life was like, her father died; and at three years old, she was removed with the dowager queen, her mother, to dwell for her most formative years away from court amid the turrets and campaniles of the city of Arévalo in the heartland of Castile.

The immediate effect of this was to confirm the direction her upbringing was already taking. She had only occasional chances to observe the martial, chivalric and exacting curriculum to which her brothers were submitted. Though her education is ill-documented, it seems to have been essentially domestic and old-fashioned, markedly dominated by the tutelary presence of her mother. Two kinds of schooling were possible for a princess of those days: that which Isabella received aimed at the cultivation of characteristically womanly virtues; the alternative, which humanistic writers were beginning to advocate, sought to bring out the qualities of princedom by means of Latin letters and classical models. Isabella's later comportment makes it clear that, judged by the high standards of those Renaissance days, her Latinity was negligible. She set herself in maturity to learn the Latin she missed as a child and managed to read it – though not more than that – after a year's hard study: when the courtly authors, echoing Pérez de Guzmán, said that 'She could speak and understand Latin, and her reading knowledge was very good', the obvious implication was that her conversation was less so. A further proof of the shortcomings of her education is that her handwriting shows no signs of humanistic influence. In an age of bad hands, Queen Isabella wrote one of the worst (see illustration following page 132). She was always an assiduous patroness of humanist scholars but was incapable of conversing with them at their own level. The only Latin she ever quoted came from the Vulgate or Liturgy, not the classics. The account by Hieronymus Münzer, the scholarly German physician and traveller, of the linguistic ability of her court is related in so dead-pan a fashion and so full of the glibness of the flatterer's art, that it is hard to know whether its intent is serious or ironic:

When I made my little speech, their royal Majesties, who understand Latin very well, but *pro gravitate* rarely speak it, ordered a prior of the Order of Santiago to reply ... Their second daughter ... greatly cultivated letters. Her teacher ... suggested to me that I hear her recite ... but I could not tarry longer. But their only son, the most serene John, a

youth of seventeen years, is so good at Latin, and such an
orator for his age, that it is a wonder. I delivered a short
Latin speech to his serenity, to which he listened with great
diligence and earnestness. I also believe that he wished to
reply in person at once, but because of a hurt he had suffered,
from which his swollen lower lip and tongue had not yet
recovered, in order that the reply might be more quickly
delivered, he gave his reply through his tutor and showed
himself ready and willing throughout.... The Spanish
language is closer to Latin than is Italian and a Spaniard
understands Latin with ease. And therefore they have not
hitherto troubled to learn Latin. Now however eloquence is
beginning to be very prominently practised by the magnates
and nobles of Spain.

Despite Prince John's disappointing performance, Isabella's
daughters were able Latinists, and the care she took over their
schooling shows that she had received humanistic ideas of what
an education should be and regretted the shortcomings of her
own upbringing. Münzer's observations on the beginnings of
Latin studies among the nobility were accurate and reflected a
phenomenon that was the result of the Queen's patronage. She
stimulated courtly imitation by teaching herself and practising
with an erudite *bas bleu*, Beatriz de Galindo. Among the
reasons she urged on the grammarian Nebrija for compiling a
Castilian-Latin dictionary, the queen objected that women had
until then been obliged to learn their Latin from men. Isabella
also paid Peter Martyr of Anghiera, one of the outstanding
stylists of the day, to teach her courtiers with the sonorous title
of 'professor of the nobility in the court', because, she said, it
would keep the young men occupied and distract them from
amorous vanities.

Although her upbringing did not conform to Renaissance
ideas of princely education, Isabella's isolation with her mother
in Arévalo and the infrequency of her contacts with the royal
court produced in her another singularity which perhaps better
equipped her to be queen than would a superior command of
the Latin tongue. For in a monarch's spouse the gravity of
unchastity outweighed that of all other sins in combination:
the slightest suspicion that the queen's child was not the king's
legitimate heir was enough to cause a civil war. It was precisely

in such circumstances that Isabella herself was preferred to the heiress apparent, Juana, from 1468, on the alleged grounds that Juana was the fruit of an illicit union. And adultery by a queen was accounted a particularly serious form of treason. Isabella already in her lifetime acquired a reputation for rigorous adherence to the forms of sexual propriety. She lived in a time when, to judge from the romances penned by fashionable literati, the chivalric ideal of high medieval literature was in decline: lovers who in older poems often served out a lifetime for love of their ladies without gratification now increasingly in poems of the new sort found their efforts swiftly recompensed. Isabella's attitude therefore seemed old-fashioned and, to use a pertinent anachronism, Quixotic. Among the anecdotes which circulated in her court was that concerning Diego Osorio, a Galician cavalier, young, hot-blooded and sprung from a family of congenitally excitable temperament, much given to feuds and rebellions. Aroused perhaps by the warm climate of the south, during a visit by the court to the magnificent city of Seville, as well as by the beauty of one of the well-born damsels who attended the queen, he was apprehended one evening at the foot of a tower of the palace-fortress where the court resided, beneath the window of the lady's chamber, a rope ladder in his hand. Isabella at once had him locked in the turret-cell of the Tower of Gold and ordered that he be beheaded in the morning. If her aim was more to frighten him into better behaviour than to deprive him of his life, her punishment had its intended effect, for before morning came he so took fright that his hair lost all its colour, and it was an easy matter for the royal counsellors who interceded on his behalf to obtain a reprieve for him before the planned execution took place. There can be no doubt that Diego's intentions, though picaresque, were scarcely sufficient to merit the severity of his chastisement: the maidens in Isabella's train slept communally in dormitory conditions which presented any intending seducer with scant prospect of success. But the sternness of Isabella's reaction was characteristic, and Diego Osorio was by no means the only courtier to be imprisoned and to experience fear of his life for inconsequential amorous misdemeanours.

There is, however, room to ask how much this strict sexual propriety on which the Queen insisted tells us of her own character, or to what extent it was an illusion or a matter of policy. In part, contemporaries certainly noticed the change which overtook courtly comportment, compared with the lax and dissolute days of her brother, Henry IV, simply because the court now had a woman at its head instead of a man: there were no pressures upon a king, as there were upon a queen, to preserve inviolate the exclusivity of the matrimonial bond; a multitude of love affairs was looked on as one of the perks of a king's job. It would have been ludicrous for Henry IV to insist upon the good behaviour of his courtiers while lacing his own bed with a wide selection of ladies of the court and women of the town; and even those detractors of Henry's who alleged that he was impotent did not deny the affairs of which he boasted, but merely said that the King took women out of fetishism without being able to consummate his relations with them. It will readily be seen that Isabella's position was the exact reverse of Henry's. Let us suppose for a moment that her personal inclinations were not chaste: it would still be politically necessary for her to cultivate the semblance of propriety in order to avoid a repetition of the contest of pretensions to the succession that had disturbed Castile in her brother's reign. This purpose, in turn, required that she impose strict behaviour on her court. Indeed, I hope to suggest that the Queen was certainly capable of flirtation, though there is no evidence that she was ever unfaithful, and that as much, perhaps, as to her personal criteria of morality, the standards she demanded of her courtiers were owed to political necessity and to the adoption of a double standard. The double standard – particularly in sexual matters among persons with authority over others or responsibility for them – is so common that it would not be surprising if it operated in Isabella. She was the defenceless victim of the infidelities of her husband; she was surrounded by a sexually permissive society while she was herself confined by her queenly dignity within a narrow circlet of exacted chastity. We know a little – to which we shall return in a moment – of her jealousy of her husband and her efforts to separate him from his paramours; there is a possibility that her interventions in the sex life of the court were a projection of that jealousy onto a wider screen and scale, combined with envy of the liberty in which her courtiers were relatively free to indulge. An envious disposition may also have been the result of her own plainness; for she was chinless and puddingvisaged with a pouting mouth and sad eyes, and for most of her life of graceless figure too. It must also be remembered that Isabella spent her childhood under her mother's influence: that may be a source of a psychological explanation of her attitude. What is impossible to accept without qualification is that the atmosphere she inculcated at court and the impeccable reputation she acquired can be explained by reference to her personally chaste disposition alone: this will become more clearly apparent when we return to the story of her own amours.

Isabella's character seems already to have been formed to a remarkable degree by the time the King, her brother, decided to wrench her from the surveillance of her mother and place her under his own eye again at court. In the late 1450s King Henry was already encountering menacing truculence among the magnates of the realm and was apprehensive of the prospects of rebellion should either Isabella or her younger brother, Prince Alfonso, fall into the hands of a recalcitrant nobleman. It seems probable that Isabella was briefly in the King's keeping in 1475 when she was six or seven years old, but was then restored to her mother's care at the insistence of Henry's nobles and counsellors, only to be apprehended anew three years later when the dangers of civil war were growing again. For about the next six years she was habitually under the supervision of the king's wife, Queen Juana, who seems to have filled her with genuine horror and revulsion; later, Isabella claimed to have feared for her life at the time, but this seems to have been a rationalization after the event, for such a fear would be uncharacteristic in a little girl of only nine or ten years. It is certain, however, that she felt a clash of personality with the Queen, who was a far laxer and less inhibited person, and that Isabella sorely missed her mother; for although Juana was strictly speaking her sister-in-law, Isabella, used to compare her to a proverbial wicked stepmother. And it is at least possible that the young Princess had genuine cause for alarm when in 1461 the Queen became pregnant: from now on, the royal infants, Isabella and Alfonso, were Juana's natural enemies as possible contenders for the throne against the child she herself was to bear. Prospectively the siblings and their unborn niece were rivals for the 'fat inheritance' – as Isabella called it – the Crown of Castile.

It was not long before that rivalry became explicit; for a

party among the magnates and prelates was anxious for a civil war as a means of increasing its own lands and jurisdictions at royal expense; and were avid for a serviceable pretext. At least, many were looking for a threat whereby they could intimidate the King into releasing wealth and power into their hands; or, if he would not co-operate, they hoped to be able to play him off against a rival for the crown. Ever since the dissolution of his first marriage with Blanche of Navarre, on grounds of its non-consummation, Henry IV had been a victim of allegations of impotence, which had spread and been increasingly canvassed by his enemies during the fifteen years of his two fruitless marriages and countless sterile affairs. The Queen's unexpected pregnancy therefore provoked an inevitable and widespread presumption that her child was not the legitimate heir to the throne. The baby, born a girl and christened Juana, became known to her foes as '*la Beltraneja*' in token of the alleged parentage of the King's closest friend and counsellor, Don Beltran de la Cueva. Her birth, and the King's insistence on her legitimacy, provoked a movement among the barons to substitute Prince Alfonso first as heir, and then, on grounds of Henry's incapacity to rule, as king. A pretext was at hand to turn ten years' accumulating fears and threats into open civil war.

The immediate importance of the war, from our point of view, was that it drew the young Isabella for the first time into politics. She had as yet no concrete political prospects of her own. It was still not suspected that she would ever be queen and the war was being waged in her brother's, Alfonso's, name, not in her own. But she was now obliged to weigh political considerations for the first time and, though she was only about fifteen years old, to make a decision that might have an important effect upon the destiny of Castile. For although within the country Alfonso's party was stronger than Henry's, it was the King's policy to engage foreign help with which to crush the rebellion, and there was no inducement more powerful than a princess of marriageable age to draw a foreign prince into a reliable alliance.

Isabella's decision to side with her younger rather than her elder brother seems to have been made spontaneously for personal reasons, rather than based on a calculation of the respective advantages and disadvantages or – as she later claimed – of the rights and wrongs of the case. She remembered that Henry had insisted on removing her from the care of her mother; she had hated the hostile and unfamiliar atmosphere of Juana's household; she welcomed Alfonso's rebellion as a chance to escape. The imagery in which she later expressed the terrors and experiences of these dangerous years which so sharply contrasted with the time of security in infancy with her mother at Arévalo, suggests that she saw herself as a character in a fairy-tale, half a prisoner in the fortress-city of Segovia, set in the mountains of central Castile, awed by the gothic skyline, chilled by the icy climate, obscured by the shadow of her wicked 'stepmother', awaiting rescue by the chivalrous knights in Alfonso's party. Her chance to regain her freedom did not come until 1466. Henry was in the north, struggling to secure the great towns of that region against the rebels and attempting to invoke the aid of Portugal, while Juana and her household, including Princess Isabella and Princess Juana, oblivious still at the age of four of the consequences of her contentious status, remained in Segovia. The municipal and military authorities of that city now decided to join the rebellion. At a single stroke Henry lost his favourite city, his most beloved retreat in peace and strongest fortress in war, together with his mightiest military arsenal and, in the person of Isabella, his most powerful diplomatic weapon. Queen Juana and her daughter found an Udolpho refuge in the gothic castle, of fairy form but sufficiently solid substance, that commands the approach to the city while Isabella remained below with the rebels.

Over the previous year Henry had already suffered a number of lesser but in themselves serious blows: the most important cities and strongholds of northern Castile had fallen or defected to the rebels; worst of all, Burgos, universally acknowledged as the most important city of the kingdom, had rebelled in June 1465, Henry's own lieutenant, Pedro de Velasco, defecting to lead the revolt because of the overwhelming strength of the opposition to his administration. The Marquess of Santillana, one of the king's staunchest friends among the nobility, had also changed sides. Henry therefore decided to trade honour for survival; he realized that it was worth his while to make any concession, if only he could retain the means to reverse the situation later.

It is impossible to know the whole truth about Henry's character or even whether the girl for whose rights he staked his own position was really his daughter: it may be that his impotence, along with his cruelty, irreligion, depravity and incompetence, is a myth written into history by chroniclers in his enemies' pay. It seems that he was certainly lazy, ill-equipped to exercise power and disinclined to discharge its responsibilities; rather than struggle against adversity and accept toil and hardship, he worshipped with resignation the malignant star of his own fortune; he tended to shy from his admittedly daunting difficulties by temporization and micawberisms, or at least to meet them deviously with subtlety and intrigue rather than confront them directly by force of arms. The spring of his motivation was a peculiar kind of pride, itself a reaction to the deeply resented humiliation and calumny, the ignominious smear of impotence. Henry was not a man of strong convictions, but seems to have been a material-ist in the sense of willingly sacrificing words – even words like honour and dignity – to real advantage; this made him a politi-cal chameleon, a man of opal heart and short-lived loyalties; but if he was resolved in one thing, or if his life had any unifying principle, it was to vindicate his manhood and re-furbish his self-respect against first the insinuation and then the allegation that he was impotent.

It was natural that he should feel the injustice of this charge. Not even his greatest enemies denied that he had sexual rela-tions of some sort with a kingly number of women, both high and low, but only disputed the extent to which those relations were consummated. One of his most dedicated detractors Hernán de Pulgar, court chronicler of Ferdinand and Isabella, accuses him of immorality by saying that 'in his youth he gave himself up to certain excesses which youth tends to demand and modesty ought to forego'; but since Pulgar also insists that Henry's impotence resulted from an inability to complete the sexual act, the implication is that Henry's excesses were a particularly perverse and disgusting form of sexual fetishism. Henry admitted, in the process of procuring an anulment of his first marriage, that he had been unable to consummate his relations with Blanche of Navarre, but to the imputation that this was explicable in terms of his impotence he replied with fervent accounts of his sexual prowess, on which – since he was obviously an interested party – as little reliance can be placed as on the testimony of the gaggle of whores whom he called on in his support, and whose word was doubtless as saleable as their bodies. On the other hand there was no issue among contemporaries that he did purchase both those commodities, as well as maintaining noble mistresses at court, the most notable of whom, Doña Guiomar, had a feud with the Queen as a result, culminating in a feminine fracas fought with sharpened finger-nails.

Alonso de Palencia, the most vituperative of Henry's literary adversaries and another pensioner of Ferdinand's and Isabella's, who is therefore usually quite unreliable in what he says about Henry, perhaps lets fall the truth without meaning to when he says that Henry was incapable of sex 'with any woman, especially with virgins': now this is an obvious contradiction; if Henry's incapacity was the same for all women, there cannot logically have been anything special about his relations with virgins. But it may be that his trouble was in fact exclusive to virgins. He said in the process of his divorce that the incompleteness of his intimacy with Blanche of Navarre was attributable to 'bewitchment'; not impossibly, he was merely making an oblique reference to her intact condition. He suffered perhaps rather from a sort of sexual debility than from total impotence. His detractors again came near to acknowledging this in a graphic – though not necessarily true – story which circulated among doctors in the court of Ferdinand and Isabella, according to which Henry's physicians, in the course of investigating his impediment, resorted to manipulating him; with difficulty they produced an ejaculation of discouragingly weak dimensions and loose consistency. Again, his difficulty may have been psychological. Henry IV of Castile would not be the only man in history to find it impossible to make love to a virtuous wife but easy with a mistress or prostitute. There can be no doubt that witchcraft was a paradigm much used in Henry's time to explain phenomena which nowadays would be regarded as psychological abnormalities. What is certain, whether or not he was capable of fathering the Princess Juana, is that his resolute defence of her legitimacy is psychologically explicable as a reaction – intelligible in any man – against the imputation of impotence. The stories of his wife's infidelities are less credible than those of his own disabilities, for they derive exclusively from sources hostile to the King; in particular it is impossible to put any reliance on the tale that the Queen had second and third bastards – variously by a groom, an archbishop and the archbishop's nephew – who thereafter seem to disappear from history.

Compelled to acknowledge his impotence in the field, if not in other contexts, Henry had now to make the best of his defeat in the civil war. Most ignominiously of all, in order to recover the treasure he had lost in the revolt of Segovia, he had to surrender the Queen as a hostage to his enemies. Powerless and reviled, retaining the name without the substance of a king, he was left to strut about Castile, still proud but for the time being defeated, from city to city until finally establishing himself in Toledo.

Isabella returned to the bosom of her mother, and to the company of the pretender, her brother, Alfonso, at Arévalo. Meanwhile, the destiny of her future husband, Ferdinand, Prince of Aragon, was drawing closer to her own as he waged a battle for his own rights in the kingdom which bordered Castile to the east. Ferdinand was born a little less than a year after Isabella on 10 March, 1452. Thereafter his preparation was for the most part very different from hers: instead of the sedentary, domestic existence Isabella had under her mother's frail aegis, Ferdinand led a peripatetic life in two courts, bearing a shield of his own and learning the exercise of arms; at the age of seventeen, when he married Isabella, he was already a king in his own right, the hero of two wars and the father of a child.

His own judgement on his education was that he had 'seen much but read little': the picture this implies appealed to contemporaries – a warrior prince rich in practical experience of the present but heavily reliant for the lessons of the past on the learned counsel of his humanistic advisers. It flattered the vanity of the humanists, particularly Alonso de Palencia, to whom we owe the record of this phrase of Ferdinand's, and Lucio Marineo Siculo, whose history of the monarchs' reign is pejorative about the king's Latinity, to feel that they and their prince each played complementary roles in the government of the kingdom. It is undoubtedly true that Ferdinand had little time past early childhood to amplify his knowledge; but by the age of ten when the civil wars of the Crown of Aragon intervened to disturb his fate, he had certainly already absorbed the basis of classical learning. Even after that time his father was careful to provide him with humanistic tutorship, and gave him Francisco Vidal de Noya for his Latin master. But Ferdinand seems to have spent more time in the saddle than at his schoolbooks and had his own horse from the age of eight.

His education was more up-to-date and, in the Renaissance sense of the word, more 'princely' than his wife's precisely because he was designated from birth for an actively political role. Like Isabella, Ferdinand was not the heir apparent to his father's crown: John II's elder son by a previous marriage was Don Carlos, Prince of Viana, but the continual dissensions between the King and his first-born over the inheritance of the kingdom of Navarre ensured for Ferdinand the prospect of greatness as a rival of his brother. From the 1450s King John favoured Ferdinand with a series of honours and jurisdictions to spite or weaken Don Carlos. Much has been written of John's 'love' for Ferdinand, but the truth is that the favours the youngster enjoyed are intelligible in political terms. Love did not run in the family. Ferdinand took after his father in what was really an inability to love – an exclusion of the mawkish and a total dedication to the politically realistic. This was another source of his difference of temperament from the sentimental and romantic Isabella. The influence of Ferdinand's mother, too, must have been very different from that of Isabella's. Juana Enríquez, of the blood of Castile in a collateral line, was more ambitious and more active than the dowager Isabella, perhaps because she was not born to, but only acquired, her queenly dignity. And it was naturally on her son that her ambitions were centred. She made a painful journey in the last stages of her pregnancy in order to ensure that Ferdinand was born on Aragonese soil. After the death of Don Carlos of Viana she played a masculine role in the civil wars, defending against the rebels her husband's throne and her child's acquired 'birthright'. On the other hand, there is no evidence to support the rumours that she was hostile to Don Carlos in his lifetime and complicit in his death; he seems on the contrary to have trusted and respected his stepmother.

Naturally the death of the Prince of Viana in 1461 greatly enhanced Ferdinand's position: he became 'primogenit' – 'first-born' or, as we should say, heir apparent. But the same event

A statue of King Ferdinand, carved by Felipe Vigarny, in the chapel royal, Granada

Queen Isabella, a portrait now in Windsor Castle

Don Juan, son of
Ferdinand and Isabella.
Detail from the painting
*The Madonna of the
Catholic Kings*

Left King Ferdinand in fu
armour on horseback

Below The silver crow
worn by Queen Isabella

brought an increase of danger. The elements in the kingdom (above all the urban patriciate of Barcelona and other important centres) which had supported Don Carlos in his disputes with the King, now had no recourse but open rebellion. The same source from which Ferdinand derived his hopes of inheritance also therefore contributed to the outbreak of the civil war that imperilled it.

In 1468, Ferdinand's mother died, but although he owed all his past success to her exertions in his cause, he probably did not now greatly feel her loss. He was firmly in control of his destiny. Sicily was secure. The Crown of Aragon was pacified. Affection for his mother had already been displaced in his breast by another kind of sentiment for women. His first illegitimate son, Don Alfonso, was born in the year after his mother's death; King John supplicated the pope to launch this infant on a prodigious career in the Church: he subsequently became Archbishop of Zaragoza. The number and identity of Ferdinand's paramours at this time are uncertain, but they seem, like those of Henry iv and King John his father, to have represented a wide social range. Yet procreative power was wasted in a bachelor-prince. Ferdinand had to be married.

Meanwhile Isabella's potential fertility was similarly redundant on the far side of the Castilian border. We have seen how King John had been considering the possibility of marrying his son to that princess for some time; the marriage seems to have had a place in popular aspirations too, as well as precedents in the longstanding close relations and blood-ties between Aragon and Castile; the remaining events of 1468 in Castile brought the union of Ferdinand and Isabella irresistibly nearer. Henry iv had considerably improved his position since the loss of Segovia. The surrender of the Queen into the hands of the Marquess of Villena had marked the beginning of what was in effect an uneasy alliance between the Marquess and the King. As Villena was also Master of Santiago, this was a considerable accession of strength to the monarch's side; moreover Henry had saved his treasure from the Segovian débâcle, and he still had custody of the Princess Juana. She was potentially useful in two possible ways. If he were successful in defending her birthright, Henry could bait his line with her to fish for a marriageable foreign prince to help him, whether in the calm Mediterranean waters of Aragon (also the most difficult of access), the more dangerous Atlantic shores of Portugal, or, stormiest of all, in the Bay of Biscay, where swam a fat fish in the form of the French King's brother. On the other hand, if Juana's cause did not prevail, at least for the time being, she could still be useful as a hostage for the support of a great magnate dynasty. Henry appears to have been contemplating the Mendozas with this in mind.

By 1468, Prince Alfonso and his party seem to have decided to come to terms. But the finger of death was already pointed at the Prince. He had eluded its mark in Arévalo, where he and Isabella had just spent a torrid summer amid a lethal plague. But it caught him one day riding out of Segovia and struck him from his horse. 'The most excellent King Alfonso xII', as his supporters preposterously styled him, could dispute his brother's throne no more. When the rebels confronted Henry at the meeting at Guisando, south of Avila, amid the great stone bull-images that have stood there mysteriously since ancient times, it was Isabella who was at their head.

The results of her brother's death were the most significant events that had yet befallen Isabella; suddenly she became, in the usage of her supporters, queen in name, without ever having anticipated such a dignity; and she was faced with prospects of power, and political problems, for which she was totally unprepared. The traditional picture of her reaction is that, urged by the Archbishop of Toledo to claim the succession and continue the war, she took a strong moral line of her own, insisting on a peaceful settlement which would allow Henry to remain a king in his lifetime. The notion is attractive, and almost all authors have succumbed to its allure. But it is one of the most successful as well as one of the most palpable false-hoods of history, coined by Isabella in her own account of these events two years later and then widely disseminated by chroniclers in her pay. The truth is that her reaction was not firm but vacillating; not moral but opportunist; and not independent but reflective of the different advice she received in successive moments. Her first inclination, under the influence of the Archbishop of Toledo, was at once to claim the crown. She circulated the localities, using the title of queen, to claim the oaths of allegiance of the subordinate authorities of the kingdom. 'You already know that from the moment when Our Lord disposed otherwise of (Alfonso's) life, the succession of these kingdoms and lordships of Castile and León belong to me as his rightful heiress and successor.' But then she changed her mind, and came to pin her hopes on a compromise, whereby Henry would retain the style of king in his lifetime, but she, Isabella, be named to succeed him.

The explanation of this change is undocumented and can only be approached by reasoning. In part, Isabella was compelled to it by circumstances, for Alfonso's death had caused defections to Henry's band and the Princess was without sufficient means to continue the war. In part, she was probably persuaded to it by counsel: the advice of the Mendozas no doubt played a role for they had been an important part of Alfonso's faction since the Marquess of Santillana led his clan into the rebel camp, and Isabella could not help but heed their word. They favoured an accommodation with Henry for two reasons: Archbishop Mendoza of Seville was the necessary rival in the ecclesiastical hierarchy of Archbishop Carrillo of Toledo; moreover they could hope to profit from peace by securing custody of the Princess Juana. On the other hand, the Mendozas were so obviously an interested party that Isabella would be likely to look for genuinely objective and friendly counsel too. This seems, indeed, to have been the first of a number of occasions to which Andrés de Cabrera intervened decisively in her history. His wife, Beatriz de Bobadilla, Isabella's longstanding friend, was in the Princess's company at the time. Cabrera was in the service of the King who had appointed him to rule in Segovia after the rebellion, because he was loyal to Henry but also acceptable to the Villena faction. Throughout the rest of the civil wars, Cabrera's aim was to profit from his connexions with both sides. The idea of a compromise whereby he would enjoy Henry's present favour and Isabella's future thanks, was distinctly his own policy.

Exactly what respective concessions were made at the Guisando meeting remains unclear to this day. The graphic quality of the chronicler's version of the opening of the meeting, with Isabella dismounting to kiss Henry's hand in homage while the Archbishop of Toledo sat haughtily on his horse, is an unreliable guide to what might have followed. But it is certain at least that Isabella's party withdrew in one highly important respect from its previous position: Henry was acknowledged as King. There is also no doubt that Henry accepted Isabella as his prospective successor. Implicit in this, it is true, was the illegitimacy of Princess Juana, but it was a significant fact in that age of subtle distinctions that the King refrained from explicitly acknowledging any such compromising circumstance. The version of the Pact of Guisando in which he appeared to do so was a forgery concocted by Isabella's partisans and publicized by her circulars and chroniclers: the necessity of such a forgery makes it clear that in the original Pact Juana was not explicitly illegitimized. Now if Juana was not illegitimate, Henry would be free to argue that the part of the Pact which named Isabella his successor was automatically void, since the laws of succession were such that not even the king could dispense. It was probably with this in mind that Henry wrote to the Pope within two months of signing the Pact, asking him to refuse to ratify it in this respect.

The reply of Juana's friends to the Pact of Guisando was swift: even before the Pact was signed, the Mendoza Count of Tendilla, who had Juana in his care, denounced Isabella's elevation above his ward as 'a great and enormous hurt, affront and injustice . . . nul and of no value or effect'. He argued that Juana was by common knowledge princess and heiress and had been sworn as such by all the parties to the Guisando arrangement; that Isabella's elevation was contrary to custom and without the consent of the *Cortes* and had been effected in defiance of Juana's rights, with no opportunity for the aggrieved party to be heard. He added forcefully that Juana was 'legitimate daughter of the said lord king, born of legitimate matrimony', approved by the pope.

Juana herself remained committed to the care of the Mendozas, but this was not necessarily a disadvantage for Henry since custody of the child made the family remarkably responsive to the argument that she was the true heir. The Pact of Guisando had thus left everything still to be settled. On balance, Isabella emerged weaker than she had been beforehand. In order to stop the flow of defections to Henry's banner and to draw new strength to her cause, she had to contrive a decisive stroke in her favour. Her greatest advantage was her personal liberty, for it enabled her to marry as she wished. And the best prospective husband for a pretender to the Castilian throne – the man, that is, who could attract most support within Castile – was Ferdinand of Aragon. Henry's hopes of marrying Juana to that prince, when her legitimacy had been implicitly besmirched in the Pact of Guisando, and when she was in the keeping of an independent noble faction, cannot have been sanguine, but he did hope to apprehend Isabella and marry her off relatively harmlessly in France, 'a country abhorrent to our Castilian nation', as Isabella expostulated. In the months after the Guisando encounter, Isabella was therefore literally a fugitive, avoiding places controlled by the King or his partisans, travelling incessantly to elude the spread of Henry's net. On visiting Madrigal de las Altas Torres, her own birthplace, she found it in enemy hands and was obliged to take refuge in a convent outside the walls.

Valladolid offered her a temporary respite at the moment when her envoys achieved agreement with Aragon – a political agreement between John II and the magnates in Isabella's faction, which would bring Isabella a husband and find Ferdinand a wife.

It is strange at first glance that John II and Ferdinand should be willing to contract an alliance as close and indissoluble as marriage with a fugitive princess of uncertain prospects. Moreover, as we saw in the first chapter, the Aragonese accepted a marriage settlement that gave Ferdinand little independent influence in Castile: in other words, they did not attempt to take advantage of Isabella's critical position to insist on favourable terms. The most likely explanation is that King John realized that the marriage could only be a political success if Ferdinand found large-scale support inside Isabella's future realm; this in turn could only be assured by respecting Castilian customs and laws.

Isabella was said to have been looking out longingly from her chamber window when Ferdinand approached and, though she had never seen him before, to have recognized him at once from among his eight companions, crying 'That is he! That is he!' If she indeed picked him out so accurately, the youth she must have seen was strongly built and of medium height, whose pale, serious face was marked by clear eyes and a small but full-lipped and red mouth. Ferdinand was in no sense handsome – his features were too small for his large and inelegant head, but his future queen seems to have found him instantly attractive. The haste with which this marriage was celebrated was, in a sense, literally indecent, for Ferdinand and

Isabella, who shared a great-grandfather, were related within the degrees of consanguinity forbidden by the Church. Papal dispensation was not difficult to arrange, but it would have cost more time than King John and Archbishop Carrillo had at their disposal. Isabella's partisans had already indulged in lies and forgery in her cause and their's at the time of the Pact of Guisando; they did not now hesitate to take another step along that primrose road. With the connivance of King John, Carrillo produced forged papal bulls of dispensation while genuine ones were being obtained in Rome. Thus Isabella, the future guardian of public morality and champion of courtly chastity, began her married life technically living in sin.

Much less than of the Pope, Isabella had not asked the permission of Henry IV to contract marriage; Henry had a legal case, which he soon brought out in argument, that Isabella was his ward and that she could not marry without his consent, both by virtue of his position as head of the house and because, in respect of marriage, the heir to the throne was naturally the king's ward. The real reason why Isabella had not consulted him was of course quite simple : Henry would never have given permission for Isabella to make an alliance which he desired for Juana and which would severely compromise all his hopes and plans; but Isabella had to find the answers in legal terms to the King's arguments. Moreover, she had not, as was usual in the case of royal marriages, sought the advice of the Royal Council – that is, the magnates and prelates together with the king's picked, lettered counsellors – but merely relied on the urgings of the faction clustered about her. In a justification addressed to Henry, which achieved wide circulation, Ferdinand and Isabella sought to explain their conduct :

We are joined in matrimony as the Holy Mother Church of Rome commands and should have waited till seeing your Grace's consent and the vows and counsels of all the prelates and great men ... but ... so clear and manifest was it ... that were it necessary to wait for everyone's accord and consent this would be very difficult to obtain or else so much time would have passed that in these realms great peril would arise because of the absence of children to continue the succession ... therefore ... we decided to contract our

aforesaid marriage as much without scandal as we could . . .
and without favouring any foreigners.

They went on to say that they hoped to serve Henry 'in the
dignity of his estate' to bring 'concord and peace' to Castile and
'with all our might to favour justice, which because of recent
disturbances is in a weak condition'. One could almost call this
document an ill-concealed self-indictment: first came the
understated admission that it would be 'very difficult' to obtain
the necessary consent for the steps Ferdinand and Isabella had
taken; followed by the further admission that their marriage
had been a source of 'scandal', and a reference to their own
greatest weakness – the fear among Castilians that Ferdinand
would favour foreigners. At the same time the newly-weds
propounded the essential pragmatism of their policy: the aim
of their marriage was to ensure the continuity of the succession; if they fulfilled the half-promise of this declaration by
producing an heir, that would be a weighty argument in their
favour in their bid for the crown.

Already in their childhood and the earliest days of their
marriage, even before the war of succession in which they
clawed their way to the crown, Ferdinand and Isabella had
learned the right blend of boldness and circumspection, un-
scrupulousness and meticulousness, commitment to their own
ambitions and indifference to political adversity, that would
serve them well both in the civil wars that spanned their
succession and in the future problems of their reign. In his last
years, Henry IV never became fully reconciled to their marriage, though at times, influenced by Mendoza or Cabrera, he
was inclined to favour their right to succeed him for reasons of
state. Most of the time, however, personal considerations disposed him more favourably towards the Princess Juana, whom
he sought to marry to the King of Portugal; the policy, as we
have seen, was realized after his death with disastrous consequences for the realm of Castile. It was partly thanks to the
fluctuations of Henry's resolve and the mutations of his mind
that Ferdinand and Isabella gained ground from their relative
isolation of 1468 to the position of strength they occupied
when the old king died; the patronage resources of the Crown
of Aragon and the advantages their cause represented for its
followers completed their hand.

We have still to ask what was the nature of the crown they struggled for so tenaciously, what and over what the power they gained by it, how they used it, and what – finally – were the achievements they realized with it.

Some points in justification of Chapter 2

The succession was established according to indefeasible hereditary right of the nearest legitimate heir; priority within the same degree of relationship to the deceased monarch was determined by sex. On one occasion in 1471, Isabella alleged that her rival, Princess Juana, was illegitimate because her parents' marriage was uncanonical. Recent investigations have confirmed that there are arguments both for and against that point of view – see L. Súarez Fernández and V. Rodríguez Valencia, *Matrimonio y derecho sucesorio de Isabel la Católica* (Valladolid, 1960) pp. 90-3 and T. de Azcona, *Isabel la Católica* (Madrid, 1964) pp. 32-4. But since contemporaries barely noticed this canonical discrepancy, which remained unproven at the time, and since Isabella's case rested on the allegation, equally unproven, that Juana was not the King's daughter, it is fair to say that Isabella's accession was contrary to law. To adduce points in her favour which were unperceived at the time would be strictly correct, if history were a law-court and biographers wore wigs, but smacks too strongly of anachronism to be admitted here. The case for the lawfulness of Isabella's own wedding depends on the supposition that Paul II had secretly authorized her marriage in January 1469. (v. J. Meseguer Fernández, 'Dispensa de consanguineidad', *Archivo Ibero-americano*, xxvii [1967].)

Isabella's Latinity is a point on which her eulogists have wasted much ink, by accepting uncritically the distortions of her contemporary flatterers. The limits in which her recorded use of Latin were confined show that she never became skilled in this accomplishment. She had begun to learn the language by 1482, when Púlgar wrote enquiring after her progress. The tradition that Isabella was taught by Beatriz de Galindo is based on a misunderstanding (see A. de la Torre,

'Beatriz de Galindo', *Hispania*, xvii [1957]), but the Queen probably conversed with her and learned from her.

My somewhat deprecating physical description of Isabella is
based on the contemporary portraits (or near-contemporary
copies thereof) in Windsor and Madrid, done realistically in the
Flemish style. The family devotional painting in the Prado,
though more nearly idealized, shows recognizably the same
face. It is ridiculous to reject this evidence on the *a priori*
grounds that Isabella must have been beautiful (v. Silió, *Isabel la
Católica* [1967], p. 83). My account is broadly compatible with
the statements of her courtiers that she was 'fair' and 'of
comely aspect' if due allowance is made for their otiose
flattery: compared with their encomia of her character,
panegyrists were remarkably reticent about her looks – this
reticence, I think, is eloquent enough. The only really ir-
reconcilable point is Pulgar's statement that her countenance
was 'gay' – which accords ill with my insistence on her sad
eyes. No doubt this was in part a matter of mood, but her
portraits show her with sad eyes and I include them because
they suit her serious personality. Pulgar's physiognomies tend
to be stereotyped and he gives smiling eyes to almost anyone
whom he found personally sympathetic – or who paid him
well. I suggest a psychological explanation of the effects of
Isabella's plainness, linking it with envy. Prudery is often said to
be a consequence of plainness and one wonders whether there
was any natural connexion between the two in Isabella's
case.

The opinion, finally, of some authors that Henry IV was
indifferent to allegations that he was impotent is nonsense. The
contrary may be proved from the evidence even of his enemy,
Pulgar (i, 5, 9, 12), if that of his friend, Enríquez del Castillo, is
doubted. Pulgar also admits that he upheld Juana's legitimacy
to the very moment of his death (i, 64). But a further explanation of his attitude towards Juana could be that he upheld her
legitimacy simply to use her marriage prospects as a diplomatic
lure whereby foreign support might be gained in his wars
against his nobles. The political and psychological explanations
are not mutually exclusive.

3
Kingship and the Court

A monarch in those days was the apex of society; yet he did not merely straddle its summit passively, but sustained it and gave it unity and cohesion, so that the apex was as essential a part of the structure as was its base in the people and the soil. When Isabella and Ferdinand came to the throne, Castile was still emerging from a gruelling proof of the necessity of monarchy, for a weak king or doubtful succession had been shown to be the inevitable harbinger of disorder and dissolution. One of the monarchs' servants defined the kingly dignity thus;

> The office of king is the highest and greatest of all, because, under God, the most exalted place is his and he must be assisted and served and obediently revered and feared both with much loyalty and in all truth and obeyed in all things, alike in presence and in absence, with entire purity of intent, for thereby God is served, and thereto are we his subjects bound from the very moment of our birth, when we emerge from our mother's womb or, at the least, from as soon as a man begins to acquire knowledge; and this is the second doctrine which every father must teach his son, after that of God. And this office of king, as it is the greatest and best of all, so it is the most difficult and hazardous in the same

measure, so that we are all obliged to pray God give him life and understanding to govern himself well and rule his kingdoms.

Here was a clear expression of one of the greatest bases of monarchical power – the subject's sense of duty. But the most eloquent and comprehensive statement of the theory of kingship was Ferdinand's and Isabella's own, with which they prefaced some of the most important documents to emanate from their chancery. It was of course the work of their *letrados*, the university-trained administrators who staffed the Royal Council, but there can be no doubt that it reflected faithfully not only Castilian royal traditions but also the monarchs' own views:

God is called King over all kings because from him they derive their name and by him they reign and he governs and maintains them and they are his viceregents, each one in his kingdom, placed by him over the nations to preserve them in justice and truth temporally; which is shown perfectly in two ways, one spiritual, as the prophets and saints have shown to whom our Lord gave grace to have accurate knowledge of things and to cause them to be understood; the other is according to nature as the wise men who know the things of nature have shown.

And the Saints said that the king is set on earth in the place of God to fulfill justice and give to each man his right and therefore they call him heart and soul of the people and as the soul is in the heart of man and thereby the body lives and is maintained, so justice reposes in the king which is life and sustance to the people of his lordship; and as the heart is one and from it all the limbs are one and make one body, even so all the people of a kingdom, however many they be, yet are one for the king must be and is one; so too must all unite with him to follow him and help him in those things which he has to do; and according to nature have the wise men said that kings are the heads of their kingdoms, because as in the head the senses have their origin whereby all the limbs of the body are ruled, even so by the command which emanates from the king, who is lord and head of all the people of the kingdom, must they be ordered and governed and they must obey; and the right to power of kings is as great as the laws which they have beneath their sway, because they hold that power not from men but from God, whose place they keep in temporal matters, and it is a chief part of their power among other things to love, advantage and preserve their people.

Ferdinand and Isabella and their contemporaries thought of monarchy not primarily as we do today in terms of supreme power in the state or of unlimited legislative capacity, but as a relationship to God. In their image of the universe, the king, at the summit of a mountain-shaped society, was in a sense physically close to God, as a fountain above a terraced garden is closest to the sky. This proximity was limited to temporal matters because of the pope's headship in the spiritual sphere and because kings, despite periodic attempts during the Middle Ages, had never succeeded in showing that they were ministers of God in the spiritual sense that was the domain of the sacerdotal class. But Ferdinand and Isabella were careful to point out that each king was sovereign in his own kingdom; there could be no question of their allowing the pope or any foreign power jurisdiction in their realms.

It must be remembered that Ferdinand and Isabella almost never called their power by the modern name of sovereignty. The paradigms of feudalism, in which kingship was a superior kind of lordship – suzerainty rather than sovereignty – were still predominant. So was the idea that the monarch's high dignity was in the nature of things. The king and queen were 'natural lords' of every man. Their leadership was as the head's over the limbs of the human body – and everyone knew the correspondences between the physical nature of man and the universe of which he was a microcosm. The image was already a traditional one in Castile and had characterized documents ever since its appearance in the collection of laws assembled in the thirteenth century by King Alfonso the Wise. The manifest hierarchy of nature could easily be gauged by a cursory examination of the different creatures and natural phenomena; and it was clear from sacred writings and the traditions of mystical theology that a similar establishment prevailed in heaven among God and the different ranks of angels. It was thus easily comprehensible that the same state could characterize the affairs of men.

An element in Ferdinand's and Isabella's kingship which was more readily intelligible in our terms was its co-extension with the right to make laws. It had long been accepted in Castile that the king could make laws on his own initiative, but there remained issues down to the days of the Catholic Monarchs about the more precise definition of his right; whether, for instance, the laws the king proclaimed on his own were different in quality from those made at the representative assemblies, or *Cortes*, where the king met the deputies of the nobles and important towns; whether the king could override or alter existing law; and in particular whether the crown and the king's decree could exercise a transmutative control over the local laws and customs in which the Spanish monarchies abounded. Over the previous two centuries the kings had repeatedly been compelled by the towns and great churchmen not to break certain 'fundamental' laws – those governing the succession and forbidding the dispersal of the royal patrimony – for if either of these were tampered with, the monarchy would be weakened and internal order put at risk. In practice, Ferdinand and Isabella continued to exceed the law in granting away royal lands, but they did recognize that they were bound in theory by the existing code and did make some effort to obey it: they succeeded in restoring to the crown a small part of earlier alienations, and when Isabella died she ordered that her own excesses in this respect be revoked for the sake of her conscience. There can be no doubt that the Catholic Monarchs insisted upon a very high degree of legislative liberty for themselves: they made wide use of a phrase which strongly evoked the traditions of Roman Law in which many of the jurists whom they grouped around their throne in their Council and Secretaryships were trained – 'my royal absolute power'; their chancery wielded freely in their proclamations the injunction upon all who heard them to obey them 'as if promulgated in the *Cortes*', and 'with the force of law'; and frequently asserted the monarchs' right to suspend or dispense with any law that might run contrary to their commands, even a law of the *Cortes*.

They were not, however, absolute rulers in the modern sense; though overlain by some Renaissance ideas, the fundament of their kingship was thoroughly medieval. The divine origins and connotations of their power tended to limit rather than extend its exercise. They were restrained in the first place by the fear of hell-fire: as the humanist Canon of Toledo, Alonso Ortiz, warned, 'Monarchs have only God to fear, and if ever that fear is overcome, they fall headlong into the abyss of vice'. Above all, their actions were strictly related to popular advantage: they could do only what conduced to the public good, and accorded with justice and the preservation of their people in peace. This was again connected with their relationship to God, for Pulgar could still quote the old medieval adage, 'The voice of the people is the voice of God'. Therefore their government, though not necessarily *by consent*, was *with advice*. Ferdinand and Isabella made only dwindling use of the traditional representative institution of Castile, the *Cortes*, partly because it was cumbrous and expensive and partly because they were apprehensive that this organ of advice should attempt to arrogate to itself the privilege of consent; but they continued to heed petitions and take the counsel of their magnates and chosen advisers. The monarchs were obliged to take counsel only with those subjects who were directly beneath them in the feudal hierarchy; there were no institutions for consultation with peasants save through their lords, nor the townsfolk save through their oligarchic corporations. But the monarchs received the supplications of folk at all social levels on particular matters. An old tradition of Castilian jurisprudence, which the great jurist Montalvo placed prominently in the collection of laws he compiled for Ferdinand and Isabella, said that 'the King must show generous faith in hearing the petitions and plaints of all who come to his court to ask for justice'.

As well as by the conscious pursuit of the public good, the monarchs were limited by the fundamental laws of the realm, and by the prescriptions of divine and natural law, of which they were joint guardians with the Church; and in theory – though Ferdinand and Isabella never provoked such an occurrence – had they committed some overt crime, or been guilty of such an offence as heresy or blasphemy, spiritual sanctions could have been applied or a foreign prince justly acted to constrain them. The Church actually broke the royal monopoly of jurisdictional power by having its own courts and penalties, where alone Churchmen could be tried. Such cases might be appealed outside the frontiers of the realm, to Rome; where other monarchs of the time resented the jurisdiction of the pope and tried to limit or abolish such appeals, Ferdinand and Isabella exploited it deftly, allowing cases to leave Castile but using their diplomatic influence at the papal court to obtain a result favourable to their interests, or else inducing their bishops to keep appeals within the realm. Generally, jurisdiction was for contemporaries a function even more important than legislation, which was thought of more as a static legacy, to be particularized and modified, collected and codified, rather than as an area of continuous innovation. That the king was the source of 'justice' in the land constituted a vital contribution to his essential nature – 'the king', as Pulgar said, 'has only God for judge'. The chief ingredient of his superiority in the kingdom was still thought to be this ultimate nature of his temporal jurisdiction – though here too the king was circumscribed, at least in theory, by the demands of justice, and it was explicit in the laws that the monarch could not pronounce judgement in a case during its trial or make a valid ruling which deprived one party of equity. On the other hand, there was no institution to oversee the king's conduct in this respect.

Royal power was in a sense tempered by the inchoately fashionable Renaissance idea that the most effective remedy for despotism was a princely education. The notion was still in its infancy in the days of the Catholic Monarchs, but was voiced by Alonso Ortiz, a canon of Toledo who wrote a treatise on the upbringing of their son (although as we shall see, the prince's education was deficient by Renaissance standards). The principle was that a proper schooling would make a prince wise and temperate and that study of the classics would give him understanding both of his own Augustan dignity and of the fates of tyrants. Similar views seem to have been expressed by Peter Martyr and his correspondent, Diego de Muros. It was strongly felt that the judgement of posterity was a factor in moulding a king's conduct, comparable with the effort to achieve the increase of his own estate and realm in his day; hence Ferdinand and Isabella spent generously on historians and poets to chronicle their deeds for them.

Finally beyond the theory – and perhaps more important – were the practical realities of power. The monarch commanded the military allegiance of every man in the kingdom and material and financial help in time of need; he could 'make mercies' (as the current phrase was) or donate lands, titles and offices in patronage; he possessed a widespread network of castles, whose command and garrison were in his gift; he controlled the issue of money; and he enjoyed the income of the royal estates, which, albeit much reduced by Ferdinand's and Isabella's day, was formidable still. He was directly the lord of many of his subjects, without any intervening seigneur, including categories as important as the tax-paying townsmen – 'the royal arm' as they were called – the Jews and Castilian Moors and foreign merchants. The obverse of the king's 'mercy' was his 'anger', and by withdrawing favour or threatening to do so he could do much to regulate the loyalty of his magnates. Similarly, the most significant check on the monarchs was a material one: they never had more money than was barely sufficient for their needs, and frequently had only much less; their powers of taxation and the fiscal resources of the state were negligible by modern standards, and much of the history of their reign is a tale of expedients devised to make ends meet, expand their income or find patronage resources that could be used as a substitute for cash.

A good deal of what we have said of kingship applies only to Castile. As King of Aragon, Ferdinand had to cope with a quite different set of institutions and traditions, which allowed the monarch nothing like the degree of pre-eminence he enjoyed in Castile. An alternative theory of the relationship of the monarch to God was that royal power derived from God not directly but only by way of the polity: the king wielded it as though by a pact with his people, which constrained both parties. It was this kind of theory which was most faithfully reflected in the institutions of Aragon (although it is as well to remember that not even in Castile was the ruler yet habitually styled 'majesty' or 'by the grace of God'.) Above all the King of Aragon ruled by consent; to some extent, he even reigned by consent, for the oath of allegiance of his magnates was expressly conditional on his upholding their customs and liberties. He was trammelled up by a variety of representative institutions; and finally he was hampered by the strength and diversity of local laws, partly customary and partly codified. In Castile, Ferdinand and Isabella re-affirmed the principle for which their predecessors had struggled with varying degrees of success since the thirteenth century, that in cases of conflict the *Fuero Real* or law of the kingdom, was superior to the local *fueros*. Such *fueros* as they themselves issued during their reign were all royal grants, not pacts between the monarchs and the localities, and were concerned with administration rather than law; moreover they tended to extend rather than limit royal influence in appointments to offices.

Although Aragon and Castile remained separate states, the monarchy of Ferdinand and Isabella derived a new and exalted dignity from the union of the monarchs. They reigned in a time of aggressive religious fervour, induced by the alarming territorial gains made in previous years by Islam, whose waxing crescent filled the southern and eastern Mediterranean and whose horns protruded ominously from Constantinople into central Europe and from Granada into Spain. It was natural that Ferdinand's Aragonese counsellors, who had been bred up in secular fear of the Turks, should brim over with excitement at the hope that their master's new Castilian connexion would bring the accession of strength they needed to strike a decisive counter-blow for Christendom; while the Castilians in their turn expected Aragonese help to be valuable in the continuing war against the Moors. Mingled with these expectations was a millenial fever, fed by the approach of the new century, and a renewal of a belief, long persistent in the Middle Ages, that a Last World Emperor would appear, whose reign would be marked by the defeat of Islam and the commencement either of a resurgence of Antichrist in some unspeakable form or alternatively of a blissful 'Age of the Holy Spirit'. Poets close to Ferdinand wrote of him in such terms during the wars of succession that spanned his mounting of the Castilian throne. Christopher Columbus shortly echoed the refrain. And the chronicler Diego de Valera assured the king, 'You shall hold the monarchy of all the Spains and shall renew the imperial seat of the matchless blood of the Goths, from whence you come'. Valera was undoubtedly influenced by the tradition that the ruler of the whole of Spain was entitled to the style of emperor, a departure from the notion dominant in millenarian thought that Christendom was a single empire and successor of Rome. Of the union of Ferdinand and Isabella, the curate-chronicler Bernáldez declared in a similar vein, 'With this conjuncture of two royal sceptres, Our Lord Jesus Christ took vengeance on his enemies and destroyed him who slays and curses'.

C

In all their dominions the King and Queen were so prominent in public life that they had little of the privacy which modern constitutional monarchs enjoy. It was fitting that the first of the institutions by which they ruled their realms was also the household and environment in which their daily life was led: the royal court.

The court, though its facets were many, was above all an aristocratic institution and the monarchs' first means of regulating their relations with the nobility. That was how Galíndez de Carbajal characterized it, who owed his own place at court not to refined blood but to refinement of education in the university, which equipped him to be among the most favoured of the monarchs' lettered counsellors. He wrote:

> They kept a great household and court, accompanied by Grandees and leading barons, whom they honoured and elevated according to the quality of their degree, keeping them occupied in ways wherein they could be of service, and when occasion arose, mindful to serve in the government of the kingdom and the Royal Council. The monarchs were most careful to place men of prudence and ability to serve, even though such were of the middling sort rather than great men from the noblest houses.

Of course the new men were merely added to the old aristocracy in the Royal Council and never excluded the noblemen from it or outnumbered them. On the other hand, few nobles spent more than a short time at court; although in one contemporary opinion, a cavalier who never went to court was like a priest who never went to Rome, and although the monarchs made great use of minor nobles who, under the name of *continos*, dwelt continuously at court (except when a commission from the monarchs took them to a distant locality in the royal service), Ferdinand and Isabella never created a true courtly nobility. Despite the usefulness of the court in restraining magnates from rebellion and discontent, the local power of the aristocracy was little impaired by their increased attendance on the royal persons.

Of the personnel of the court the near contemporary Fernán Pérez de Guzmán wrote that they were 'well informed, discreet and subtle'. But he was thinking particularly of the men of letters, the university-trained administrators whom monarchs especially liked to employ, because usually having no great inherited power of their own, they depended upon royal favour and so in turn could be relied on by their masters. They were often trained jurists; some of them, as was almost traditional among the servants of the kings of Castile, had Jewish blood. Their functions were mainly to propound the royal theory of kingship and devise ways of expressing it; to assist the monarchs in the dispensation of justice; and to make the most of the royal finances. Other men of the same class not permanently attached to the court were used on administrative and judicial missions to the localities. The most important of these courtier-bureaucrats of Castile were the *contadores* or officers of the royal counting-house, who handled receipts; the treasury officials, who kept the treasure and made disbursements; the working chancellors and secretaries, who played key roles in drafting the diplomata of the royal chancery; and the judicial members of the Royal Council. Often an aristocratic sinecurist was in theory their superior, but merely received part of the profits of the office (so that his loyalty to the monarchs should be assured) while the monarchs' servant did all the real work. The bureaucracy of the Catholic sovereigns was still merely a small group of men – not yet a system of government as it would be in Philip II's day – but Ferdinand and Isabella were fortunate in being served therein by men who combined skill in their fields with a generally high sense of duty to their master and mistress, and a strong leavening of professionalism in their methods. The disadvantage of employing such men was that they were necessarily corrupt. The monarchs could never afford to pay them as their talents deserved, and they had to live largely from the 'profits' of their offices. Any applicant soliciting a royal favour, or even a litigant demanding justice, had to make the appropriate payment to the right official, as well as the authorized fee, of which the royal servant concerned also received a proportion, before anything could be done. Treasury officials, like Luis Santángel of Aragon, went further and speculated on their own behalfs with royal funds. The monarchs were generous in making periodic, irregular settlements on the officials – trading and mining concessions, for instance, in new areas of Castilian expansion, monopolies and commanderships of the Military Orders – but the bureaucrats all aspired to lead an aristocratic and expensive life-style and to marry into the nobility or found great houses of their own. It would be wrong to see them as a 'modern' or 'bourgeois' element in the Catholic Monarchs' government. By taste and aspiration and finally by adoption they belonged to the aristocracy, and they were by no means hostile to the interests of the traditional leaders of society.

Among the longer established nobles the vacuum left by the decline of the chivalric ideal had not yet been filled in Spain by the Renaissance concept of the perfect courtier, and standards of conduct among the nobility and at court remained mixed. One of the most barbarous cases on record concerned Don Fernando de Velasco, the Lord Constable's brother, who burned to death some yokels who, in their drunkenness, had taken him for a Jewish rent collector and abused him accordingly. The King replied to subsequent complaints that he regretted the wretches' deaths, without benefit of prior confession, but that Velasco had acted nobly in exacting satisfaction for the outrage they had committed against him.

The most conspicuous instances however, are not always the most typical. Although it would be quite wrong to speak of a transformation of the nobility, there were signs in some cases of a pacification of their habits, part of which was owed to the influence of court life. Even the fiery Rodrigo de Osorio tempered his insurgent inclinations with love of music, and the sons of the great began to be seen in the universities. In the next reign Gutierre de Toledo, Pedro Fernández de Velasco and Alonso Manrique all completed academic careers which they had begun under Ferdinand and Isabella. Nobles indulged increasingly in the peaceful distractions of luxury and embellishment of their persons and their houses. Alonso Manrique, the knight of Salamanca, was exceptional in vaunting the motto he coined,

> My lineage is for me enough,
> Content to live without expensive stuff.

With the expansion of taste came an increased interest in the accumulation of wealth. Some nobles even went into business. The Admiral of Castile (whose title was an hereditary dignity, not a naval office) obtained a dyestuffs monopoly from the monarchs, though the produce was disposed of for him by the wealthy Genoese merchant house of Riberol in Seville. The

Dukes of Medina Celi had their own merchant marine fleet, and their noble colleagues of Medina Sidonia invested heavily in another contemporary 'growth industry' – sugar production. Even the less enterprising nobles rose to new heights of estate management, especially stimulated by the need to match rising prices, which were beginning to be a permanent feature of the economy. We know that the Medina Celi dextrously increased their income from food-rents and seigneurial taxes, and although much work remains to be done on other cases, recent research has revealed how monastic and clerical lordships also increased their incomes to keep pace with rising costs.

Although they spread their wings economically and culturally, the nobles remained true to the traditions of their class. Medina Sidonia himself was one of the most rebellious and warlike of Ferdinand's and Isabella's vassals. The nobles remained a military class, whose chief virtue was prowess and whose pursuit was power. As Pulgar wrote to a magnate wounded in battle with the Moors, 'The profession you make in the order of chivalry (that is, the noble class) obliges you to undergo more perils than common men, just as you merit more honour than they, because if you had no more spirit than the rest in the face of such affrights, then we should all be equals'. Those words would have made sense to men throughout the Middle Ages: then, more characteristically of the Catholic Monarchs' reign, Pulgar added, 'But we must be happy, for you serve God with devotion, the King with loyalty, and the fatherland with love. And, after all, you were not captured. God be praised for it, and His Glorious Virgin Mother!' Side by side with a sense of the traditional qualities of the aristocracy, Pulgar displayed his belief in a strong, pre-eminent monarchy and his patriotism. Another eloquent statement of the elusive ethos of the Spanish nobility of the day was Alonso de Palencia's treatise on Knightly Perfection, in which Chivalric Practice, personified as a Spanish gentleman, sets off in search of Discretion, whom he finally encounters – interestingly enough – in Italy, the homeland of humanism. Other writers questioned the true nature of nobility, pointing out, under the influence of Aristotle and his commentators, whose works were widely diffused at a popular level in fifteenth-century Spain, that gentility lay in the cultivation of virtue. 'God made men, not Lineages', was a theme of Gomez Manrique's and

Pulgar's, meaning not that all men were social equals, but that humble men could wield power if they possessed the requisite merit and that the king should be able to ennoble those who deserved it. Diego de Valera put forward a concept in which elements of nobility were linked with intellectual distinction: 'I know', he declared, 'how to serve my Prince not only with the strengths of my body but also with those of my mind and intellect'.

An institution separate from but analogous to the royal court was the Court of Prince John, the heir to the throne, which the monarchs established in Almazan in 1496, when the Prince was about eighteen years old. This court was an odd body both in its head and members – a dull, weak, almost mentally retarded boy, attended by some of the most distinguished and powerful men in Castile, amid a precious ritual. It was in this ambience that Gonzalo Fernández de Oviedo, the future chronicler and natural historian of the Indies, began his long and distinguished career in royal service. He left a glib account of Prince John's court, between the lines of which much can be read of the Prince's character and the customs of the times. The personnel of the Prince's train was brilliant. Among the administrative staff were some of the most promising of the lettered men, of relatively humble origin but august preparation in the university, such as Gonzalo de Baeza, treasurer of the Prince's court, who was later advanced to a corresponding position in the household of the Queen, and Juan Velázquez de Cuellar, the *contador mayor* or keeper of accounts, who subsequently became *contador mayor* of the whole kingdom. These financial officials were no mere cyphers, like the figures they manipulated, but powerful men in their own right, key links in the chain of patronage by which monarchs sought to increase their power. Opportunities for the exploitation of patronage in the Prince's court were limited, for if there was one respect in which that body was not independent of the court of the monarchs, it was that its personnel was paid directly by the royal secretary, Francisco de Madrid: even so, as Oviedo discreetly remarked, 'The *contadores mayores* can bring profit to many in the exercise of their office'. Alongside the officials were the Prince's 'companions', divided into those of his own generation, for his company and amusement, and a body of older men for his surveillance and improvement: what they had in common was their lofty birth. The younger set included Hernán Gómez de Avila, and the older Nicolás de Ovando, future governor of the Indies. The Prince's own household staff was of barely less noble composition: the chamberlains at its head came from the best families in Castile; the pages were all of aristocratic birth and even the humbler grooms like Oviedo himself, who performed menial services at the prince's meals or *toilette*, were well born and educated. The last, and, from some aspects, most important of the permanent members of the court was the Prince's tutor. Fray Diego Deza, of the Dominican order, was called from his theology lectures in the University of Salamanca to take charge of John's education; the preparation of the future king was more important than that of the nation's future bishops. Deza, albeit an expert Latinist, was no humanist of the new school, and the Prince's education at his hands was not characteristically of the Renaissance, though it embraced study of the classics, but concentrated rather on religious knowledge and the inculcation of a particularly narrow and intolerant attitude – a 'catholic' attitude, as it was then inappropriately named. John's tutor was a noted Thomist, later to be Grand Inquisitor of Spain and the advocate of a severe line in the treatment of heretics and recalcitrant neophytes. The Prince's preparation left him – to take up Oviedo's words – 'very well learned in all that which was proper to his royal person; especially was he a very catholic and great christian'. The Prince's mind was inelastic and superficial, and this was the only part of his studies for which he showed any aptitude. Diego Deza's work was assisted by the whole atmosphere of John's court. Said Fernández de Oviedo, 'In the time of the Prince, my master, at his table and in his closet, in his kitchen or at his cup or buttery, or in any office whatsoever that was exercised anywhere in the palace from its very threshhold, there was room for no man that was not of pure lineage, a nobleman of refined and unmixed blood or at the very least from a family which had always been Christian save for two or three whom I prefer not to name and whom the Queen had appointed before the Prince had a household and accounts of his own; and even these were well known to be strangers to the Prince, out of his grace and favour'.

Oviedo also claimed with less emphasis that John 'emerged a good Latinist', but the truth is that he was incapable of conversing in Latin, or indeed of any intellectually demanding activity whatever. He was more at home risking small bets at games of chance or sharing his hairdresser's banal jokes than with the serious Diego Deza at his daily lessons; on the other hand his bathroom furniture did include a chess set, and it must be presumed that he was not averse to a little mental exercise while gaining physical relief. He was childish long beyond his boyhood: this reflected his need for security in an atmosphere redolent with responsibility and expectations of greatness to be, which far exceeded his modest capacities, and which seem to have filled him with subconscious anxieties. He never slept without a nightlight; he had an insatiable sweet tooth, and his closet was always stocked with sweetmeats for him to suck, especially fruit preserves, stiff quince jelly from Valencia, ethereal concoctions of egg-yolk and sugar, and aniseed balls. This may have been an inherited taste, for his parents are known to have gorged themselves on sweets on at least one royal visit to Valencia. All the monarchs' children appear to have been brought up on syrup flavoured with roses, for sugar was an expensive commodity, grown in small quantities in the irrigated gardens of Valencia, Sicily and Granada (until in the next three decades the Atlantic Islands were developed for that purpose) and the quantities consumed by the royal infants were prominent in Isabella's household accounts. The Prince as a boy was capable annually of downing syrup of sufficient value to maintain a soldier in arms for a year; and dulcet savours were generally more highly praised then than now. But in John's case, his abnormal greediness for confections clearly accords with his other infantile traits. His problems were aggravated by the fact that Isabella's queenly responsibilities separated John from the motherly affection he needed so much. The result was an exaggerated love for his childhood nurse, Juana de Avila, and a curious relationship with her, animated by sexual fantasy, and the imagery of mother-substitutes: 'you must have me for your husband more than anyone else', he wrote to her in a typical letter.

Around this weak little boy, average in height, colouring, and physiognomy and middling in capabilities, revolved a glittering courtly ritual, like bright rays around a spent sun. The Prince's daily round began when three chamber-servants called to assist him dress and wash in two silver basins. A 'groom of arms' buckled on the princely sword and dagger. His barber and shoemaker were called in and shared their unsophisticated sense of humour with the Prince: 'sometimes the barber coined absurdities and other ridiculous jokes at which the Prince would laugh and all who heard them'. John attended to his prayers, heard Mass, and finally shut himself up with Diego Deza and tedious works of classical lore and strict devotion. When there was no court event or hunt on, and the Prince's court was away from that of his parents, John's recreation was a modest flutter at the gaming-table or a distribution of alms to paupers and petitioners and tips to tradesmen and menials. His biggest expenditure was on clothes, and no doubt he often had something new to try on or something in the making to be fitted. At his evening *toilette*, when he washed his hands, the water was poured onto them by the aristocratic chamberlain, Juan de Calatayud, or, if present, one of the grandees of Castile in the following, unalterable, order of precedence: the Lord High Constable of Castile; the Lord High Admiral; the Duke of Medina Sidonia; the Duke of the Infantado; the Marquess of Villena; the Count of Benavente. At last he would deal with any petitions or memoranda of the day while undressing.

The monarchs did not establish this court for their son's comfort, but a political purpose. Nor was it a purpose exclusively proper to them, but common to many monarchs of that period. In particular, the cultivation of court ritual, with the consequent ideas that it was an honour to serve the king and that his dignity was of a superior quality to that even of the loftiest noble, were widespread devices among the courts of Europe, and shortly would be taken up in England under Henry VII and France under Francis I. Even basic functions like eating, washing, dressing and undressing were given ritual form and symbolic meaning. Finally, the multiplication of courts and offices and honours increased the scope of royal patronage and so added to the reality of monarchical power as well as to the opportunities for its symbolic expression.

Partly because so many members of the court were redundant – the aristocratic attendants, the quasi-hostages, the sinecurists, the fops – its recreations were an important part of its life. Daytime relaxations, which were reserved for festivals and special occasions, were chiefly the tourney and the hunt, and at times the court would assist at a more popular spectacle, the bullfight; this last had not yet evolved into the highly esoteric ritual practised in Spanish bullrings today, but consisted in a headlong career of mingled young men and bulls precipitated perilously through the streets, such as is still loosed in Pamplona and Ciudad Rodrigo on the day of Saint Fermín. It was not an entertainment to Isabella's taste. She found its cruelty disgusting and its levity offensive. On one occasion in Arévalo she ordered the horns of dead bulls to be tied back-to-front to those of the beasts that were to participate in the bullfight: this had the effect of blunting their prongs, diminishing the bloodiness of the sport and, apparently, provoking unreserved mirth among all the onlookers. Isabella roundly declared that she would never watch the bulls again, except under the same conditions. Another time, her confessor touched her conscience by writing and urging her to ban the sport from the kingdom. Isabella replied sharing his sentiments and promising never again to assist in person, though she declined to outlaw the spectacle altogether, since that would be to interfere with the enjoyment of others.

The joust, on the other hand, was a sport of unsurpassed nobility, beyond all criticism; and it not infrequently had a political utility too. One of the best described was celebrated in the midst of the war with Portugal at Valladolid in April 1475. The *Cronicón de Valladolid* records that

a tourney was held in Valladolid where jousted the King, Don Ferdinand, and the Dukes of Alba and Alburquerque and the Counts of Benavente and Salinas and the Admiral of Castile and Don Enrique Enríquez and Don Pedro Pimentel and Don Sancho de Velasco and Juan de Velasco ... provided hospitality that night for the King and Queen and ladies and dames. The master of the joust was the Duke of Alba: he likewise provided hospitality for the aforesaid lords and other counts who were present at the time, and for the Cardinal and Bishop who were also present.... The festivities indoors lasted till sunset on the day after their commencement.... On the Friday, the Duke of Alba had fallen armed from his horse on his way to risk himself at the tilt and was rendered dumb, unable to speak and he hurt his head and they bled him: yet he still came out armed and jousted twice. This was the most magnificent tourney that had ever been seen, men said, for fifty years and more. The Queen was dressed in brocade and wore a crown and all her ladies had tabards, half in green brocade and half in light-brown velvet and all embroidered with crowns ... fourteen ladies were so dressed. The Queen was borne on a mount decked with a coverlet and its mane and breast-leather and false bridle and halter all embellished with silver and flowerets of gold. The King wore devised upon his helm a yoke or anvil. In this joust the Catholic King bore a motto which read

> I suffer without making sound
> For as long as I am bound.

Beyond its value as a recreation, the joust exercised noble-men in the profession of arms, to which their social duty bound them, and helped to keep their class in trim for its martial role. For the monarch in particular, the tourney was an opportunity to receive or renew the homage of his lords; Hernán de Pulgar was too shrewd not to observe how that was the purpose of the Valladolid festivities of 1475, when Ferdinand and Isabella were anxious to know who was with them or who with the rebels. On the other hand, the magnates had their political uses for the tourney too, and according to the chronicler Palencia intended to exploit the occasion to distract Ferdinand from matters of state and lure him into expenditure and concessions.

The evenings at court were whiled away at table and in music and dancing. It appears to have been the practice for men and women to be segregated at meals, but Isabella some-times allowed them to dine together, at least when ambassadors were being received, because, she said, it was the French, Burgundian, Portuguese and English custom. The royal family habitually ate alone, but on festive occasions would allow the whole court to join them in the Burgundian fashion, while music was played or poetry declaimed. Münzer on his visit was impressed with the modernity, sophistication and cleanliness of the monarchs' table, compared with that of John of Portugal, who dined alone, handled his food excessively, was surrounded by minions and boys instead of noblemen and dignified retainers, and allowed them to finish off the scraps under the table.

Dancing was an activity in which both sexes joined, though it was usual for women to dance with one another. We know from the account by Roger Machado, the English ambassador's interpreter, that Princess Katherine's favourite partner was a Portuguese damsel in her train.

The children were encouraged to make friends with their own little courtiers, and had their favourites like any king. It was an age of demonstrative emotion, and the children were allowed to show their affection for their playmates by dancing and embracing. On another occasion, we know that the Princess Isabella, the monarchs' eldest daughter, organized a dance herself with thirty-one companions. Serious-minded ecclesiastics considered dancing frivolous and licentious and Isabella professed to dislike it. It was untrue that she danced at *fiestas*, she protested to her confessor, who had no doubt upbraided her for it – 'there could not be anything further from my mind'.

Ostentation and pageantry were an important part of court life. The monarchs had learnt from Burgundy, and from the northern artists they employed at court, the importance of a rich and impressive display in affairs of state and the usefulness of pageants which emphasized symbolically the pre-eminence of the king. It is not by accident that large numbers of observers have left us detailed descriptions of the royal apparel on different occasions, for every golden stitch was significant. It is curious, on the other hand, that Isabella felt guilty about the opulence of her garb, and it was the relative simplicity of her dresses that she stressed. 'I wore only a simple dress of silk with three gold hem-bands', she boasted on one occasion to Hernando de Talavera.

The court had an intimate side too. The life of the private household of the monarchs and their children is highlighted by Isabella's personal accounts. Her biggest expenditure was on materials for clothing and furnishing; in particular prodigious quantities of black velvet were used for mourning clothes. Furniture and jewels figure largely in her accounts too, especially those of a sacred nature. From 1488 Isabella's chapel must have been a veritable thesaurus of jewelled crosses of gold, encrusted with diamonds and rubies, for she bought 190 ducats' worth of them in that year. Political expenditure thrust its way into these intimate ledgers too; for instance, when Granada was conquered, Isabella contributed to the campaign for the forcible acculturation of the Moors by providing cash for them to be re-clothed in Castilian fashion; when the King of Granada's son was a prisoner in 1488, 106,000 *maravedis* went on equipping him with the right clothes. The Queen would also give fat tips to foreign ambassadors. The English envoys who negotiated the Treaty of Medina del Campo in 1498, together with a Scottish representative who happened to be present, took 248,290 *maravedis'* worth of personal presents away with them: it sounds as though they made an excellent bargain, since Isabella's treasurer laconically remarked that the Englishmen had only brought 'hats and other things' for their royal hosts. The town of Antequera, famous in the history of Isabella's house, received 50,000 *mrs* for the repairs of its walls in 1482. And seven of those bolts of black velvet went to the messenger who brought the news that Ferdinand had captured Loja in 1486. Alongside this sort of expenditure, one finds the record of purchases of sweets for the children, wages for the masters who taught them Latin and the upkeep of a painter to do their portraits. Isabella and Ferdinand liked to keep Christmas as a family occasion; they would stock up with quince jelly well in advance and buy presents to exchange. In 1492 Granada was conquered, the New World discovered, the Jews converted – and Ferdinand gave painted dolls to his daughters for Christmas; and very fine dolls they were with changeable blouses and skirts. Prince John who, as manchild and heir to the throne was no doubt meant to be above such things, got an embroidered purse and Isabella four dozen bolts of finely spun material for veils. For the family generally, Ferdinand supplemented their Christmas sweetmeats with lemon preserves.

As far as its use in government was concerned, no feature of the court was more important than its mobility. The Catholic Monarchs ruled not as the later kings of Spain from a fixed, central capital, but led a peripatetic existence as they crossed the country from town to town, taking the court with them like a menagerie on a lead. In the course of their reign, the monarchs traversed most of their realm in this way, though some areas were better frequented than others, according to their importance. They spent most time in the heartlands of old Castile between the central *cordillera* and the Duero, but often visited New Castile and Andalucia. They would go to Extremadura when Portuguese affairs were prominent, but Aragon they visited comparatively rarely. In this way not only was the monarchs' contact with their subjects and personal role in government maintained, but the burdensome cost of entertaining the court, which fell on the localities where the court resided or the lords who hosted it, was spread across the realm. But the monarchs had to meet the cost of transporting their own cumbrous and colourful caravan: on one occasion in 1481, Isabella paid out to 'The procurators of the commune and the land of the town of Medina del Campo', 14,477 *maravedis* which they had advanced for the hire of sixty-two carts to take 'the baggage belonging to her highness's and the Prince's chambers, and that of the Infanta, the lady Juana, from Medina del Campo to Valladolid'.

4

Government and the Economy

Ferdinand and Isabella repeatedly declared their intention to establish peace and justice at home. But the Castile they ruled was a state permanently organized for external war. Hostilities with Portugal occupied the first five years of the reign. The 1480s were largely absorbed by the conquest of Granada. The Granada war closed amid rumours of conflict with France. And while sporadic fighting broke out against the Turks, the Moors of Africa and the Indians of the New World, the monarchs imposed in their realms an extraordinary degree of economic and political control, not out of a conscious desire to create a 'modern' or 'absolutist' state but because of the emergency conditions arising from the circumstances in which they seized the crown, and continuing from the interminable strain imposed by war. The examples of opposition to Ferdinand and Isabella in their day arose from the effects of war on the economy and on the pockets of their subjects. In Medina the *corregidor*, or royal administrator, García Sarimento, was reported to have denounced the monarchs as 'tyrants' for having held men in oppression. Queen Isabella because of her ill government was in hell and the King of Aragon 'with her never did anything save rob and dissipate these kingdoms'. In 1489 verses appeared denouncing the Granada war in these terms, addressed to the King:

> If you should your intent declare
> The better for your sheep to care
> Or to exalt your law more high
> Or make your pastures broader lie,
> And call well spent the wealth employed
> To see the mountain realm destroyed
> We'd say, What good's this extra land
> With our herds dying by your hand?

Popular reactions of this kind, and the evidence from Bernáldez's pages of the heavy fiscal burden on the common people, show how deeply Castilian society was touched by the tensions of war. Nothing in the government or economy of Castile under Ferdinand and Isabella can be understood except against an awareness of this background.

The population of about seven million souls was widely distributed in hamlets in the north and tiny rural towns in the south. Within Castile, except in the seventeen royal corporate towns, there was no distinctly urban life and no concentration of population of more than eight or ten thousand people. Virtually all the land was owned by the nobility as individuals or by the chivalric Orders and the Church, and was organized as large estates. Pastoral farming was overwhelmingly predominant, but arable *latifundia* must have employed more labour: in most cases the peasants were free of servile obligations, but worked their lord's land in return for the usufruct of an allotment of their own, or else compounded for such services with rent. Lordship was often effectively a matter of jurisdictional power. In Galicia, however, the traditions of serfdom were stronger: the peasant was tied to his holding and his lord's fiscal and personal rights were more extensive than in the rest of the country. The monarchs did not attempt to alter the fabric of society, though they favoured the free peasantry as an industrious section of society, whose freedom and mobility had to be preserved: in particular, the monarchs needed them to be able to settle the conquered lands of Granada and later the New World. In 1480 and at intervals during the rest of the reign they re-affirmed the right of their subjects to migrate and condemned efforts to restrain them on their lords' part. It was representative of the monarchs' attitude towards the free peasantry that Ferdinand should have attempted to promote the displacement of serfdom in the Crown of Aragon – though there the economic modalities of the countryside were more complex than in Castile, ranging from slave-worked *latifundia* in the southern Levant to co-operatives in the Valencian hinterland and proprietary peasant smallholdings in the north. The relaxation of the burdens of villeinage was necessitated there by a long history of social conflict and villeins' revolts.

It was not social but economic regulation by which the monarchs sought to increase the fiscality and therefore the power of their realms. They encouraged what they regarded as productive activities, capital accumulation, large-scale estate management and commerce (because it was an important source of revenue). In no sphere was this more obvious than in their promotion of the *Mesta*, the great corporate organization which controlled Castilian sheep-farming and wool-marketing. In the past, wool exports had been viewed with suspicion and subjected to heavy tolls, but in the opinion of the outstanding authority on the *Mesta*, under Ferdinand and Isabella 'the policy of aggressively promoting wool exports became the keynote of the commercial programme of those royal devotees of mercantilism . . . Every possible device of the new government was turned to the task of concentrating the energies and resources of Castile to sheep-farming'. The monarchs were attracted to the *Mesta* because it was fiscally remunerative and relatively easy to control, with a ready-made and widespread organization. They attached the presidency of the *Mesta* ex officio to the senior member of the Royal Council, staffed its lower echelons with their officials and defended its interests in their courts. The royal machinery of local judicial investigation was used to curb corruption among the receivers to whom the *Mesta* entrusted the collection of its revenues, and, in some ways most important of all, a uniform rate of tolls on grazing and herding sheep was imposed throughout the country: as trade tended to follow the routes of pastoral migrations and markets to coincide with sheep-fairs, this measure was of great assistance to internal commerce; similarly, the monarchs exempted the *Mesta* from internal tolls on the transportation of foodstuffs. For the control of the wool-trade, a register was established at Burgos to allocate ships to the merchants and keep count of the amount, value and destination of their cargoes. Wool production was not only a direct source of exports but also fed the manufacture of cloth, which in turn aroused the rivalry of wool-exporting towns like Burgos with centres of manufacture like Segovia, Toledo and Cuenca. Despite a probable overall rise in output of cloth, Castile – indeed, the whole peninsula – remained a net importer of that commodity. The monarchs opposed enclosures in favour of extending pasture and in 1492 actually ordained that a member of the *Mesta* could not be denied access to a field where his sheep had grazed, nor could his rent be increased, and if he grazed undiscovered by the owner for a season he was to have perpetual grazing rights free of rent. Historians have often criticized the Catholic Monarchs' pastoral bias. The Castilian economy was unbalanced and the arable sector neglected. Shortage of grain, which was sporadic in the early years of the reign and almost continuous from 1506, was no doubt made worse. But in the conditions of war and emergency under which Ferdinand and Isabella laboured, it was essential to cultivate an area of the economy which ensured a high fiscal return and a strong measure of royal control.

Economic regulation under Ferdinand and Isabella meant above all regulation of trade. Out of the civil emergency and Portuguese war which complicated their accession they developed the rudiments of the system which would preserve royal control of trade throughout their reign, by licensing commercial voyages and establishing a corps of ships' scriveners to represent the royal interest and verify the value of the goods carried. Collectors were located in important ports to receive the dues and remit them to the treasury. This system, set up between 1475 and 1480 for ventures in West Africa and the Canaries, was greatly streamlined when the New World commerce opened in earnest. The monarchs then fixed arrival and departure points, and ordered the registering and warehousing of cargoes under supervision of their own administrators in Seville and Cadiz – but a description of the genesis of the institution in Seville which operated this control belongs in another chapter (page 144 below). The restoration of internal trade, which must have been impaired by the civil war, was assisted by renewal of the privileges of the annual fairs and markets, and the gradual unification of the coinage of Castile, which, because of widely varying values, sizes and metal contents, had not favoured the confidence of trade. This appears to be one area in which Castilian practice followed that of Aragon; in 1497, the movement towards a rationalized monetary system began in Valencia and spread from there to the other kingdoms of the Aragonese crown. In the wider context of economic policy, to promote trade and encourage any kind of productive economic activity, the monarchs had to favour the holders of capital – and in particular this meant supporting the alien merchant minorities, of whom the largest were the Genoese and the Jews. The Jews' importance as financiers is evidenced by the longstanding Castilian royal legislation which Ferdinand and Isabella confirmed, exempting them from possible imprisonment for debt. The monarchs' protection of them lasted throughout the Granada war – despite growing pressure for the revocation of their privileges and their expulsion from the kingdom – precisely because of their fiscal usefulness. And from pardons and quittances which the monarchs issued to the Hebrew leader, Isaac Abrabanel, when the Jews finally were driven out, it is evident that his own private fortune ran into millions, and that debts owed to him amounted to more than one million *maravedis*. However, where the financing of large projects was concerned, the Genoese capitalists exceeded even the Jews in importance. Castilian overseas expansion would have been impossible without their support, for it was Genoese merchants who supplied much of the cash for the conquest of the Canary Islands and the voyages of Columbus to America. When Ferdinand confirmed their privileges at the start of the reign for a biennial period which was repeatedly renewed, he admitted,

I understand it to be of advantage in my service and to the increase of my rents, levies and dues ... that they should be allowed to stay and do stay in these my said Kingdoms in order to trade in their goods and articles and merchandise and receive and charge whatever should be owed them by virtue of their said transactions.

It is curious to record that there was almost as much opposition to the privileged position of Genoese merchants as to that of the Jews. Increasingly during the 1490s Ferdinand and

Isabella received petitions and supplications asking them to limit the property-holdings of foreigners in their empire and particularly of Genoese. Lawsuits multiplied as Genoese merchants who had acquired the rights of residents in the townships of the realms were challenged or impugned by locals who wanted them ejected from the offices in which they served. In the 1480s, 1492 and 1498, the monarchs issued ordinances exposing Genoese property to forfeiting or limiting the size of foreign holdings: though these were rarely applied, and many Genoese purchased immunity, it remained a useful weapon in localities where the foreigners were particularly hated, or an individual gave cause for offence; above all it was a useful lever for extortion. Some of the prevailing dislike of foreigners can be detected in the opposition to Columbus: he himself complained of being impugned 'as a poor foreigner', and among the allegations made against him in 1499, for which he was subjected to imprisonment and royal judicial investigation, was the charge that he had planned to give Hispaniola to the Genoese. A representative figure of the Genoese minority was Francesco da Rivarolo (Francisco de Riberol in the Spanish rendering) of Seville. He made his fortune in banking and commerce, in dyestuffs, sugar and cloth, and was so wealthy that one of his debtors asked the monarchs to excuse him on the grounds that 'the Riberol are so rich that it would make no difference'. Francesco had subscribed to Columbus's voyages, the establishment of sugar refining in the Canaries, and the conquest of La Palma; but he suffered most disheartening obstacles to his business. His right to local office in Seville was challenged on grounds of his foreign origin; he was sued for more money than he originally contracted to pay for his dyestuffs monopoly. His colleague and countryman, Francesco Palomar, who had contributed financially to Castilian expansion in the Atlantic, was similarly victimized. Palomar's sugar-mill in Gran Canaria was confiscated under the law limiting foreign property-holdings, although he had paid heavily for exemption and confirmation of his right; and he was heavily fined for transferring money between Castile and Valencia because it was an action technically in breach of the laws against the export of specie. It is remarkable that men like Riberol and Palomar found it profitable to operate in Castile. The fines and forfeits they and their colleagues incurred were in a sense the equivalents of modern taxation: Ferdinand's and Isabella's fiscally primitive state had no other means of levying a fair proportion of the profits of trade.

The nature and aims alike of Ferdinand's and Isabella's economic controls are apparent from the fields in which they showed an interest: shipbuilding, arms manufacture and horse-breeding, for example, because of Castile's war needs. They actually banned the use of mules for riding (exceptions were made for women, friars and the old and sick) in case they should displace horses to the peril of the war effort. They attempted to reduce imports and keep specie inside the country by encouraging a regime of austerity – an early example of deflationary policy. In 1494 they condemned gilding and the use of expensive foreign luxuries as 'an universal source of damage' and declared,

> These brocades and cloths of gold are brought to these our said kingdoms by foreigners who take out gold and silver in the amount for which they sell their wares and thus it leaves our kingdoms. And in the same way in gilding and silvering much gold and much silver are lost without any greater advantage being got therefrom.

The export of specie was specifically prohibited, and as we have seen, merchants could be heavily penalized merely for transferring money from Castile to Valencia.

All royal interventions in the working of the Castilian economy had either a directly bellicose or, more generally, a fiscal purpose. And it was with the same objects in view that Ferdinand and Isabella reformed the financial institutions of government. We shall examine in greater detail in the next chapter the means whereby the monarchs met the costs of the Granada war, but their whole reign was characterized by a continuing and growing expenditure. Royal income was traditionally based on the demesne, which had been much diminished and which Ferdinand and Isabella expanded again, together with the profits of coining, salt taxes, port tolls, levies on livestocks and the profits of justice. Only on the Jews and the Moors could the monarchs impose regular taxes as of right. They supplemented these sources by obtaining subsidies from the towns of the *Cortes*, cash commutations of feudal services from other municipal communities, and grants from the clergy.

Of special importance were the profits on the sale of papal indulgences and the proportions of church tithes granted to Ferdinand and Isabella by the popes. Originally intended to make a contribution to the Granada war, these monies continued to sustain the royal treasury. In the opinion of Francisco Guicciardini, the contemporary Florentine traveller to Spain, they were the monarchs' main support for the rest of the reign.

The royal financial returns at the end of the Granada war have been closely scrutinized and it appears that up to that time a precarious balance was maintained between income and expenditure; but two striking features of royal financial administration are inescapable: its wastefulness, and the monarchs' effective reliance on loans based on anticipations of uncollected revenue. Ferdinand and Isabella neither possessed nor had the time to create a bureaucracy large or specialized enough to manage the fiscal problems which an enormously increased rate both of income and outlay entailed. The core of their financial institutions was the traditional *hacienda*. At its nominal head was the *mayordomo mayor* whose office was a mere sinecure or patronage device. The effective running of their finances was in the hands of the *contadores mayores*, their own lettered nominees who received and accounted for all income and apportioned expenditure. In localities where receipts or disbursements were high – in large ports, for instance – there would be a salaried royal receiver on the spot, whose accounts were made and attested before a public notary, then referred to the *contaduría* for vetting. After approval, the *contadores* then authorized disbursements, which had to be receipted again before a public notary. In addition, the accounts of royal receivers generally had to be annually approved by the nearest royal judicial representative. Even this kind of framework allowed loopholes for corruption. Ferdinand and Isabella were able, however, to do much to reduce losses within the *contaduría* not so much from direct peculation as from the abuse of patronage by their officials, who could build up clienteles of their own by issuing illicit exemptions from taxation or forged receipts. By ordinances of 1476, 1478 and 1484 the monarchs attempted to purge the administration of such practices, including the 'scribeship of rents' in which office the demesne accounts were kept. And in

1478 they appointed their most reliable treasury officials, Alonso de Quintanilla and Díaz de Alcocer, to supervise the others in this respect. Of course 'legitimate' forms of corruption persisted, like levying personal charges on tax farmers and receivers in return for concession of office or approval of accounts: these were regarded as 'fringe benefits' are of certain jobs today. It is remarkable that the monarchs borrowed substantial sums from their own treasury officials – in 1480, for instance, Alonso de Quintanilla pledged money received for the conquest of Gran Canaria, and the contribution by Luís de Santángel, who was in charge of the demesne receipts of the Crown of Aragon, for Columbus's first voyage in 1492 is well known. Gabriel Sánchez, who also helped Columbus, underwrote the monarchs' loans from Barcelona and Valencia at the height of the Granada war. These contributions were based on anticipation of revenues the officials expected to handle for the monarchs, so that a large part of the entire royal financial administration seemed effectively to be farmed out rather than under royal control. Furthermore, it must be remembered that the royal receivers were few and far between: the collection of almost every type of revenue was in the hands of tax farmers and Jews who merely sent lump sums to the *contaduría* and did not have their accounts vetted as the receivers did.

Finally, business was habitually discharged by means of loans, and revenue largely absorbed in repayments. The monarchs' own subjects were obliged to aid them free of interest – but this did not apply in practice to the nobles. The royal source of interest-free revenue thus coincided largely with the taxable wealth of the kingdom and was consequently heavily committed. Ferdinand and Isabella did raise loans of this kind, but were perforce dependent on foreign loans, raised in Germany, Italy and the Low Countries, and on *juros* or pledges of interest sold to nobles for lump sums.

The deficiencies of royal finance had to be met from the exploitation of patronage. Instead of employing all its officials on salaries, as states do today, Ferdinand and Isabella had to win the support of the individuals and classes whose co-operation in government they required – the *letrados*, nobility and clergy. *Letrados* could be readily satisfied with positions of profit in the royal administration supplemented with grants of land and the concessions of monopolies – usually in trade or mining – which they could turn over at a profit to eager merchants. Occasionally, a noble marriage with a royal ward or a family which the monarchs were in a position to influence, would be used to reward a professional administrator. The clergy had to be controlled through relations with the papacy, the pursuit of policies – like the crusade against Moors and Turks – of which they approved, and the use of ecclesiastical appointments in the royal gift, to harness the hierarchy in the royal cause. Regulation of the nobility, however, was a more complex problem, as well as in a sense a more important one because of the size and power of that class. Moreover, owing to the long-popular belief that the Catholic Monarchs 'controlled' their nobles and limited their influences, the question demands close attention. The overwhelming trend of the most recent investigation shows that Ferdinand and Isabella favoured and fostered the nobility. Far from seeking to eliminate them from government and creating, in this respect, a 'modern' state, the monarchs aimed at partnership with the nobility, on whose support their government in fact greatly depended. All one can say on this subject relates to the highest rank of the nobility – those with titles and conspicuous concentrations of jurisdiction and wealth – because they can be readily identified in the sources and information about them is plentiful. It must be remembered, however, that the nobility formed a diverse and disparate class, and it may be that the lesser nobles were worse off under Ferdinand and Isabella than is suggested by some of the examples of veritably great magnates whom we shall meet in these pages. In particular, extensions of royal jurisdiction may have occurred at the expense of lesser seigneurs, and small estates – especially under the pressure of rising prices, which were beginning to tell on the economy – are unlikely to have found conditions as favourable as the vast *latifundia*.

The power of the great nobles had grown continuously since the time of Henry II because of the alienation or usurpation of royal lands and jurisdictions. It would not be misleading to think in terms of a struggle for power between the crown and the aristocracy, in which neither party conceived of excluding the other but in which each sought a dominant role. The general tendency of the kings was towards a greater degree of independence of magnate counsel, and a larger share of local jurisdictions and revenues, while that of the magnates was towards feudal devolution, the passing of royal power in their localities to their own hands and the constraint of royal policy within the limits of their own advice. The nobility was never united in opposition to the king, since there were inevitable clashes of interest, like those we discussed in the first chapter, between regionally powerful families or rivals in the Military Orders, or else some noblemen would find it convenient to support the king at times in order to obtain particular concessions for themselves. It greatly exceeds the evidence, and imposes anachronistic terms on a period of history where such concepts have no place, to represent the fifteenth-century struggles between crown and magnates as a clash of 'absolutism' with 'constitutionalism'.

By the end of Henry IV's reign the struggle was no longer fruitful for either party. The nobles who supported Ferdinand and Isabella did so, as we have argued, because they were ready for a period of peace and retrenchment to enjoy the gains they had made in the civil war, while the Catholic Monarchs on their part needed noble support for their struggle for the crown and were willing to issue considerable rewards to the individuals on their side, as well as making extensive economic and political concessions to the class. The seigneurial regime (that both of lay lords and ecclesiastical) was in many ways strengthened by the reign of Ferdinand and Isabella; conversely, because they won noble support and co-operation, the monarchs were in no danger of finding contractual features intrude by force upon their monarchy nor of losing the large degree of central control of the country which, under the shell of the civil war of 1474–80, they were able to build up. The reality of such dangers had been emphasized in the previous reign, when the magnate coalition had attempted to depose Henry IV; it had been advertised in France, where the King was menacingly opposed by the League of the Public Weal, in Germany by the growing territorial autonomy of the princes and in England by the Wars of the Roses and the power of Parliament. Ferdinand and Isabella were kept mindful of it by instances of the truculence of individual nobles, which we shall describe in a moment, and general demonstrations on the magnates' part, such as their reluctance in 1497 to swear allegiance to the Princess Isabel as heiress presumptive to the crown.

It is therefore not surprising that the monarchs in the *Cortes* of Toledo of 1480, far from destroying the great nobility, as used to be claimed, in fact confirmed them in their dominant social and economic position. It is clear from the work of Vicens Vives and his pupils that throughout Ferdinand's and Isabella's reign and for a long time afterwards the nobles' economic interests were in perfect harmony with those of the monarchs, which may be summarized as the development of the pastoral sector of the economy, and the increased internal circulation of goods. Noble economic power was growing during the reign from increased rents and probably an increase in seigneurial imposts (from work done by Bartolomé Benassar this seems to be true of monastic lordships and is likely to apply more generally). It appears that over the reigns of the Catholic Monarchs and Charles v as a whole, the income of the great nobles kept pace with rising prices. Despite the old view that Ferdinand and Isabella 'destroyed' the nobles, almost the entire surface area of Aragon and Castile remained in noble hands or under seigneurial jurisdiction. Thanks to Vicens Vives, it is now known that the *Cortes* of Toledo contributed to this situation: gifts and hereditary pensions granted to the nobles in the last years of Henry iv's reign were cancelled to the value of about thirty million *maravedis*, but the magnates remained in possession of more than half the total income they had usurped or obtained from the crown in the period covered by these revocations – and they were specifically confirmed in the enjoyment of all the grants they had received in the lavish years of Henry ii and John ii. The monarchs reclaimed certain fiscal rights, such as the grazing taxes, but it is untrue to say that royal finances were restored at the nobles' expense. Dues from trade and papal concessions continued to account for nearly all the funds of the *Hacienda Real*.

Already before the *Cortes* of Toledo the royal patrimony had grown through the forfeitures of the losers of the civil war; but much of this was redistributed to nobles who had sided with Ferdinand and Isabella, or else was later restored to its erstwhile proprietors. Not even the absorption of the enormous Marquessate of Villena into the crown lands could prevent its subsequent partial restoration to the Marquesses. Moreover the Catholic Monarchs actually made quite new alienations from the demesne and lands of the royal towns – the grant of Moya to the Cabreras became a subject of regret in Isabella's will and she stipulated that their gains be restored to the royal patrimony in exchange for compensation elsewhere. The Cabreras seem to have received lands belonging to Segovia, as did the Duke of Infantado (formerly Marquess of Santillana), and the Duke of Alba appears to have acquired the usufruct of royal lands in Avila. The Catholic Monarchs upheld and imparted new significance to the longstanding distinction in Castilian law between land inherited by the monarch, which was inalienable, and that acquired by conquest, which could be granted away. In this way, by distributing as much as half the conquered land of Granada among the nobles, they could actually dispose of land in patronage without diminishing the royal patrimony. Further conquests in Italy, Africa, the Canaries and the New World vastly increased their patronage resources, although in remoter areas their right of dividing the soil was at first useful only in promoting settlement, and later as a source of rewards for royal servants; but the distant wilderness was largely unwanted by the established nobility.

As well as defending the nobles' economic interests, Ferdinand and Isabella tried to preserve the aristocratic 'lineages' – the survival of great families and the unity of their patrimonies. As the researches of Roger Highfield and Luís Suárez Fernández have shown, there were two means of advancing this policy: they encouraged marriages between noble houses and rising families of conspicuous loyalty or wealth, and helped to prevent the break-up of inheritances by means of *mayorazgos* – that is, entails of their estates – in favour of noblemen's eldest-born sons. In 1489, for instance, Pedro Manrique was forbidden from alienating any part of the *mayorazgo* of his lands as count of Treviño from his eldest son. In the same year the monarchs assisted the lord of Robles in setting up a *mayorazgo* for his eldest. It would be tedious to cite too many examples, but the history of the *mayorazgo* of the Canary Islands may be related for its singularity and because it was a jurisdiction noteworthy for its traditions of independence.

In 1476 Diego de Herrera and Inés Peraza were authorized to create a *mayorazgo* of their Canarian lordship, apparently on the assumption that the beneficiary would be their eldest son, Pedro García Herrera, although a younger son, Hernán, was in fact higher in his parents' favour and was administering the isle of Gomera for them. He seems to have been particularly his mother's favourite, named after her branch of the family; when Diego authorized his wife in 1480 to set up the *mayorazgo* on her own initiative, there can have been little doubt that it would be Hernán who would benefit. At this time, he was only his parents' deputy, exercising lordship and administering its incidence on their behalf. In 1484, however, his father died, and his mother, anxious – it seems – to prevent the patrimony from falling into the hands of Pedro, who had rebelled against his parents' authority, and perhaps desirous of freeing herself of some of the burdens of government, soon began to turn Hernán into a seigneur in his own right. In 1486 and 1488, Hierro and Gomera were turned into *mayorazgos* for him and he obtained immediate usufruct, together with the disposal on his own behalf of various prerogatives which had been his parents', and the assurance that on his mother's death all would pass to him save the 'superior lordship' reserved to the crown. Moreover, in the case of Gomera the transmission of the grant by succession was carefully regulated so as to exclude the line of Pedro de Herrera. On the extinction of Hernán's line, the gift was to pass to the line of the youngest son, Sancho. These large subinfeudations by Inés Peraza in favour of her favourite child illustrate the royal policy of favouring the nobles with *mayorazgo*-grants (for the original grant may have been intended as compensation for loss of rights elsewhere) and the working-out of such a grant under the buffetting of circumstance. The original plan – the transmission of the seigneury to the eldest son – was frustrated. But the essential point – the conservation of the patrimony – emerged unscathed.

The promotion of *mayorazgos* was strikingly to the advantage both of the nobility and the crown. For apart from land-grants it was the form in which royal patronage was most sought after by the nobles and therefore one of the principle means whereby the monarchs obtained their support. By implanting primogeniture in certain favoured families, the use of the *mayorazgo* also created a body of younger sons who depended on other forms of royal patronage and of whom some entered the royal service. The Catholic Monarchs also made great play with the right to create noble titles; it was by no means universally accepted that they possessed such a right, and they had to win their point as the kings of the previous century had been obliged to struggle for the exclusive prerogative of creating *mayorazgos*. But Ferdinand and Isabella vindicated their prerogatives in these respects by using them in many cases to the advantage of the existing nobility: five marquesses or counts became dukes – including the Marquess of Cadiz and Count of Medina Celi. Among creations of marquesses and counts the Catholic Monarchs took the opportunity to use their patronage to favour cadet lines and to introduce loyal supporters like Andrés de Cabrera into the titled nobility for the first time.

One source of power and patronage within the noble class was the masterships of the Military Orders, which also involved the control of great wealth. Struggles for the masterships had been a disruptive influence in the past and had helped to cause the disaffection of the Marquess of Villena and Rodrigo Tellez Girón at the start of the monarchs' reign. The fact that the Reconquest, the raison d'être of the Orders, was drawing to a close seems to have affected the members of them and to have created the feeling that the active phase of their history was over. In 1485, at the monarchs' suggestion, the Order of Calatrava decided to elect no new master and to allow the administration of the mastership to pass to the king in perpetuity; in the same year, Ferdinand secured patronage over the two most important priories of the Order of Santiago. In 1493, when the Master, Alonso de Cárdenas, died, who had been the monarchs' nominee during the dispute over the mastership in which the reign began, Ferdinand was elected to succeed him and annexed the administration of the Order to the crown. In 1494 the last master of the Order of Alcántara was induced to renounce his office and Ferdinand again took up the administration: incorporation was in this case deferred for a few years. The process was completed in 1501 when the monarchs obtained a papal bull confirming these changes and allowing Isabella, whose sex precluded her from holding the masterships, to continue the royal administration should her husband pre-decease her.

A word must now be risked in conclusion on the relations between the Catholic Monarchs and their nobles. There seems to have been a period of co-operation caused partly by mutual fear but more effectively by community of interest. But the magnates lost neither their potential for rebellion nor their taste for it. The Dukes of Medina Sidonia, who had flexed their muscles during Isabella's reign, but generally found sufficient employment for their aggression in the Moorish war and expansion overseas, reverted to type after the Queen's death, when a new break in the smooth flow of the succession revived the tendencies to rebellion and self-seeking that had been so evident at the start of the monarchs' reign, thirty years previously. The turbulence which broke out under Isabella's successor Philip the Fair, was so great and the confusion so damaging that it took Ferdinand, returning to take up the regency of Castile following Philip's death in 1506, nearly two years to quell it. The magnates of Andalucia, led by Medina Sidonia, were in frank revolt in the hope of preventing Ferdinand's resumption of power. 'The upheaval is so great', wrote Alonso de Lugo. 'that each man takes what he can get'.

Beyond the spheres of the economy, finance and patronage, Ferdinand and Isabella had to construct a royal judicial and administrative system throughout the country to resolve the crisis prevailing at the start of their reign, to preserve the conditions of internal order which were necessary for the success of foreign war, and to ensure that the military and fiscal potential of the kingdoms was maximized. What one might call the emergency situation amid which they ruled required considerable institutional innovation and extemporization. In the first place, the fact that the heiress of Castile was a woman created problems exacerbated by the conflicting pretensions of Ferdinand and Isabella; we have seen how this situation was met by the marriage contract and the agreements worked out in the first months of their reign. But this meant that the monarch was now two persons – in itself a new and challenging situation.

The government of Ferdinand and Isabella in Castile was joint government – but so articulated that the monarchs could act separately and, in Ferdinand's case, specialize. Pulgar's observation that 'the King and Queen have no political favourites ... know that the King's favourite is the Queen and the Queen's is the King', was not strictly true, for they had other favourites too; but each of the royal couple exerted a strong

political influence in the other's closet. Peter Martyr described
their united government thus:

> If ever it was permitted among mortal men to say that one
> spirit might infuse two bodies, these are two bodies which by
> one spirit and one will are ruled ... they have disposed that
> the Queen should govern in such a fashion that she shall be
> seen to govern jointly with her husband.

Alonso Ortiz repeated the image of the two monarchs 'sharing
a single mind'.

It has frequently been noticed that their chroniclers so often
refer to Ferdinand and Isabella jointly and ascribe all their
actions to 'the King and the Queen,' as though they were a kind
of syncretism, that from these sources alone it is almost impossible to distinguish between the monarchs. This indicates
that Ferdinand and Isabella actively desired to be thought of as
acting in unison. That 'deep love and conformity' to which
they often confessed was not personal affection but a political
necessity – even an institutional structure. On 14 April 1481,
Ferdinand took the momentous step of extending the institution of joint rule to Aragon. Just as Isabella had made him her
'proctor' in Castile and invested him with her legal persona, he
now appointed his wife 'Co-regent, Governor and Administrator General in the kingdoms of the Crown of Aragon ... *in
our presence* and absence alike'. Thus although in almost all
other respects the two parts of Spain remained separate, two
institutions embraced the whole: joint monarchy, and the
Spanish Inquisition (of which we shall speak in its turn). In
practice, Isabella made no independent interventions in
Aragonese affairs, but the measure Ferdinand had taken was
important in helping to create a virtually unexceptionable
impression of joint rule and making it acceptable in all the
monarchs' dominions. Similarly, although technically empowered to do so, Ferdinand never acted individually as king of
Castile without his wife's consent. By an accident of Spanish
history the paradigms of joint rule continued to be appropriate
for fifty years after Isabella's death: first in the case of the
monarchs' daughter, Juana, and her husband, Philip the Fair;
then after Philip's death of Juana and Ferdinand; and finally of
Juana and her son, the Emperor Charles v. But only under the
Catholic Monarchs was joint rule a reality. Isabella's will laid

down that, after her, Ferdinand's participation in Castilian government was to continue, if necessary, by means of a regency vested in him in place of the proctoral powers which had been devised for him in the harum-scarum of the succession war and which he had enjoyed in her time. It may be instructive to reflect that although its usefulness long endured, the idea of joint rule, like the other institutional innovations of Ferdinand and Isabella, was originally an extemporization to meet the emergency in which their reign opened.

The monarch was not a figure remote from the common people, but linked by ties of popular awe and direct jurisdiction to every part of society. The first means of royal contact with the realm was the progress. The court was continually moving from place to place so that the King and Queen should see and be seen throughout the country. On arrival they would accept the hospitality of the great men of the locale and take the chance of improving their amity with them; they would receive the homage of their servants in ecclesiastical, administrative or judicial offices; they would inspect any royal estates in the vicinity. They would continue wherever they were to attend to the daily business of governing the kingdom, legislating by decree, communicating their will by writ to the authorities of other localities, and hearing pleas and petitions arising from litigation up and down the country. Often the plaintiff or appellant sent his proctor to present his case, or commissioned someone already at court to do his pleading for him; but local men, when the monarchs were in their part of the country, might appear before the Royal Council in person.

The weight of business was too great for the monarchs to deal with it all themselves: their council would divide the business among its members, to enable several cases to be heard at once, and permanent chanceries were established at Valladolid and later Granada where appeals could always be entertained. As time went on, the monarchs took an increasingly severe line with local judges who referred trivial or simple cases to them, and referred them back with strict instructions to make a swift judgement. Generally, the cases which ended in the royal courts were never insignificant, but often concerned humble people or reflected the preoccupations of the lowliest levels of society. In an appeal case of the first year of their reign, the monarchs ordered 'Francisco de Solis and his men' to restore 2,000 head of cattle which they had taken unlawfully from 'Pascual and Pedro Garcia, citizens of Lumbreros'.

Central institutions of justice were valueless without local judges, and means of enforcement and policing. We have suggested how in the course of the civil war in which they began to reign, Ferdinand and Isabella introduced representatives into the localities, who formed the cadres of a strong royal presence and participation once peace was restored. The characteristic royal administrative official was the *corregidor*, whose powers lay in the supervision of justice and of the ordinances of the municipal councils: during their tenure, the local authorities actually handed over their powers and were confined to an advisory role. From 1480 the *corregidores* became ubiquitous in the towns of Castile, and the importance the monarchs attached to them may be judged from Púlgar's description of them as a 'divine provision'. Further or alternatively, the monarchs appointed *asistentes* to sit on town authorities, with varying powers: in Burgos, for instance, Rodrigo de Ulloa could expel members of the council, who might not meet without his approval. In the reconquered towns, the monarchs imposed administrations which kept important local offices in their own gift. Despite this policy, towns remained difficult to govern: there was the rebellion of Segovia against the Cabreras, already described; in 1478 Burgos refused to admit Andrés Ribera as governor of the castle and actually provoked a public difference of opinion between Ferdinand, who wished to appease the town, and Isabella, who was unshakable for her nominee; in 1483 Jeréz rebelled against its *corregidor* and obliged the monarchs to accede to the town's demands. Lesser demonstrations against the *corregidores* were legion. When towns were not resisting the monarchs, they were often the foci of other forms of discontent – riots against Jews or foreign merchants, risings of the common townsmen against the urban patricians, legal disputes between trade organizations, turbulence of journeymen and apprentices.

An instance when not only a town but a provincial authority defied the crown occurred in September 1483, outside Vitoria, where the gates were closed in Isabella's face by agreement between the municipality and the 'general junta' of the province of Alava. The Basque provinces enjoyed a special status

D

which they were anxious to conserve and were no doubt suspicious of the elements in Isabella's entourage and policies that were generally hostile to local liberties. Isabella rode up with her prelates and courtiers to verify for herself the fact of the locked portals and was met by all the local judicial officers, the city councillors and even the deputies of the provincial *hermandad* (the citizen-gendarmerie which was usually most loyal to the monarchs), who asked her to confirm the privileges of Alava. In the circumstances she was happy to comply.

Generally the truculence of the towns cannot be ascribed to noble influence in their government. Seville was certainly an exceptional case, where noblemen had threatened to monopolize the council and the brute force of the Marquesses of Cadiz and sometimes the Dukes of Medina Sidonia made themselves felt: in 1478 Ferdinand and Isabella resurrected an old and defunct ordinance forbidding the vassals or dependants of nobles from holding office in the city. The administration of Toledo had also suffered noble encroachment, but the *corregidor*, Gomez Manrique, cut the Gordian knot by ruling in the royal name from 1477 to 1490. There are also frequent examples – at Burgos, Avila, Segovia, Córdoba – of co-operation between the monarchs and the nobles in administering the towns, and opposition nearly always came from the town fathers or communes, who hated outside interference whether its source was royal or aristocratic and were particularly resentful of the spread of a uniform royal administrative system. But it should be remembered that many localities of a municipal type were wholly subject to a seigneurial regime, while even the larger communities and royal towns involved their resident nobility in their governments: holders of judicial offices in Medina del Campo, for instance, had to be local noblemen.

Complementary with the reclamation of jurisdiction and administration was the monarchs' effort to simplify the law and establish a pre-eminent royal law, which would serve to resolve conflicts between the multiplicity of local customs and codes. Legists were still much despised. Joanot Martonell spoke representatively when he likened them to women and said that he preferred action to words. And Tomás Mieres noted that 'knights are full of hatred for the men of the law'; but as we have already seen, Ferdinand and Isabella relied heavily on jurists to help them rule Castile. It is impossible to be sure about the effects of the introduction of printing in the broad spheres of intellectual and institutional history, but it seems incontrovertible that the spread of the press in Spain greatly stimulated the diffusion and stimulated the rise to eminence of the royal law. The great work of codification that Ferdinand and Isabella entrusted to Alonso de Montalvo was disseminated in this way. Many – perhaps a disproportionate number – of Spain's other incunables were juridical works; and royal writs began to be printed in the 1470s. So were Castilian versions of papal bulls, often with judicious alterations or interpolations by the monarchs' servants. As a consequence, the work of the royal chancery was greatly expedited and increased in efficiency. It was with the severely practical aim of training legists and administrators to staff the Church and bureaucracy that Ferdinand and Isabella fostered the universities and favoured new foundations.

A final word must be said of the monarchs' remarkable organ of enforcement, the *Santa Hermandad* – or 'Holy Brotherhood' as it would be literally rendered in English – which doubled as a means of military mobilization. Ever since the thirteenth century a multitude of *hermandades* had existed in different localities as peacekeeping forces, vigilante-style units, or private armies of municipalities in their struggles with their lords. The decayed state of local justice and the lamentable rate of violent crime which prevailed at the death of Henry IV and during the civil wars created the right conditions for a centrally organized and uniform *Hermandad* to be established throughout the country : an attempt to set up such an institution had already been frustrated in the previous reign, but the convening of the *Cortes* of Madrigal in 1476, combined with the organizing talents of two of their administrative servants, Alonso de Quintanilla and Juan de Ortega, gave Ferdinand and Isabella the opportunity to make a new effort successful. A central junta to regulate the local 'branches' was to sit in Toledo. The taxpayers of every town would contribute or be liable for service. The *Hermandad* had jurisdictional and police powers throughout the countryside and small villages and was empowered to execute wrongdoers – brigands, rebels, fugitives from justice – summarily upon apprehension by shooting with arrows. Even within the towns and private jurisdictions, the

Hermandad had the same powers in cases of violent crimes, like murder and rape. Increasingly as the interior of the country was reduced to order by these draconian measures, the *hermandades* became sources of soldiery for the monarchs' use, a kind of permanent citizen militia – almost the cadre of a regular army – and was employed in the conquests of Granada and the Canary Islands. The *Hermandad* excellently illustrates how the emergency conditions in which Ferdinand and Isabella seized the crown promoted the creation of strong institutions of government and so in the long run increased royal power.

The *Hermandad* became assimilated into the war organization of the Castilian state; in 1498 it was re-organized on more military lines and some of its police functions were curtailed. But this official reform had already occurred in practice. What was more, when the French war broke out in 1495 the monarchs formally militarized the Castilian people by ordering every man to equip himself to fight, only men of the cloth being exempted. This was a radical innovation, since it was only the knightly class that by tradition permanently bore arms, supplemented at need by mercenaries and representatives of the townspeople. Research has not yet uncovered the practical implications of this measure, but it remains an interesting glimpse into a society overshadowed by war. Our next task is to examine the wars to which Ferdinand and Isabella committed Castile.

5
The Conquest of Granada

Contemporaries had no doubt that the greatest achievement of
Ferdinand and Isabella was the conquest of the last Moorish
state on Spanish soil – the kingdom of Granada. 'It is the
extinction of Spain's calamities', exclaimed Peter Martyr. 'Will
there ever be an age so thankless', asked Alonso Ortiz, 'as will
not hold you in eternal gratitude?' An eye-witness of the
capture of Granada declared it, 'the most distinguished and
blessed day there has ever been in Spain'. The monarchs of
Europe tendered their congratulations; the University of Paris
sent an encomium; and the Pope bestowed the title, 'Catholic
Monarchs' on Ferdinand and Isabella, calling them 'athletes of
Christ'.

The significance of the Christian victory in Granada
appeared so marked partly because the division of the known
world of the day between Christendom and Islam was not
unlike the confrontation of our own times between the Com-
munist bloc and 'the West'. Two mutually incompatible and
hostile ideologies clawed at one another across the Mediterranean each committed to the other's destruction or conversion,
at times overtly waging war, at others merely struggling to win
the outlying and uncommitted peoples of the world to their
cause. The local victories of one side or the other therefore
seemed to have global importance. Recounting the monarchs'

intention of conquering Granada, the Basque Bartolomé de Zuloaga, for instance, declared that Isabella had 'redeemed Spain, indeed all Europe'. Although in Spain the moon of Islam, which had almost filled the peninsula in the eighth century, had gradually waned to the tenuous crescent it now occupied in the south, no progress had been made in the Christian Reconquest for more than a century, when in 1481 the Catholic Monarchs decided that the crescent should finally be eclipsed. Although Henry IV had announced a crusade against the Moors and had raised funds for the purpose, the money had been spent on other internal needs and the promised war had not been put in hand. Now Granada was enjoying a St Martin's summer in the winter of its life. Its King, Mulay Abu al-Hassan, was famous for his wealth; his soldiers notorious for their contempt of their Christian neighbours. Judged, however, by the standard of the combined might of Castile and Aragon, Granada remained extremely vulnerable. When the Christians were at peace among themselves, the Moors survived by their sufferance alone. Granada was a tributary state, buying its continued independence from Castile with annual *parias*, that is, tributes, of gold. The prosperity of Granada depended on the stability of this arrangement. But when the Catholic Monarchs came to rule in Castile, the Granadines found themselves at last confronted by opponents who would find war more profitable than 'selling protection.'

Ferdinand's and Isabella's own justification of the Moorish war, addressed to the Pope, is of the highest interest.

We neither are nor have been persuaded – they wrote – to undertake this war by desire to acquire greater rents nor the wish to lay up treasure; for had we wanted to increase our lordships and augment our income with far less peril, travail and expense, we should have been able to do so. But the desire which we have to serve God and our zeal for the holy Catholic faith has induced us to set aside our own interests and ignore the continual hardships and dangers to which this cause commits us; and thus can we hope both that the holy Catholic faith may be spread and Christendom quit of so unremitting a menace as abides here at our gates, until these infidels of the kingdom of Granada are uprooted and expelled from Spain.

In a sense what they said was true, for they could indeed have been saved the costs of the war and still have exacted a handsome and permanent tribute from the Moors. However, there were other considerations, impelling them towards war, of a more material nature than those they admitted to the Pope. The wealth of Granada was represented not only by tribute but also by trade and land. The Granadines controlled part of the Saharan gold traffic operated by their co-religionists in the Mahgrib; now, while the demand for gold in the Christian lands was increasing, the usefulness of these intermediaries was dwindling in men's estimation. The volume of trade in silk was even greater than that in gold and its value comparable. Of still deeper significance for Ferdinand and Isabella were the patronage resources they could add to their crown by the conquest of Granada. Since their war of succession many nobles had remained insufficiently rewarded or inadequately appeased. The monarchs had contracted further obligations to their servants, and the existing resources of their kingdoms allowed them little leeway to make up the deficit. The royal patrimony had been critically diminished in the previous reigns and the monarchs were painstakingly attempting to restore a part of it : they did not wish to make any further grants from it to the great men of the realm. They had already exceeded their legal powers in diminishing the royal lands for the Cabreras' benefit, but there was little further scope for more donations of the same sort. Their attempts to take land from the municipalities to use in patronage, had been resolutely opposed by the towns, and experiments of that kind would not be repeated. However, the acquisition of the soil of Granada would resolve the monarchs' difficulties. According to the laws, a monarch's inherited patrimony could not be dispersed, but any lands he acquired by conquest could be freely bestowed on whoever pleased him. That was precisely the destiny which Ferdinand and Isabella envisaged for the kingdom of Granada. By the end of the conquest, more than half its surface area had been distributed among their nobles.

The war was not only a matter of the dilation of Castile's own borders, but had to be considered in the context of the struggle against Islam, where Aragonese interests, and those of Christendom generally, would also play a part. It seems clear that on the eve of its extinction, under Mulay Hassan, Granada was enjoying a revival. The increased demand for silk and specie in Europe may have been a contributing factor, but in any case it was clear that the wealth and strength of the Moors, and their ability to defy and attack their Christian neighbours, were greater now than for a long time previously. Spaniards responded with mingled fear and aggression. The pressure of Islam on the frontiers of Christendom had been grievously felt since the mid-century, when the Turks captured Constantinople. Since then the Ottoman Empire had enormously increased its naval effectiveness in the Mediterranean and developed relations with the Muslims of North Africa and Granada. Ferdinand of Aragon, as King of Sicily, ally and soon king of Naples, and protector of Catalonian trading interests in the East, was particularly apprehensive of the advance of Islam and eager to clear the Muslim bridgehead in Spain from its perilous proximity. Meanwhile, each side in the potential conflict was succouring the other's enemies. Many rebel refugees from Ferdinand's and Isabella's vengeance took shelter at Mulay Hassan's court. At the same time Ferdinand encouraged and negotiated secretly with the dissidents of the kingdom of Granada. For Mulay Hassan's crown too was disputed and doubts of the propriety of his succession disturbed the scruples of other members of his dynasty: he was bedevilled by court intrigue in which the politics of the seraglio embroiled so many Muslim monarchs and had already once been shaken by a rebellion among a portion of his own military nobility – the knights called 'saddlers' from the humility of their lineage.

Finally among the causes of conflict, Ferdinand and Isabella hoped that a remunerative war against the Moors would distract the Andalucian nobles from their own squabbles and so help to bring internal peace to Castile; nor were they disappointed of such expectations, for once the fighting had begun in earnest, even such inveterate foes as the Marquess of Cadiz and the Duke of Medina Sidonia – 'my enemy incarnate', as Cadiz called him – joined forces, and exerted themselves in each other's support. Pulgar reminded Isabella that Tullus Hostilius had made unprovoked war merely in order to keep his soldiery occupied and commended the enterprise against the Moors for 'exercising the chivalry of the realm'.

Although Ferdinand and Isabella ascended the throne with hostile intentions towards the Moors, the struggle with

Portugal forced them to postpone the projected reckoning. Between 1473 and 1478 they were compelled to apply humiliatingly to Granada for a series of truces in which the traditional tribute was probably waived. Certainly in the last and most extensive truce, which was fixed for three years' duration, the Castilians expressly forewent their tribute. The employment of the Count of Cabra in negotiating the truces was significant for he had already contracted and used friendship with the Moors in the course of his private feud against the house of Aguilar. Although in the opinion of at least one chronicler, Christians who made allies of the Moors 'deserved to die for it', and although the law expressly forbade it, yet the practice was common and the private wars of the Andalucian aristocracy throve on the exotic diet of infidel support.

Despite the official peace, border incidents continued unabated, and while the Portuguese confrontation with Castile endured, the Moors took the opportunity to profit from their enemies' differences. 'They were more astute in taking advantage of the truce than the Christians', as Alonso de Palencia observed. Both sides appointed arbitrators as part of the terms of the peace to settle disputes arising from breaches of the truce, but this machinery appears to have been ineffective, for instances were repeatedly referred to the monarchs, who could respond only by making diplomatic representations to the Granadine king; and he, on the Moorish side, was one of the worst offenders in the matter of truce-breaking.

Mulay Abu al-Hassan commited his greatest outrage when he sacked the Murcian town of Cieza in April 1478, putting eighty inhabitants to the sword and carrying off the rest. The helplessness of Ferdinand and Isabella in the face of such action was disturbing: they were unable to obtain the hostages' release by diplomacy and could not afford to ransom them. But to those families who were too poor to meet the price, the monarchs gave permission to beg alms for their ransoms, and relieved them of the need to pay dues, tolls and taxes on the money sent to Granada to obtain the Ciezans' release.

Both sides continued to offend the truce, and Ferdinand and Isabella had repeatedly to admonish belligerents on the Castilian side. On the other hand, once the war with Portugal was concluded, the monarchs introduced a more marked tone of aggression into the circulars with which they plied the

D*

affected areas. At the same time they made diplomatic representations to Pope Sixtus IV for his help in the coming war:
the popes had traditionally conferred the status of crusades
upon wars against the Moors, by associating spiritual benefits
with them. Participants in the fighting could earn remission of
the temporal penalties for their sins, or if they died on
campaign, could be assured of the crown of martyrdom. Those
who did not actually fight could obtain the same reward by
way of a cash commutation: the proceeds from the sale of
such indulgences could, by papal bulls of November 1479, be
employed by the monarchs for the expenses of the war.

When hostilities began in earnest, the non-payment of
tribute by the Moors was at best a pretext on the Castilians'
part and perhaps involved an element of falsification by the
Catholic Monarchs. In his original version of his chronicle,
Hernán de Pulgar said that Mulay Hassan was excused tribute
for three years from 1478 'on account of the war with the King
of Portugal': only in his later version did he say that the war
began over the tribute issue. The sonorous message attributed
to Mulay Hassan, who is supposed to have challenged
Ferdinand and Isabella with the taunt, 'the coffers of Granada
contain no more gold but steel!' is probably apocryphal.

Thus although Ferdinand and Isabella had already decided on
war, and had begun to take counsel with their servants in the
area on how best to unite the Andalucian aristocracy for the
enterprise, the actual commencement of hostilities arose from
the interaction between the truce-breaking on both sides with
the local feuding among the magnates, which had so complicated the war of succession in the south. And it was from the
Moors' side that the first attack came. For the Marquess of
Cadiz, exasperated by the way in which his secular enemy, the
Duke of Medina Sidonia, had recruited help from Granada in
the course of their private war, launched a raid on the Moorish
town of Ronda, an ancient seat of petty Moorish kings, famous
for its bandits and its deep ravine, in 1481. This was the most
spectacular instance of truce-breaking yet. Partly in reprisal
and partly no doubt because they felt the imminence of full-
scale war, the Moors decided to seize strongholds on the
Christian side of the frontier. On a moonless and unsettled
December night of 1481 they lunged forward against Zahara
and other fortified places. The Christians were unprepared for

an attack which was no longer any mere raid but an attempt to invest permanently the assailants' objectives. At Zahara, at least, the Moors were successful; as the house chronicler of the Marquesses of Cadiz wrote,

> They scaled the castle and took and killed all the Christians whom they found within, save the commander, whom they imprisoned. And when it was day they sallied forth and opened the gates of the castle and descended to the town and made captive one hundred and fifty Christian men, women and children, and sent them bound to Ronda.

The response of Ferdinand and Isabella, contrasted with the mildness of their reactions to earlier border raids, is eloquent enough:

> And if it can be said that we take pleasure in what has passed, we say so only because it gives us the chance to put in hand forthwith what has long been in our minds, and by mere chance had been delayed awhile. But now that this last event has happened, we are taking counsel to determine how war shall be waged against the Moors on every side in such fashion that we hope in God that very soon not only shall the town be regained that has been lost but that others will be won in which Our Lord may be served and His holy faith increased and thereby we too shall receive much service.

Even this was an understatement of their war aims. In 1481 Ferdinand remarked to the *adelantado* of Galicia that he would be satisfied with no less than the total expulsion of the Moors from Spain:

> With great earnestness we now intend to put ourselves in readiness to toil with all our strength for the time when we shall conquer that kingdom of Granada and expel from all Spain the enemies of the Catholic Faith and dedicate Spain to the service of God.

The conduct of the war represents the highest point of 'conformity' between Ferdinand and Isabella. Castilian and Aragonese interests were well matched, and while it was necessarily Castile which bore the brunt of the war effort, the Aragonese contribution was important. Above all, Ferdinand himself led the Spanish armies and Isabella deferred to him on all military matters: it is curious that on one occasion when Isabella dared to dissent from her husband's strategy, she prefaced her criticism with words of exculpation – 'May your Lordship pardon me for speaking of things which I do not understand'. The contemporary poet, Juan del Encina, celebrated the difference between Ferdinand's contribution to the war and Isabella's:

> She with her prayers,
> He with many armed men.

One point at which Castilian and Aragonese interests diverged or, at least, failed to coincide in this connexion was the problem of the Pyrenean passes between France and Aragon: Ferdinand's aim was permanently to annexe the counties of Roussillon and Cerdagne in order to close the routes of access to his realm from the north; these two counties had formed part of the Crown of Aragon until 1462, when they were entrusted to French hands as a pledge, but had not been recovered. Now the start of the Granadine war, requiring Ferdinand's attention and forces to be committed in the south, obliged him temporarily to postpone the realization of his policy. Isabella seems to have prevailed upon him to make the brief sacrifice. In fact, within two years of the end of the Moorish War, Charles VIII of France was to cede Rousillon and Cerdagne to Ferdinand.

In some ways for Ferdinand and Isabella, financial stringency was a more formidable problem than the Moors. Even with a wide variety of sources of finance, radical measures were always necessary. Diego de Valera advised the king 'to eat from earthenware if necessary, and melt down your tableware, sell your jewels and appropriate the silver of the monasteries and churches and even sell off your land'. To follow this advice literally would have meant the utter ruin of the monarchy, but fortunately Ferdinand and Isabella found sufficient alternatives.

Papal indulgences though important were in themselves insufficient to pay the costs of sustained war. After the failures of Henry IV's reign, Pope Sixtus was understandably reluctant to invest in Ferdinand's and Isabella's crusade until he had clear proof of the sincerity of their intentions. The bull of 1479 had a limited term of effectiveness, and the revenues it produced were to be divided between the monarchs and the Pope. But early Christian victories in the war convinced Sixtus, and from 1482 he renewed the concessions until the war should end. The Church in other ways too was naturally a willing source of subsidies for so holy an enterprise. Though not obliged to pay taxes, the clergy were generous in helping the King and Queen with portions of their income for particular purposes. Specifically for the Moorish war the monarchs could use their 'royal thirds', the portion of ecclesiastical tithes which the Pope had set aside for the crown's wars with the infidels. And the clergy contributed a further subsidy called the 'tenth' because it was in theory reckoned at a tenth of the Church's income. In fact, however, fixed sums were agreed between the monarchs and the contributors, for the sake of administrative facility. In the opinion of the latest investigator of these revenues and of the expenses of the war, the indulgence funds and tenth accounted for the greater part of the crown's outlay. But they were never alone sufficient. The popes took a third share of the revenues, ostensibly for use against the Turks; more stuck to the fingers of tax-farmers and royal servants. Ferdinand and Isabella had to meet their remaining needs by raising loans and exploiting all available sources of taxation and recruitment. The Jews, for instance, who paid heavy taxes anyway, had to contribute a special levy for the war against their fellow infidels; together with the *mudéjars* – the Moorish subjects of the monarchs – they were exempt from service in the war but made more valuable contributions in cash than they could have rendered in arms.

The monarchs' own subjects were obliged to aid them with loans free of interest, and sums were raised from rich individuals, churches, religious houses, chivalric orders and secular corporations. Above all, the monarchs borrowed from the municipalities, whose ruling bodies would levy the sums required from their residents, each according to his capacity. Generally, the borrowings were made in anticipation of other revenues and were repaid within a year. In the acutely stringent days of 1489, however, the monarchs raised two loans from the townships within a twelvemonth and the term of repayment was much delayed. As security for the sum raised from Valencia, Isabella deposited a crown of gold and diamonds and a jewelled necklace with the municipal authorities that year. At intervals, sums were borrowed abroad, in anticipation of domestic loans, though in these cases interest usually of between nine and twelve per cent had to be paid.

At least in part, or in a restricted sense, medieval wars could pay for themselves. For booty was a further important source of finance. In Castile a fifth of all booty taken belonged to the crown, whilst the rest was divided among the captains responsible for its capture. Thus something was accomplished to satisfy the nobles who served in the war without pay, while the monarchs received money which could be ploughed back into the war effort. The capture of Alhama, the first Christian sortie of the war, yielded 'infinite riches in gold and silver and pearls and silks and clothes of silk and striped silk and taffeta and many kinds of gem and horses and mules and infinite corn and fodder and oil and honey and almonds and many bolts of cloth and furnishings for horses'.

Another item of booty was prisoners, whom their captor could hold to ransom for cash. The scale of a victory was assessed by the size of the booty, and no chronicler's account of an action was complete without a relation of the things and people captured. Movable plunder, however, was unreliable. None might be yielded, or the means might be lacking to carry it off. It was a stricture, not pure praise, that Alonso de Palencia passed on the Marquess of Cadiz when he said that the victory brought that nobleman 'more glory than booty'. This source of recompense for partakers in the war had to be supplemented from the immovable resources of the kingdom of Granada, from the land which the aristocracy coveted and which the monarchs, should they conquer it, would be free to grant away.

Only noblemen and their retinues served for such rewards: most of the soldiery was on wages; some belonged to the *Santa Hermandad* and were paid from local funds; other contingents were levied and paid by royal places as part of their feudal service to the monarchs, much in the same way as a nobleman serving in the war maintained the retainers who accompanied him. Despite the diversity of the sources of funds, their quantity was never sufficient. Pay was frequently in arrears, or met in kind or, especially in besieged places where no kind of payment was available, by way of tokens or promissory notes. During the siege of Alhama the Count of Tendilla issued his men with tokens, whose value he guaranteed and which circulated like paper money for the first time in European history.

In fact, although the greater bulk of their forces served for wages, it was feudal obligations in one form or another which supplied nearly all the monarchs' military needs. The troops directly in their pay were bound to them by vassalic obligations in return for their wages (a relationship similar to that called Bastard Feudalism in England); the nobles and their retinues served by virtue of their duty towards the monarchs as their lords. Above all, the biggest single source of troops was the municipalities, who collectively owed military service to be discharged by those residents of the townships who were members of the municipal communal assembly; it was never necessary to arm an entire town: the assembly either sent volunteers or nominated some of its members. This soldiery was paid from the commune's funds by means of contributions from all the residents, levied, according to their capacity, by agreement. Men served on horse or foot according to their estate and the availability of funds; the total numbers in each arm were determined by the forms of the royal summons to arms. Andalucia brought forth the greatest numbers of troops; the municipalities of other regions in some cases sent their own contingents, but often compounded with cash or hired mercenaries. As well as from the towns, the monarchs obtained troops from the *Santa Hermandad* – generally from outside Andalucia, where the population was already sufficiently burdened with the expenses and manpower requirements of the war. The *Hermandades* supplied mounted forces maintained from provincial tributes, and crossbowmen out of their regular forces; these were paid from grants voted specially by the local committees, as the Moorish war was outside the *Hermandad's* normal peacekeeping functions and terms of reference. Finally, the royal forces were cheaply swelled by arrivals who served without pay in return for a pardon: but their contribution was of small significance, never apparently rising above a thousand men. At the height of the war, Ferdinand had 50,000 foot and 10,000 horse under his command, formidable numbers in the context of medieval warfare. There were no standardized units: men fought with their lords, or their colleagues from their own municipal assembly or *hermandad*, as they had been recruited; their armament was such as they could afford or fitted their social status. *Hermandad* units had standard equipment, and it was an obligation of society for wealthy men to maintain a horse and arms. In addition, the monarchs purchased artillery trains and hired gunners from their own resources, for the war would predominantly be one of sieges.

The course of the war is best summarized in an anecdote which later circulated at the Catholic Monarchs' court. According to this tale, Mulay Hassan one day summoned his sages and in their presence placed a gold platter of great wealth in the centre of one of the large carpets that adorned his palace. He said that he would make a present of the platter to anyone who could lay hands on it without stepping on the carpet. After consideration, all the wise men agreed that it could not be done. The King thereupon rolled up the carpet by hand on either side until only the central area bearing the plate remained unfurled. He lifted the plate, saying that it represented the city of Granada, and the carpet the rest of the kingdom, and that Ferdinand would defeat the Moors by seizing the seaports which gave them succour and the hinterland which yielded their wealth, and end by besieging Granada, when the city should stand alone and all its impregnability avail it nothing. The story is probably apocryphal, but it is accurate enough as a brief statement of the strategy Ferdinand adopted.

The first two years' campaigning, on the other hand, contributed little to the fulfilment of Mulay Hassan's fabled prophecy. The fighting began uncharacteristically and spontaneously with action by the Andalucian nobles in which the monarchs played little part; continued with over-ambitious and generally unsuccessful thrusts by the Christians into the heartlands of the Moorish kingdoms; and ended by proving four things; that the war would be a long one; that Castile had sufficient resources and depth of territory to sustain defeats, whereas the Moors had not; that the Spaniards would rely heavily on exploiting disunity among their foes; and that they could only hope to make progress gradually by conquering the extremities of the realm first and gradually isolating Granada.

The Andalucian nobles achieved an instantaneous and hardly expected unity in the face of the common foe. They embarked on the fighting even before Ferdinand could move south to join them or complete his preparations. The decision by the

Marquess of Cadiz to open the war on the Castilian side by advancing deep into Moorish territory and capturing the town of Alhama committed the Christians to a more or less fixed course of action for the next two years; for Alhama was by no means an undesirable objective: it gave ready access to the Moorish capital itself, menaced the Moors' communication with their westerly provinces around Málaga, and more than compensated for the loss of Zahara. On the other hand it was too deep inside enemy territory to be easily defensible and required the capture of other strongholds, and above all of Loja, nearer the border to the north-east, to make it secure. Thus, although Ferdinand welcomed the seizure of Alhama and encouraged and supplemented the Andalucians' efforts to re-inforce the place, much of the Castilians' energy in the next phase of the war was wasted in defending Alhama and making fruitless efforts to add Loja to their prizes.

The most important issue of the first phase of the war was the capture by the Christians of the rebellious Moorish prince, Abu abd-Allah, or Boabdil, as the Spaniards called him. Boabdil was the plaything of seraglio politics, whose opposition to the King, his father, was inspired and fomented by his mother because of her estrangement from the King. His support came initially from one of the most powerful of the habitually-feuding clans of Granada, the Ibn al-Sarrah, or Abencerrajes in the Spanish rendering, but rapidly acquired a popular basis as Moorish failures in the war vexed the patience of the populace. Thus ironically, the political divisions within the kingdom of Granada were exacerbated by the war with which Abu al-Hassan had hoped to quell them. By a combined palace revolution and popular rising, Mulay Hassan was driven away to Málaga and Boabdil installed in his place in Granada; but his triumph was short-lived, for the Moors were only further weakened by these mutations, and far from reversing the war's unfavourable course, Boabdil brought further military failures and ended by falling into the Castilians' hands after a disastrous action at Lucena in 1483.

The Spaniards called Boabdil 'the young king', from his nineteen years, and 'Boabdil the small' from his diminutive stature. His ingenuousness matched his youth and size. He had of course little bargaining power in his negotiations with Ferdinand for his release: yet the terms to which he agreed in the Treaty of Córdoba of 1483 amounted to a far worse disaster for Granada than his own capture had been. Boabdil recovered his personal liberty and obtained Ferdinand's guarantee of help in his callow efforts to keep his throne. But in return he swore an oath of vassalage to Ferdinand and committed the realm of Granada to a future existence as a mere vassal-state of Castile. This in itself might have been no great calamity – Granada had always been a tributary kingdom, though owing Castile no other obligations in the recent past. Once he had successfully used Castilian help in his own cause, Boabdil might have intended to break his promise (on the grounds that it was made under duress to a non-believer) and restore the full independence of Granada. But the real peril in his compromise with Ferdinand – and the aspect of the situation which Boabdil failed to perceive – was that the Spaniards were no longer willing to tolerate the existence of Granada, even in vassalage. The treaty and release of Boabdil were mere devices on Ferdinand's part to foment civil strife among the Moors and sap the strength of their state in its moment of trial. The Spanish King had tempted Boabdil into unwilling collaboration in what Ferdinand himself called frankly 'the division and perdition of that kingdom of Granada'.

Boabdil was resisted by his father, Mulay Hassan and half-brother Abd-Allah Mohammed, called el Zagal, in whose favour Mulay Hassan abdicated, while the Christians continued to make advances under cover of the Moorish civil war. When Boabdil made some advances in the north along the Christian frontier with Spanish help, and agreed with el Zagal to partition the kingdom, the Spaniards took the opportunity to assail his rear and at last capture Loja. The victory was important to the Christians for two reasons. In the first place Boabdil fell once more into their hands and Ferdinand was able to impose even harsher terms on 'the young king', according to which Granada would be ceded to Castile when Boabdil recaptured his throne, and the Moorish state reduced to the town of Guadix and its environs. It is hard to believe that Boabdil can ever have intended to keep such harsh terms, or that Ferdinand proposed them for any other reason than to prolong the Moorish civil war; but for the present, the new agreement served both subscribers' terms. In the second place the capture of Loja completed the fulfilment of the strategy Ferdinand had pursued since the start of the war and freed his hand to adopt the course his advisers had long urged on him – to conquer the kingdom of Granada bit by bit from its extremities, working menacingly towards the capital. The most important early success of the new stage of the war was the capture of Málaga in 1487. The effort was costly enough. As Bernáldez lamented, 'The villagers were drained by the tax-gatherers because of the vast expenses of that siege'! But the rewards were considerable. Men and supplies could now reach the zone of the fighting by sea; the Moors' communications with their co-religionists across the Mediterranean were significantly affected by the loss of the port; and the whole western extension of the kingdom of Granada had now fallen to the Christians.

Even in the face of Ferdinand's advance, the Moors could not end their internal differences. But Boabdil's partial defeat of el Zagal and return to Granada, with Spanish help, had the paradoxical effect of strengthening Moorish resistance, although Boabdil's was the weaker character and the weaker party. For once Granada was in his power he found it impossible to honour his treaty with Ferdinand and surrender the city into Spanish hands: nor was it prudent for him to do so, once the Spaniards had bereft el Zagal of his territories and power. Boabdil now was chiefly influenced by the militant mood of the inhabitants of Granada and the ferocity with which they would resist any attempt to introduce the Christians. Thus the efforts of Boabdil, which so far had been exerted in effect in the Spaniards' favour against his own compatriots, were henceforth bent toward the defence of Granada and the defeat of Ferdinand. Even in the last months of 1491, when the Spaniards had closed around the walls of Granada and Boabdil had personally resolved, as he did that November, to capitulate, still the indomitable mood of the inhabitants delayed surrender until January 1492. The true terms of the surrender had to be kept secret, and the Spanish troops introduced by a stratagem into the citadel by night, in order to avoid the 'much scandal' – that is, the needless bloodshed – which it was feared the Moors would otherwise cause by a desperate last resistance.

Every stage of the conquest had brought new problems for Ferdinand and Isabella – problems of the fate of the conquered population, the disposal, settlement and exploitation of the

land, the government and taxation of the towns, the security of
the coasts, the assimilation and administration of the conflicting systems of law which the Castilians on the one hand
brought and the Moors on the other maintained, and finally the
difficulties arising from the religious differences between the
two peoples. The monarchs' policy was governed by the traditions of benevolence towards the conquered Moors and co-
existence between the different races, inherited from earlier
medieval practice; but the danger represented by the large
concentration of an alien population, and the compulsion
Ferdinand and Isabella felt to reapportion the land of Granada
among their followers and settle it with their own subjects, also
affected the situation. By the terms of their surrender the
conquered Moors became subjects and vassals of the monarchs,
with all the obligations that implied. Ferdinand and Isabella
even attempted to organize them for military service on the
crown's behalf and to provide coastal watches against invasion;
but that part of their policy was outrageously over-optimistic.
It was from the Muslims of Africa or from the Turks that an
invasion was feared, and most Christians were in no doubt of
whose side the Moors would favour in such circumstances. As
Cardinal Cisneros wrote during his stay in Granada, 'Since
there are Moors on the coast, which is so near to Africa, and
because they are so numerous, they could be a great source of
harm were times to change'. No attempt was made for the first
twenty years following the commencement of the Granada war
and the first conquest of Moslem populations to enforce
assimilation of the Moslem and Christian communities. The
Moors were allowed to have their own laws, under which
converts to Mohammedanism were to be allowed to live if they
so wished. All the 'capitulations' of surrender of the Moorish
townships included promises by Ferdinand and Isabella to
uphold the 'uses and customs' of the inhabitants. The monarchs
respected the leaders of Moorish society, allotting lands to
some in the area south-west of Granada and continuing local
office-holders in the positions of responsibility they created in
the towns; they made special use of this kind of patronage to
induce important Moors to embrace Christianity. On the other
hand, these conciliatory aspects of their policy were secondary
to their main aim of encouraging the Moors to emigrate. This
had the complementary advantage of reducing their potentially

hostile concentration of numbers and of freeing land for re-settlement by Castilians. The populations of fortified towns were forcibly ejected and their land confiscated; many fled to Africa. Increasingly as the conquest went on the monarchs encouraged emigration by dispensing the Moors from tolls and port-dues and even providing transport. The departure of Boabdil for Africa in 1493 did much to encourage the movement, but eventually Ferdinand and Isabella were compelled to abandon the policy of emigration for that of expulsion. That episode belongs to the tale of the failure of religious co-existence, and must be reserved for another chapter.

6

Family and Private Life

In the last two decades of their reign, Ferdinand and Isabella were much occupied with dynastic problems. Their family – its life together, the mutual relations of its members, the lives and happiness of their children and their marriages to foreign princes – was the meeting ground of their personal affairs with matters of state, and the source of the greatest strains and inner conflicts that arose from the discharge of the duties of kingship. It was not only the monarchs' dynastic policy that was shaken by the bereavements and infirmities which struck their family in these years, but Isabella's own happiness, youth and resistance to death.

The monarchs' own relationship was not uniformly happy. The Queen was jealous of the King's paramours and saddened by his infidelities. Her own chastity was an important ingredient of Isabella's reputation in her day. For Peter Martyr – that master of hyperbole – she was 'the mirror of all virtues . . . incomparable'; for the more homely Bernáldez, 'a fine example of a good wife'. The poet Montoro declared her worthy to have given birth to the son of God. And a contemporary memoir on her death extolled 'The exceptional purity of her married life . . . we may presume that never did she yield to the wicked impulse of illicit passion'.

Nevertheless, Isabella's very modesty increased her romantic appeal. Her clampdown on sexual laxity at court gave renewed scope for the traditions of courtly flirtation to flourish. Her reign was rich in courtly love-poems, in which Isabella herself featured prominently among the objects of the poets' admiration, and which recent research suggests were written in the same kind of flirtatious atmosphere as infused the court of Elizabeth I of England. The romantic conceits offered to Isabella are typified in this verse, attributed to Alvaro Bazán:

> When we part,
> Departs my heart.
> Glory hides:
> Sorrow abides.
> Victory vanishes:
> Memory languishes
> And grievous smart.

Bazán's colleague, Juan Alvarez Gato, was perhaps even more explicit:

> My soul is fasting. I appeal
> To you for aid. I'm near to dying.
> All the world knows how my weal
> Is one that you alone can heal.

Or in another verse:

> You are paramount in beauty
> Whereas I in love am first.
> Than your estate is none more great:
> While I with greatest grief am cursed.

Isabella also enjoyed the attentions of other, less literary courtiers, and though there is no evidence that she was ever unfaithful, her favourites were modestly skilled in flirtation and gallantry. According to Castiglione's *Book of the Courtier*, Gonzalo de Córdoba, the 'Great Captain' of the Italian wars, took more pleasure in the Queen's favour than in all his victories: the impression is irresistible that Ferdinand found his wife's male favourites unwelcome; he particularly disliked Gonzalo de Córdoba, whom the Queen had raised from relative obscurity in the royal household and valiant deeds in the Granadine war to supreme command in Italy. After Isabella's death, the 'Great Captain' fell from favour and was humiliated and rapidly superannuated by Ferdinand.

But if Ferdinand reacted unfavourably to his wife's favourites, where there was probably no impropriety to alarm him, Isabella was far more jealous of her husband's frank infidelities. Though Ferdinand always expressed his affection for the Queen in the right conventional language his temperament was more phlegmatic than hers and he did not give her the quality of love which she demanded. Early in the marriage, Hernando de Talavera advised the king, in a list of improvements the confessor counselled him to make to his character and conduct, to be 'far more wholehearted in the love and devotion which you owe to your excellent and very worthy wife'. Ferdinand's amorous tastes, however, were inconstant and unconcentrated. After his marriage he had at least two daughters by different mistresses; both were known as María of Aragon; both professed religion in the convent of Our Lady of Grace in Madrigal. After Isabella's death, Ferdinand petitioned the Pope to legitimize them so that they could serve their community respectively as mother superior and prioress.

Isabella's attitude to her husband's paramours is described by the contemporary humanist, Lucio Marineo: 'She loved after such a fashion, so solicitous and vigilant in jealousy, that if she felt that he looked on any lady of the court with a betrayal of desire, she would very discreetly procure ways and means to dismiss that person from the household, to her own great honour and advantage.' The most notable case was that of Beatriz de Bobadilla, not the Marchioness of Moya but her cousin of the same name (she has sometimes been mistaken for the Marchioness's daughter). She was among the loveliest and cruellest – as later events revealed – of the women of Castile, whom the King openly admired, and Isabella sought to remove. In 1480, the lord of the remotest seignury in the monarchy, Hernan Peraza, of the island of Gomera in the Canaries, came to court to answer charges of causing the death of a rival *conquistador*. The King resolved to have him pardoned in return for his participation with eighty men at his own expense in the conquest of the unsubdued Canary Islands, while the Queen seized the chance to marry Beatriz de Bobadilla to him and despatch her to the distant archipelago, out of reach of Ferdinand's affections. It is curious to record

Beatriz's subsequent career. Her new husband met a violent end in a native insurrection in 1488, to which the young widow violently responded, hanging or enslaving the miscreants. After a celebrated amorous encounter with Columbus, she then married Alonso de Lugo, greatest of the Canarian *conquistadores*, and outlived him to fight tigerishly for her children's rights in the tangled lawsuits, involving rival claimants and royal pretensions, that waylaid their inheritance.

Meanwhile, Isabella's life amid the sophistications of court continued in marked contrast to the violent wilderness of Beatriz's environment, and the Queen's admirers were poets and courtiers, while Beatriz's were captains and conquerors. The political usefulness of literary and artistic patronage was pointed in one of Isabella's replies to the strictures of her confessor. She insisted that she must accept the effusive panegyrics presented to her for reasons of state, however distasteful she might personally find them. As well as casting light on her culture, study of the books and paintings she commissioned or purchased can reveal something of her personal tastes too. It is noticeable firstly that almost all her books were in vulgar tongues, and of Latin works she often had translations too. This is not to her discredit since it suggests that she actually read her books. Bibles and biblical commentaries formed a large part of her library. Next came patristics, biographic and devotional works – not only the raw material of devotion in the form of missals and collections of homilies but also the guide-books to piety that were popular at the time, like the *Vita Christi* of Ludulph of Saxony, the Spanish version of which was written under Isabella's patronage, and the *Consolation of Life*, which was one of the Castilian translations of the *Imitation of Christ*.

To judge from her devotional reading, there was nothing exceptional or impressive about the Queen's piety. It appears rather to have been of a type which was becoming conventional among literate but unlearned laymen. As well as in the *Devotio Moderna*, she was especially interested in the new Franciscan devotional school (which overlapped with the *Devotio Moderna* in some of its characteristics but was largely independent of it despite these similarities), for she patronized versifications of Franciscan sermons and Lives of Christ. Fray Inigo de Mendoza, the *converso* Franciscan poet, produced works of both these types, as did Fray Ambrosio de Montesino, who translated Isabella's version of the *Vita Christi* of Ludulph of Saxony. It was precisely this type of piety, and often these selfsame texts, which inspired the Flemish painters whom Isabella employed.

It was the secular part of her collection of books which most faithfully reflected her interests as monarch. The largest single category featured was law, including the great canonistic glossators but most prominently displaying the law-code of Alfonso the Wise, the *Siete Partidas*. Ferdinand and Isabella continued their predecessors' efforts to enforce uniform laws in Castile, specifically ordaining that the *Siete Partidas* be upheld and commissioning Montalvo's collections, which drew heavily on the same text. Isabella also possessed copies of the local laws or *fueros* – the texts of the existing particularist structure of legal administration. It was not the monarchs' aim to abolish the *fueros* or make administration uniform; merely to establish the absolute superiority of the unified royal code. After law, history was the next weapon in the intellectual armoury of monarchy: it was to be drawn on for example, while the record of the monarchs' deeds was to be preserved for posterity in the same fashion. Isabella's books naturally dwelt on the two Spanish monarchs she most looked to for inspiration from the past: Alfonso the Wise, who ordered the *Partidas* and Saint Ferdinand, who reconquered much of Andalucia from the Moors. She had several general histories of Spain – one of them 'beginning with the Goths', others copies of rescensions of the *General Chronicle* which had been another of the important innovations of Alfonso the Wise, others still more recent chronicles. Ancient history was represented by Plutarch and Livy – neither a wide nor inspiringly humanistic selection.

One of the humanist authors in Isabella's patronage was Antonio de Nebrija, who dedicated to her his biographical masterpiece, the first Castilian grammar-book. The famous words of his preface, 'Language is the instrument of Empire', expressed the sentiment that grammar, like history, was a fitting interest for a monarch and had a part to play in government: partly this was a reflection of the importance of the court bureaucracy – administering the realm was increasingly a matter of perusing memoranda and supplications, and drafting replies, laws and judicial pronouncements; partly it was a reflection of the traditional importance of rhetoric in exchanges between princes, in the preparation of ambassadors, and in the composition of royal documents. But Nebrija actually saw beyond those limits to the use of the Castilian tongue as a unifying force in Isabella's disparate monarchy. Signs of the growing influence of this idea were the zeal with which the early Spanish colonizers sought to teach the Indians Castilian in the New World, the fact that the Emperor Charles v toyed with the idea of spreading the use of language by force, and the interesting remarks of the contemporary historian and diplomat, Guicciardini, who believed that Ferdinand aimed to unite under his sceptre all the peoples of hispanic tongue and culture in the Iberian Peninsula.

Lastly Isabella's library contained books intended for her private edification and amusement. These included two books of chivalric exercises, which were one part of the traditional preparation of a prince that Isabella, because of her sex, had missed in childhood: in the same vein she had Vegetius's military handbook. There were standard works of gnomic wisdom and moral philosophy, including the *Book of Women* of the Franciscan Francisco Jimenez and the *Virtuous Woman* of Alvaro de Luna, Cicero's *De Officiis*, and five copies of Aristotle. Like everyone who had books, she possessed the great encyclopedia of St Isidore of Seville. For light reading she had popular and not excessively demanding books of poetry, including Vergil in translation only, French song-books (French, not Italian, and therefore not humanistic), Boccaccio, entertaining and sometimes scabrous verses of the Arcipresta de Hita, and a prurient version of Æsop. When one recalls the propriety of her sexual comportment, and the strict standards she insisted on at court, it seems curious and significant that her reading was the very reverse of prudish. Above all she seems to have favoured the 'novels' of medieval chivalric romance, fantastic, sentimental and sententious – the kind of works that would later turn Don Quixote's mind. The *Trojan Histories* she possessed were of this genre rather than of genuinely historical character, as were her romances of King Arthur, Hercules and Alexander the Great. She had a taste characteristic of her time for works of physic and astrology. There was nothing heterodox about this: some areas of divination were permitted by the Church; on the other hand, Isabella's medical and astrological lore had a strongly esoteric and mystical bent. Taken together with the mysticism of the new devotional works she read, there seems to be an indication here that the influence of mysticism on Isabella was present, if not pronounced. The Queen may have been mildly hypochondriac; during the illnesses of her husband and daughter she distressed herself so much that courtiers and physicians feared more for her than for the patient – when we come to describe these events we shall see morbid and even envious elements in her reaction to the indispositions of her loved ones. The evidence of her library certainly indicates her concern with medical questions.

Taken together, the surviving lists of Isabella's books reveal cultural interests both practical and personal. On the practical side the ingredients of the syndrome of power – laws, history and grammar – are prominent. The more private contents of her library and collection of paintings show her to have been conventionally pious, but not unaffected by the modern, highly personal and semi-mystical devotion of her day. On the other hand, she showed broad-mindedness in the selection of some quite licentious reading matter. She was bookish in an unlearned and unintellectual way, a keen reader of popular and mentally undemanding works. She was nevertheless anxious about self-improvement and particularly interested in the cultivation of womanly virtues, the norms of princely conduct, and the precepts of moral philosophy.

Lack of information makes it impossible to compare Ferdinand's literary tastes with his wife's, but something can be said of the wider areas in which they bestowed artistic patronage. Ferdinand was also interested in the promotion of humanism. His Sicilian and Neapolitan connexions gave him an acquaintance with and admiration for Italian culture, and he was personally responsible for the infusion of Lucius Marineus and Antonio Geraldini into Spanish humanism. But the Castile of the Catholic Monarchs remained, as had been true throughout the later middle ages, more closely linked to Flemish than to Italian culture. Apart from a few Italianisms in the music of the court, there was no reception of Italian influence in art until the next reign was well advanced. Poetry remained wedded to traditional Castilian lyric forms, painting to the Flemish school. The humanist curriculum, as it developed in Spain, was at best selective in its absorption of Italian humanism, and was preoccupied with moral philosophy (where Spanish thought was heavily reliant on Aristotle) and in particular with the redefinition of virtue and nobility to include 'humane' or literary as well as martial and traditionally chivalric values. The cosmopolitan nature of Ferdinand's own tastes extended to an admiration for Moorish architecture, despite his abhorrence of the rest of Islamic culture. The demolition of the narrow streets of Granada which Münzer says he ordered, was perhaps less of an instance of Renaissance town planning than a measure for the preservation of public order in the hostile, conquered city. In most of their endowments of churches, religious houses and colleges, and their employment of architects and sculptors, Ferdinand and Isabella acted together. To their patronage is owed the blossoming coincidental with their reign, of the finest and most characteristic style of Spanish architecture, now called plateresque from the intricacy with which their masons, as meticulous as silversmiths, embellished the perpendicular structures. The style and the craftsmen alike were native to Spain.

For the painters they patronized, Ferdinand and Isabella looked chiefly neither to Italy nor Spain, but northwards to Flanders and followers of the Flemish school in neighbouring countries. The assembly of the royal collection was entirely Isabella's work, and the overwhelming majority of the approximately five hundred paintings of hers which survive are Flemish. Isabella's employment of northerners, the patronage they consequently found from the Church and noblemen, the pupils they took in Spain and the influence they left behind them revitalized Spanish painting at a time when it had become uninspired, derivative and uninventive, and helped to make Spain for more than a century the home of some of the world's greatest schools of art. Before Isabella's reign, the movement had started through the visits of Netherlandish masters, including Jan van Eyck and – probably – Rogier van der Weyden, of whose work the Queen went on to collect many glorious examples, but it was thanks to her that Flemish influence attained major proportions and the Hispano-Flemish style, in which native artists adopted the lessons of the Flemings, emerged. Among the painters of Isabella's court were several of quite outstanding genius. John of Flanders, in terms of amount of output, quality and numbers of pupils, was paramount in importance. Throughout the school, figure-drawing and composition tended to be somewhat uniform and stereotyped, but John of Flanders distinguished himself by the soft, alluring texture of his paintings and the vivid, translucent effect of his use of colour. John has the greatest number of safe attributions to his credit among Isabella's surviving paintings; from him she commissioned mainly religious scenes – including the greater part of a polyptich for her private devotion. This perhaps indicates that Isabella perceived his greatness and did not keep him occupied with portraits to the exclusion of more personal or creative work. It must be remembered that artists had not yet risen to a position of unqualified social eminence, but were thought of as skilled artisans. Isabella employed painters specifically to record the royal family in portraits; unfortunately, it is not in most cases possible to link the surviving portraits with the names one finds in her household accounts, but in the case of Michael Zittow, enough attributions are certain to mark him out as an artist of great merit. His use of colour was not as evocative as that of John of Flanders but he captured facial expression with intriguing fidelity and could suggest the tactile qualities of hair, fur and clothing materials.

One longs to know just what it was in Flemish art that appealed to Isabella's taste. The Flemings' work was traditional in Spain, where it had long been appreciated at a much higher social level than that of the Burghers of Flanders who patronized it at home. It was inspired by a kind of devotion akin to Isabella's own. It was not a morbid school, as is sometimes claimed, obsessed with death and decay; rather, the art exuded a quiet, pious optimism, though it was often through the portrayal of extremities of pain and suffering that the painters sought to create that mood. The Flemings were realistic in their treatment of details, particularly of the human form and features; but their realism was not 'classical' – they avoided the corporeal glorifications of Italian Renaissance figure-painting. In their landscapes and iconography they often introduced fantastic or mystical elements. Their subjects were nearly always serious and reflective, often pathetic, tearful, sad. In fact, their world, pensive and poignant, was not far from the mental world of Isabella in her later years.

More perhaps than in the areas where their tastes diverged or overlapped, the points of comparison between the temperaments of Ferdinand and Isabella can be studied by their re-actions to critical events. In 1492, for instance, when his career was apparently at its climax, Ferdinand experienced an attempt on his life. To add to the paradox, the incident did not take place in the newly-conquered and still unpacified realm of Granada, but in the King's own Catalonia, nor indeed was it con-nected in any way with the great political events in which he had been involved. Assassination was an occupational hazard of kingship not only because the great consequences which flowed from the murder of the monarch were often a sufficient inducement to his enemies but also because he was frequently exposed to the public at close quarters – dispensing justice to the poor, or receiving acclamations on progresses, festive occa-sions or *joyeuses entrées*. On the other hand, to the protective presence of many attendants was added the thick hedging of divinity that guarded the king : it was generally accepted that a monarch's life was inviolable. Only in the next century, after the great apologists of tyrannicide had done their work, did assassins achieve an appreciable rate of success. The only other instance of a murderous design against the monarchs was furnished by a fanatical Moor, during the seige of Granada, who attacked the Marquess and Marchioness of Moya by mistake. Let us look at the present incident more closely, and at how it affected the royal couple.

Ferdinand, on the occasion of his escape, was holding one of his regular Friday audiences at Barcelona for the purpose of hearing the pleas of his poorer subjects. One of them addressed to the King not a submission but the point of a dagger. Luckily his aim was as untrue as his sense of a subject's duty, for though Ferdinand was struck down, the crowd seems to have realized at once that he still lived. Peter Martyr attributed his survival to the gold chain he wore, which deflected the blow. The bystanders deferred their vengeance on the assailant in order, according to the most reliable account, to learn the motives from which he had acted; yet one doubts whether the poor of Barcelona were such sophisticated jurisprudentialists: probably the royal official who wrote this account for the information of municipal authorities up and down the kingdom was attributing to the crowd his own thoughts and those of the King's immediate entourage. As it happened, the springs of the would-be regicide's motivation proved to be singularly murky.

He was a worker from a nearby town who, says our account, was 'long crazy and out of his mind'. He claimed to have learnt in a vision directly from the Holy Spirit, that he was a king and must never go to confession – what possible connexion there is between these two pieces of information and whether it was the same source of inspiration that prompted him to attack Ferdinand remain unclear to this day. It would probably be rationalizing too much to say that the man was a heretic who sensed the hostility of the King's policies respecting the Inquisition. The interesting feature of the whole incident is not its origins in the delinquent's wayward brain but the monarchs' reactions to it. The event, guided by Ferdinand's supreme political sense, was turned into a field day for royal propagandists. In the first place, the King's attitude towards his attacker was calculated to impress; in this connexion hypocrisy was an essential part of a monarch's equipment – a show of clemency to arouse admiration had somehow to be combined with a real mercilessness rigorous enough to repress rebellion. Thus although Ferdinand humanely wished to spare the man who tried to kill him, the culprit was duly condemned by the Royal Council during the indisposition brought on by the King's wound. Moreover, in the relations of the murder attempt which the monarchs circulated throughout the land, the danger Ferdinand had undergone and the escape he enjoyed, the former at the Devil's hands and the latter at God's, were made to appear as a proof of his kingly virtues. 'It is to be believed', ran the round robin,

> that the Devil attempted by the hand of that man ... to see if he could curtail the good works which ceaselessly his Highness has performed and does perform as well in the favour and increase of our holy Catholic religion as in all else that pertains to justice and to his royal duties, and that our Lord allowed this to happen in order that before all the world should be shown forth more clearly the faith and devotion, constancy, indefatigability, amity, patience and many other and great virtues which repose in his Highness.

It is curious that notwithstanding the culpability attributed to the Devil, the blame attaching to the intending assassin was unmitigated: first he was tortured, in case his insanity was feigned; then by way of punishment his right hand with which

he had done the deed was cut off; then the feet which had
borne him to the scene of his crime; then were plucked out the
eyes with which he took his aim; and finally the heart which
first conceived the nefarious design. As Père Miguel Carbonell,
Ferdinand's archivist, confided to a friend, 'Although he was
possessed by devils, mad, lunatic, senseless, yet he had to die
most cruelly to serve as example and chastisement to the rest
. . . and he died suffering – which was a work of piety'. At last
his corpse was handed over to an indignant populace who
stoned it, burned it and reduced it to dust. It was an ironic
sequel to Ferdinand's factitious clemency.

Isabella's personal reaction was characteristically different
from her husband's. She dashed off to her confessor a letter
redolent with an excess of feminine sensitivity and penetrated
by an introspective syndrome of guilt and terror; for whereas
Ferdinand had looked outside himself to the kingdom at large
to see how he could turn the attempted assassination to his
political advantage, the horror of the event turned the Queen's
thoughts inward, and for all her expressions of sympathy and
tenderness for her spouse, it was really for herself that she most
grieved and feared; rather than to the political possibilities it
was to the advantage of her own soul that she looked by
virtuously providing ten or twelve clerks and friars to pray
incessantly throughout the eight days of the King's indisposition, by occupying herself with the prospects of the condemned would-be assassin's salvation and by taking the
opportunity for a rigorous and on the whole satisfied self-
examination. Meekly she bleated to her confessor, 'The wound
was so big – so Doctor Guadalupe says, for I hadn't the heart to
behold it – so wide and so deep that four fingers' lengths would
not equal its depth and its width was a thing of which my heart
trembles to tell . . . and it was one of the griefs I felt to see the
King suffer what I deserved, without himself deserving the
sacrifice he made, it seemed, for me – it quite destroyed me'.
Subtly, perhaps subconsciously, Isabella was making her own
sorrow seem worse than her wounded husband's. She com-
municated the same impression to those around her. Alonso
Ortiz told her – for he was a consummate flatterer who well
knew what the monarchs wished to hear – that her own suffering was 'almost greater than the king's'. She went on to
commend herself for breaking the would-be assassin's resolve

never to go to confession, even in preparation for his imminent execution: she had summoned a troop of friars to convince him that he must put his soul in order, and 'Suddenly it seemed', she told her confessor, 'that he awoke from a dream' as he acknowledged the wrongfulness of his misdeed. But most prominent among all the reactions which can be observed in Isabella's letter to her confessor was the fear that she herself might be near to death, combined with a deep unease concerning the preparedness of her own soul. Ferdinand's narrow escape convinced her, she said, 'That kings can die from any sudden disaster, the same as other men, and it is reason enough to be ready always to die well'. She then asked her confessor to prepare a list of all her sins, going back to the broken vows of the time of the civil war which brought her to the throne, and which still disquieted her conscience, in order to help her steady her errant soul for death. On the other hand, the situation caused by the attack on Ferdinand did call for political qualities from Isabella too. It is apparent from Ortiz's account that the circumstances caused mutual suspicions and recriminations between the court and the town to break out, which Isabella quelled, though by what means is unclear.

But if their tastes and temperaments sometimes divided Ferdinand and Isabella, one cause which united them more solidly than any other was the fate of their family and dynasty. Isabella inculcated in her daughters a commendable modesty which Ferdinand complemented with a remarkably generous and indulgent attitude. It is significant that Isabella revealed in a letter of 1492 that the lately widowed Princess Isabel 'remains determined not to marry and my lord, the King, promised a year ago not to force her into it'. But in the interests of the house, there were necessary limits in the exercise of such indulgence. In 1478 Pulgar had written to Isabella. 'If your Highness gives us two or three more daughters, in twenty years' time you will have the pleasure of seeing your children and grandchildren on all the thrones of Europe'. The royal family was in fact committed by the nature and traditions of monarchy to a dynastic programme of that sort.

The monarchs began to look for husbands for their daughters almost as soon as they were born. We have seen how their eldest child, the Princess Isabel, was already the subject of marriage negotiations before she had reached the age of five. At that stage her half-intended was Ferdinand, Prince of Capua, but she might also have contracted to marry the Dauphin of France or Philip of Burgundy or, if nothing were settled in the short term, have gone on to make a marriage in England. In fact, peace with Portugal intervened in 1497, when the Princess was nearly nine years old, and determined that her role would be to complement the peace by marrying into the Portuguese house; meanwhile, under the terms her mother agreed with Beatriz of Portugal, she was to be a virtual hostage for the security of the peace. It must be remembered that the birth of a male heir to Ferdinand and Isabella had in the meantime made their elder daughter, because she was no longer heiress presumptive, somewhat more disposable. Nevertheless, the Castilian royal family was still perilously small in those days of prolific infant mortality, and Ferdinand and Isabella were intending to close none of their options too soon. Moreover, details of the dowry and other terms necessarily would take a long time to arrange. Meanwhile, the continued presence in Portugal of Juana *'la Excelente Señora'*, Isabella's erstwhile rival for the crown, half-incarcerated in the monastery of Evora, made the Castilian monarchs anxious for Portuguese friendship, but naturally guarded in their attitude. It was said that negotiations were so protracted on the Castilian side that in 1482 King John of Portugal, who had succeeded Afonso 'the African', presented the Castilian ambassadors with two slips of paper, of which one bore the legend, 'Peace', the other, 'War', and invited them to choose between them. But the Portuguese caused problems on their side too, for while the settlement anticipated in the Treaty of Alcaçovas in 1479 had involved the marriage of Princess Isabel to Prince Afonso, second in line in the Portuguese succession, by 1482 there seems to have been as much interest on the Lusitianians' part in the possibility of marriage with the younger *infanta*, Doña Juana, who was born to Isabella and Ferdinand in 1480 and was closer to Afonso in years. On the whole, however, the birth of this second robust daughter to the monarchs had eased the situation, for it increased the range of future options in Castilian dynastic policy; the position was even better from March 1482, when Isabella gave birth to yet another healthy *infanta*. Within two years the final details of the marriage were worked out. The Princess was to marry Afonso with a dowry of 106,666 *doblas*;

the procedure to be followed in case the union should be annulled – an essential precaution in royal marriages – was agreed; and the necessary dispensations from Rome obtained; at last, the betrothal was solemnized. But Afonso was his betrothed's junior and still too young to wed her outright. Not until 1490 could the marriage take place. By then, although the relationship of Castile and Portugal was good, conditions were otherwise inauspicious, for an outbreak of plague interrupted the festivities.

The atmosphere of joviality and celebration which attended the wedding was prolonged for the visit of Ferdinand and Isabella to Portugal the following summer. While the rest of the court jousted, Afonso and his father went on a hunt in an informal party, but on the way back the newly-wed Prince was dashed from his horse and killed. The monarchs and their daughter turned pale at the news, and the court doffed its finery for mourning. The first peripeteia of Princess Isabel's sad life had struck. The loss of her husband after so brief a union affected her deeply. She resolved to mourn for the rest of her life and above all never again to marry; it was seven years before her distaste was dispelled by the wiles of the monarchs, the exigencies of dynastic policies and the healing course of time.

Relations between Castile and Portugal continued well despite the untimely end to the royal marriage, and the Portuguese heir – soon King, – Don Manuel, was an admirer of Castile who was also by no means unsympathetic to the thought of peninsular unification. The dynastic manoeuvres of Ferdinand and Isabella were therefore directed in the next years towards Castile's other allies, her trading friends and partners in French enmity, England and Burgundy. The last-named state was now a group of Habsburg dominions since the extinction of the line of Valois dukes in 1477, and included the Low Countries, where Castilian merchants operated a lively exchange of wool for cloth. The heir to the Habsburg dominions was Philip of Flanders, son of Emperor Maximilian; he had a sister also of marriageable age, Margaret of Austria. By the 1490s two of Ferdinand's and Isabella's children were old enough to make suitable matches for these imperial siblings. For Philip, there was Doña Juana, the monarchs' second daughter; for Margaret, there was their heir, Prince John, on whom the future of the dynasty rested, and whose early marriage, in his parents' estimation, would make the house secure by increasing its potential fertility and, hopefully, producing another male prince at some future date. The projected matrimonial exchange took place in 1496. The monarchs made the departure of Doña Juana for the north an occasion of national rejoicing, and equipped her with a splendid fleet, commensurate with the glorious marriage she was on her way to make. She was attended by Don Fadrique Enrique, Admiral of Castile, with the Marquess of Astorga and the Counts of Luna and Alba de Liste. The three thousand five hundred men of her retinue, guard and crew were divided among twenty ships. Among provisions for their sustenance were provided two hundred cattle, a thousand chickens, two thousand eggs and something approaching a quarter of a million salt fish; it is curious to note that to the four thousand barrels of wine, there were only three hundred of water – but this was because water could be shipped en route. Yet for all the expense and gaiety of the occasion, Juana's departure took her to a miserable future: past the horizon over which she sailed lay the same kind of pathetic fate as cursed the whole family of Ferdinand and Isabella.

These things, however, were still unforeseeable. The despatch of Juana, and the reception in Castile of Margaret of Austria, were joyous occasions. Yet Margaret's marriage to Prince John in 1476 was already clouded by a presentiment of disaster. Isabella's physicians pointed out that the Prince was still young, young even for his eighteen years, and of weak disposition; they questioned whether he was yet ready for the responsibility of marriage and in particular whether conjugal life was a prudent prospect for the youthful couple. The monarchs believed, however, that their diplomatic obligations to the Emperor Maximilian, with their own hope for their house, demanded an early marriage. Once that had taken place, Isabella is said to have replied to her physicians' objections, 'Those whom God hath joined together, let no man put asunder'. Contemporaries ascribed the subsequent grave sickness of the Prince to his amorous intemperance with his new bride; certainly, the amount of time they spent in bed alarmed the court physicians. But John had never been robust: there is no certain means of identifying his condition, but consumption might explain his general debility. In July 1497, his illness entered its final phase; his tutor did not yet anticipate the worst and wrote to the monarchs, 'If this sickness had only come at a time when your Highnesses had not such need of being elsewhere, your presence would be a sufficient cure of his ill'. But by August, death seemed ineluctable, and the order for the dying Prince's coffin may be read in Isabella's accounts for that month. Ferdinand did repair to their son's side, not in the hope of saving him, but consoling him at the extreme hour with words recorded by Bernáldez: they may not be authentic, but truly represent the Catholic Monarchs' vision of the royal estate:

> Very beloved son, be patient since God has called you, Who is the greatest King of any, and has other realms and lordships greater and better than this which would have been yours and for which you were prepared. He will give them to you and they shall endure for ever. And have heart to accept death, which each man must of necessity once accept, in the hope of going forever to immortality and the life of glory.

In his will John disposed that he should be buried where his parents wished and 20,000 masses said for his soul. In alms he gave a million *maravedis* to house orphans and the poor, and half as much for the ransom of Christians captured by the Moors.

For all the personal unhappiness which thus befell Ferdinand and Isabella, the hopes of the dynasty could not be allowed to die with John. Their prospect of male issue now rested with their daughters, and it was a circumstance that at once gave added poignancy and new hope to the Prince's death that his elder sister had but lately been persuaded to end her ascetic mourning for Afonso, dead now for six years, and to recant her renunciation of marriage. At the very moment of John's passing, Princess Isabel was being married to her deceased husband's brother, King Manuel of Portugal. It was a marriage not without romance, for Manuel had admired Isabella since first meeting her when escorting her to marry his brother seven years before. But the Princess seemed doomed both times to begin marriage amid death and see death quickly end it. Ferdinand tried to keep from Isabella the mournful news of their son so as not to spoil the celebration of their daughter's marriage, but the news was too sad not to be broken. 'For the rejoicing at the wedding', wrote Bernáldez, 'were exchanged lamenting and mourning for the Prince, all within a single week.'

Nor would Princess Isabel's new-found happiness with Manuel long endure. The death of her brother again made her heiress to the crown and her marriage to Manuel had aroused the prospect of peninsular unification under a Portuguese king. There was dissatisfaction with this likelihood in Castile and Aragon: in the former kingdom, the magnates swore fealty to the new inheritor in 1498; in the latter, the nobles were particularly reluctant. But when in the winter of 1499, the Princess was found to be pregnant, all three realms prayed fervently for a male heir. By summer, Ferdinand and Isabella, as is apparent from the Count of Tendilla's correspondence, were themselves gravely ill with a passing malady, so that the Princess's confinement was barely more joyful than her wedding had been. In August, the mood of fearful anticipation was cut short. The Princess had brought forth the longed-for son, but had not herself survived the birth. The monarchs had lost their two elder children; yet they could seek consolation and perceive divine mercy in their new grandson, christened Miguel after the Portuguese line. Soon, however, their hopes in him played them false. Within two years the frail princeling was dead. Ferdinand and Isabella must now have been persuaded of the ill fortune of their house. Their emotions overflowed for all around them to see. Isabella was now nearly fifty, and past child-bearing. Miguel's death, wrote Peter Martyr 'has profoundly affected his grandparents. They have evidently been unable to bear with equanimity so many strokes of fate.' John, Isabel, Miguel: 'this was the third stab of pain to pierce the Queen's heart', perceived Bernáldez. The monarchs ordered 'that no man bear mourning for him', their secretary wrote to Gonzalo de Córdoba, 'since for those of whom it is thus certain that they are going straight to heaven, it is not customary to wear it'.

Isabella had four years to live, in which she never recovered from her accumulated weight of sadness. She now had three surviving daughters, all of whom would live long, but the eldest, Juana, and the youngest, Katharine of Aragon, would have lives of almost unrelieved misery. The third, María of Portugal, had been born in 1482, one of twins of whom the other died at birth. This may not have appeared a favourable omen, but she was the only one of Ferdinand's and Isabella's children to achieve temporal felicity. When Princess Isabel died in childbirth in 1500, María was the only daugther not bespoke; it therefore fell to her to continue the dynastic alliance with Portugal and marry King Manuel, her sister's widower. Despite the uneventful nature of the rest of her life, and the many children she bore, not even María was entirely free of the ill fate of her family, for in the next generation her line was extinguished and the throne of Portugal passed to the only surviving representative of Ferdinand's and Isabella's blood, Philip II of Spain. For the present, these things stayed hidden and María of Portugal was some consolation to Isabella in her afflictions. The youngest child, Katharine, was, however, far away in cold and barbarous England. She had been intended for an English match since 1489, when she was not yet four years old; negotiations had proceeded intermittently throughout the 1490s; and in 1501 she set off to fill the role marked out for her in her parents' policy. She was rapturously received in England – 'better', so Isabella understood, 'than if she had been the saviour of the world', and married with greedy immediacy to Arthur, Prince of Wales, by King Henry VII. But Arthur, a weak child of fourteen years, was as unready for marriage to Katharine as the Catholic Monarchs' own son had been for marriage with Margaret of Austria; but the cause of Arthur's early infirmity may not have been the same. Whether or not his marriage was consummated at all became a major contention in the *cause célèbre* of the sixteenth century – the annulment proceedings between Katharine and Henry VIII; but it seems probable, as Katharine always maintained, that the young couple had no conjugal relations. Arthur's death may have been due to consumption or influenza or, as Bacon said, 'a kind of malediction', for the progeny of Ferdinand and Isabella seemed indeed pursued by a curse. In any event, the death occurred in April 1502, and thereafter Katharine suffered the indignity of being kept pendant by Henry VII on a thread of uncertainty and an inadequate allowance, a semi-hostage in Henry's diplomatic schemes. Isabella never lived to see the worse sufferings inflicted on her child after her own death, when Katharine was further humiliated by Henry VII and then tragically married to Henry VIII, but Isabella nevertheless already found a source of pain in the penurious state in which Henry kept Katharine's household, and – allegedly – the aged King's almost indecent proposal at one stage to marry the widowed princess himself.

A sharper source of grief even closer at hand was the personal decline of the Princess Juana, who, since the death of Miguel, was heiress to the throne. She had much of her mother's romantic tenderness and was similarly emotionally committed to her husband. But Philip 'the Fair' was even more extravagantly unfaithful to Juana than Ferdinand was to Isabella. In 1502 Juana bore a son and heir; a new future hope enlightened the Dynasty; *'cecidit sors super Mathiam'*, quoted Isabella in recognition of that hope. But Juana's visit to Castile in 1503 brought home to her mother the distress to which married life consigned her, and the effects it had upon her state of mind.

Juana's wretchedness resembled Isabella's own, except that it was exacerbated by mental imbalance. The Princess seems to have been a manic depressive. But the context of her melancholia was romantic dissatisfaction. The gravity of her condition, and its grim effects on the ageing Isabella, are apparent from the letters by which the Queen's physicians informed Ferdinand of these things in the summer of 1503.

> May Your Highness believe how great a danger it is to the Queen's health to live as she does in the Princess's company ... and Your Highness should not be surprised for the Princess's condition is so grave that not only to her to whom she is so important and who loves her so much does it cause much anguish, but to anyone, even to strangers. For she sleeps ill, eats little or at times nothing at all; she is very sad and very thin. At times she refuses to speak so that in this respect as at other moments when she seems to be transported, her sickness is very advanced ... so that beyond all the travails and cares which Her Highness usually has to discharge all this weighs harshly upon our lady, the Queen.

After the 'stabs of pain' Bernáldez had observed, the knife was being turned in Isabella's heart. The 1490s had been her personal decade of achievement, in which she had exercised for herself a role in the government and been prominent in dynastic and ecclesiastical affairs and in Castilian overseas expansion. But from the tragic year, 1497, events conspired to destroy her. And the fatal flaw was partly her own, for she was more involved with her family and the personal sources of happiness than a monarch ought to be. She had overcome briefly the political imbalance of her marriage with Ferdinand – the lion had emerged from behind the bars – but her tragic commitment to an ill-starred pursuit of the personal satisfactions of a wife and mother made her an inferior statesman to her husband, and an easy victim to death.

7
Dynastic and Foreign Policies

Under Ferdinand and Isabella, Castile became the most rapidly expanding realm in Christendom. But at the start of their reign, that distinction seemed more likely to belong to France. In 1453 the English had been expelled from Guienne, and retained only Calais of all their outposts in France; the unification of the French monarchy had proceeded under Louis XI, until in 1477 Charles the Rash of Burgundy was defeated and killed and the Burgundian dominions in France recovered for the French crown. Britanny was now the only territorial principality in France capable of defying the monarchy. France was the most populous and most prosperous country in western Europe, and the territorial ambitions of her kings were turning increasingly outward to Italy and the Pyrenees. Meanwhile another phenomenon of expansion was disturbing the eastern confines of Europe, where the Turks threatened the independence of Hungary and had become the major sea-power in the eastern Mediterranean. The containment and, if possible, reversal of these two centrifugal monarchies was the aim of the foreign and dynastic policy of the Catholic Monarchs. The declared obverse of this policy was 'the increase of our own realms'.

In some ways, Aragon and Castile, and therefore respectively Ferdinand and Isabella, were heirs to different traditions of international politics. For most of the late Middle Ages, the English presence in Gascony had tended to combine France and Castile against England in the Hundred Years' War, while Aragon's long frontier with France had made her the enemy of that country. Moreover, Aragonese interests in Italy, where Sicily was a dominion of the Crown of Aragon and the Kingdom of Naples was linked to the Aragonese dynasty, were no affair of Castile's, whose traditions of expansion were confined to the Iberian peninsula and Africa. Finally, the trading partners of the two countries were different. Until the Conquest of Granada Castile had little in the way of a Mediterranean seabord, and the Mediterranean trade of Cadiz and Seville was carried by the Genoese; the ports of Galicia and the Basque country were closer to northern France, England and Flanders. In the Crown of Aragon, by contrast, Barcelona and Valencia were as intimately part of the Mediterranean commercial nexus as Genoa or Venice, and Catalan or Mallorcan traders and shipping were little less prolific.

By the time of Ferdinand and Isabella, however, Aragonese and Castilian interests were drawing together. After the expulsion of England from southern France, the growth of the French monarchy had begun to appear as a threat to the security of all the Pyrenean states. It is worth recalling that Isabella had called the French 'a people abhorrent to our Castilian nation'. The danger was pointed by French attacks on the Biscay coast during Ferdinand's and Isabella's war of succession and expectations of French help for Afonso of Portugal. It was equally in the interests of both Aragon and Castile to defend the autonomy of the papacy when, later in the reign, this was threatened by France. Moreover, the menace of the Turks was felt to be a direct threat to Castile, even before the completion of the conquest of Granada; following that conquest, Castile's crusading energies were bound to be directed at least in part to the Mediterranean, and it would again be common interest, as well as the personal links which bound the Catholic Monarchs, that united Castile and Aragon in the effort to mount a Christian alliance against the Turks. Although it is true that Ferdinand involved Castile in a distinctly Aragonese foreign policy of war against France and intervention in Italy, it is also true that the matrimonial alliance between himself and Isabella was by no means the only cause of that turn in Castilian policy, but merely confirmed the existing trend of events.

At the time of the monarchs' accession in Castile, John II of Aragon, Ferdinand's father, had been labouring to create an alliance of Aragon, Naples, Burgundy and Castile against France, but the relative weakness of the members of this confederation, John's lack of a diplomatic service, the unreliability of Henry IV of Castile, and the inactivity of England frustrated his efforts. Following the distractions of the war of succession in Castile, and the defeat of Burgundy in 1477, it seemed that no effective combination against France was possible. But the bulk of the Burgundian inheritance passed to Maximilian, future King of the Romans and head of the Habsburg Empire: conceivably, Imperial Burgundy would be a more formidable opponent of France than the dominions of Charles the Rash had been. More importantly still, from an Aragonese point of view, Maximilian would be more anxious than Charles to close French routes of access to Italy, where the Empire had other fiefs and areas of influence. At the same time, English power seemed to be reviving, thanks to a temporary suspension of the Wars of the Roses. Therefore, as soon as their war of succession was concluded, Ferdinand and Isabella set about constructing an alliance of 'all who by nature are the enemies of France' – that is, in effect, the rulers of the states which bordered France: England, Imperial Burgundy, Brittany, and Aragon and Castile. The objects of this alliance were defensive: the Spanish monarchs wished to be free to wage war against the Moors, and, if possible, it remained their persistent intention to generate the energies of Christendom in conflict with the infidel rather than internecine strife. Above all they wished to close the access from France to Spain through the Basque country, Navarre, Roussillon and Cerdagne, and deter the French from attacking Italy.

Italy, however, lay like a pile of dry tinder at a spark's leap from France. Contemporaries sensed an important difference between the northern and southern halves of the Italian peninsula. The north was occupied by a medley of republics and petty despotates, which were the object of periodic attempts at unification, but remained too perfectly matched, their relations governed by tension, tempered by war. Genoa in the west was an entirely mercantile and marine power with little in the way of a hinterland and without territorial ambitions in Italy. By contrast the Duchies of Milan and Ferrara and the republic – effectively a despotate – of Florence, in the centre and south of this area, were committed to rivalry and policies of expansion: the commercial ambitions of Florence depended on whether she could dominate Pisa; those of Milan were occasionally aroused by hopes of conquering Genoa. Milan was ruled by the condottiere-dynasty of Sforza, Ferrara by the Gonzaga, who made a useful by-line of war, and Florence by the Medici, who were in perpetual danger of being unseated in favour of a reversion to communal rule. Generally the despotic houses could survive only on a diet of aggrandisement or rumour of war. Venice in the west possessed an enormous hinterland and overlooked Lombardy from the lower reaches of the Po. Thus although unwilling to extend her dominion in the peninsula, and still fully occupied by trade and the delicate balance of her relations with the Turks, she was the largest single power in northern Italy and unable to dissociate herself from the troubles of the region.

These states, and the smaller principalities and feudatories which surrounded them, had preserved for most of the previous forty years an unstable peace, which had been brought about and largely sustained by fear of the Turks or desire to preserve the independence of the papacy. Meanwhile, in the south of the peninsula, the kingdom of Naples, which Italians simply called *il Regno*, in contrast to the republics and principalities of the north, lived a different kind of life under its Aragonese dynasty, permanently perturbed by the same kind of feudal and dynastic problems as characterized the kingdoms of Spain. In particular, the rebelliousness of the Neapolitan barons found a point of focus in the claims of the House of Anjou to the throne of Naples: ominously for the diplomacy of Ferdinand and Isabella, that claim was being openly vaunted on behalf of Charles VIII of France.

Between Naples and the north, the Papal State sat like a garter on the knee-cap of Italy. But the garter was threadbare and loosely tied, in imminent danger of falling or snapping. The elective nature of the papal monarchy had hampered the pontiffs – just as the same difficulty had impeded the Holy

Roman Emperors – from controlling their magnates; it was as much the internal wars of the barons of the Papal State as the central power of the popes that prevented their lordships from becoming principalities in their own right. Ironically, the popes, whose courts heard pleas from all over Christendom, were unable to keep control of jurisdiction in their own state. And the fact that the magnates were heavily represented in the College of Cardinals, from whom the pope was elected, meant that a pontiff could hardly attain the throne without truckling to the feudal adversaries of his government, nor, save in exceptional circumstances, detach himself from the private interests of his own family or faction.

Had French ambitions unleashed themselves on Italy while Ferdinand and Isabella were still distracted by the Moorish war, the consequences for Spain would have been extremely grave. As the monarchs advised the King of England, Henry VII, in 1493, 'We should be unable to raise our hand (against France) without evident peril of losing all our conquests (in Granada)'; they went on in their instructions to their ambassador to warn Henry 'that he already knows the ways the King and dowager Queen of France are accustomed to use in creating suspicion among persons whom they wish to quit of all conformity'. That fear provides the key to the Spanish monarchs' policy in this period prior to the fall of Granada. They had to keep France occupied by diplomacy without over-extending their own commitments to hostile action. Consequently they ran the continual risk of a breakdown of trust between themselves and the allies on whom they relied to engage the French. The areas in which they chose to create trouble for France were the political struggles between the French crown and the Empire in the turbulent municipalities of Flanders and Picardy; Franco-imperial disputes over frontiers and jurisdictions in Burgundy; English pretensions to the French throne; and – above all and for a time with greatest success – the Breton struggle for continued autonomy. It was specifically over this last issue that towards the end of the 1480s Ferdinand and Isabella constructed a loose quadruple alliance with Henry VII, Maximilian and Anne of Brittany, based on the understanding that Spanish and English forces would co-operate in defending Britanny and attacking France from the north and south. But, as we have seen, this was the very moment when the Granada war most heavily burdened Castile, and the monarchs were in no position to play their part in the struggle against France. The result was a temporary rift in Anglo-Spanish relations and the break-up of the alliance in a series of separate peaces, which freed French hands for new martial enterprises. But the Catholic Monarchs' principal objective had been achieved: their isolation from their northern allies and lone confrontation with France had been delayed till the Granada war was over.

Having forced Brittany into submission and the Duchess Anne into marriage, Charles VIII of France had bought peace from Henry and Maximilian. 'At the news of peace among Christians', declared the Catholic Monarchs, 'we cannot do other than rejoice'. Their tone was perhaps begrudging – but not necessary hypocritical. The Moorish war was over by this time – the end of 1492 – and they had less to fear from France. Moreover, in the preceding years they had learned to expect a rich yield in advantage from the clever exercise of diplomacy. They had kept the French distracted not only by political sagacity in identifying the weaknesses they could exploit, but, as Mattingly showed, by the employment of a fine, professional diplomatic service such as had existed previously only within Italy, but which Ferdinand, thanks to his knowledge of Naples and Sicily, had spread to Spain. The monarchs had permanent diplomatic agents at the Papal, Venetian, Imperial and English courts, all of whom were skilled specialists. A representative figure was their English ambassador, Dr Rodrigo de la Puebla, whom Spanish visitors to England abhorred for his Jewish blood and vilified in their reports on his conduct. Characteristically, however, the monarchs trusted their judgement of men and retained de la Puebla in his post. The wide spread of their fixed diplomatic representatives marked a new departure in the conduct of diplomatic relations outside Italy, and, being rapidly emulated by other great powers, helped to make the sixteenth century a time of large and shifting international alliances recognizably akin to those of more recent times.

The nexus of diplomatic relations which Ferdinand and Isabella created in the last two decades of the century was professedly intended as the framework of an alliance of Christendom against the Turks, beyond its usefulness for the containment of France. Ferdinand envisaged himself as the champion of Christendom. To his eulogists he was the legend-

Detail from a painting of the Battle of Higueruela which took place during Ferdinand and Isabella's subjugation of the Moors

Above The triumphal entry of Ferdinand and Isabella into Granada on 2 January 1492, depicted in a bas-relief on the altar of the royal chapel

Opposite above The royal signatures

Opposite below A portrait of 'the Catholic kings' from the monastery at Madrigal de las Altas Torres, the birthplace of Isabella

... p quis deceat observari. Et cauear diligenter a contrario
... Insuper et expresse mandamus q Senus uras pramaticas ... et Indignacioem uras ac penas predictas incurr
... adeorum ... et habitatoribus ac declinantis Ineisdem ignorancia minime valeat allegari Incuius rei t
... metue del campo Decimo septimo die mensis february Septime Indicionis Anno Anativitate dom
... eutesimo quarto

Domini Rex et Regina mandarut
michi Michaelt perez dalmaca

Ju parte ...

The tomb of Ferdinand and Isabella in Granada Cathedral

ary Last World Emperor; to Columbus, 'the chief of the Christians'. In a style he and Isabella frequently used he was 'King of Jerusalem', and though the monarchs had received smilingly Columbus's plans for the conquest of Jerusalem, by the end of his reign Ferdinand was putting similar projects before the *Cortes* as a serious objective. Turkish pressure made the crusade an appealing image throughout Christendom in the late fifteenth century, but differences among Christian powers frustrated the design. And in the period which most particularly concerns us, the jealousy of Charles VIII and Maximilian, both in their own ways as anxious as Ferdinand to lead the movement, helped to prevent its launching. Most English historians have followed Machiavelli in doubting Ferdinand's sincerity; but this is the consequence of a misunderstanding of Machiavelli's cristicism of Ferdinand as 'a prince who breaks his word'. The Catholic Monarchs saw the pursuit of power by secular means as an essential part of their divine duty as rulers. 'God's service and ours' were always coupled in their diplomata. It is true that they sometimes distinguished between their own interests and those of the Church – but always in order to show that it was the latter rather than the former that they were pursuing. In January 1496 for instance, they sought in these terms to justify the French war to their ambassador in England:

> You know already that this war we have with the King of France is not for any interest of our own but to aid the Pope in order that the King of France may restore what he has taken from the Church by force; and he presumes to occupy and make war on the kingdom of Naples which is a feudatory of the Church and as all Christian princes must defend the Pope and the lands of the Church, we, in order to fulfill that obligation and obey the Pope's commands ... opened this war with France.

This statement was strictly incompatible with the admission which the ambassadors of Ferdinand and Isabella had been instructed to make to the French King in December 1494 that *'the war of Naples touches only their own interests whereas that of Granada was chiefly God's cause'* but it is important to make one allowance for the Catholic Monarchs. In the first place, there were two aspects of the Naples war, which they had in mind at different times : their opposition was, on the one hand, a protective gesture to safeguard the independence of the papacy; on the other, as we shall see an affirmation variously of their own right or that of their Neopolitan Cousins against the French King's pretensions to the crown of Naples. Secondly, the monarchs and all their contemporaries recognized a distinction between acts which positively and directly favoured the Church – such as in this case the war against France – and actions in support of dynastic rights, which, while not specifically to the Church's advantage, were nevertheless just in their agent's eyes and therefore consistent with the service of God. It is true that the Catholic Monarchs frequently broke undertakings or construed them in whatever wholly improbable sense most conduced to their own interest. Their intervention in the Naples war was again a prime example, for having promised in the Treaty of Barcelona to support the French King 'in his just pretensions in the realm of Naples', Ferdinand and Isabella excused themselves from compliance on the ground that none of Charles viii's claims in Naples were in fact just. But this was verbal pedantry rather than dishonesty – and thoroughly characteristic of the epoch. Ferdinand was certainly conscientiously capable of committing moral outrages, like his callous partition of Naples in 1500 or unprovoked attack on Navarre in 1512 – but all were cases where he was convinced of the viability of his own claims in law, and where he felt justified by the fact that the broad lines of his policy – defence of papal independence against France and hostility to Islam – were genuinely and undeniably in the general interests of Christendom, however much they happened to benefit Spain in particular. Immediately after the fall of Granada, the prospects of a concert of Christendom and a crusade against the Turks seemed very real to contemporaries. Maximilian, Ferdinand and Charles viii all promised in letters to Pope Alexander that they would take arms in person, and – the Pope wrote to Charles – 'We also, out of zeal to propagate the faith and defend the Lord's flock entrusted to our care, promptly offered with an ardent spirit not only our own faculties and those of the apostolic see but also our own body and spirit in person, to set out against the enemies of our Saviour'.

A strategic plan was actually worked out, involving simultaneous descents through Poland and Hungary and Germany,

Croatia and Greece, with a naval expedition launched from Italy by the Pope and Spain. The final French refusal to co-operate, and the provocation by France of an internecine war in Christendom by France, shocked men far more than any of Ferdinand's particular departures from the ideal code of princely conduct. Ferdinand and Isabella were on strong ground when they complained to Charles VIII, 'It seems to us that your Majesty ought to pursue the enterprise against the infidels, which would do no damage and much good to Christendom'. One observer exclaimed that the French 'were as detested in Naples as the Turks', and the Catholic Monarchs complained that the French treated the deposed Neapolitan royalty 'worse than Moors'. Such expressions are indications of the feeling that France had betrayed Christendom. The pattern established under Ferdinand and Isabella was sustained throughout the sixteenth century: the kings of Spain representing themselves as Christian champions and trying to achieve unity against heretics and infidels; the French demurring precisely because a Christian concert would favour Spain, and later actually allying with the Protestants and the Turks.

In the early 1490s the tempo of events in Italy quickened. The death of Innocent VIII was followed by the election of Alexander VI to St Peter's see. He came to the papal throne with a reputation for wordliness and nepotism which his pontificate did nothing to dispel. Although, according to Peter Martyr of Anghiera, his election was echoed in Spain by fears for the wellbeing of the Church – fears which Ferdinand and Isabella shared and which the pallor of their cheeks attested – there were nevertheless grounds for thinking that the new Pope would favour Aragon and Castile. In the first place, as a Borgia from the eminent Valencian family of the Dukes of Gandia, Alexander was by birth a subject of Ferdinand's. He had been papal legate in Castile and was on close terms with the monarchs. And outside the curia most of the offices by which he had advanced his career had been in the Spanish Church: in not a few cases Ferdinand's patronage had played a part in his promotion. Nor were Ferdinand and Isabella disappointed in the hopes they must have had of the Borgia Pope, for not only did he quickly confirm their shares of Church revenue and extend their power and patronage over the Spanish Church, but he also at once adopted an international policy after their own hearts: that of trying to achieve a concert of Christendom against the Turks; during 1493 he proposed this course to the monarchs of France and Spain, and actually suggested to Ferdinand and Isabella that the Turkish peril was so great in Italy as to require Spanish military presence. It may be, however, that Alexander was thinking as much of the threat of French as of Turkish invasion. On informing Isabella of his election as Pope in August 1492, Alexander seems already to have anticipated this in exhorting the Queen, 'Your serenity, as greatly befits a monarch, from whom others must copy the example of virtuous living, desires to protect and defend the Catholic faith and the patrimony (*honorem*) and liberty of the Church by authority of the apostolic see'.

Ironically, however, the new Pope's policy within the confines of the Papal State helped to provoke a French invasion. Alexander desired, partly as a result of his fears for the independence of the papacy and partly because of his ambitions for his own family, to strengthen his temporal power and create a strong monarchical authority over the disparate seigneuries of the patrimony of Peter. The effect of his rigorous line with his barons, combined with the disappointment of some of them at the result of the papal election, was a rebellion by two of the most powerful 'patrician' families in 1494, and the defection of the port of Ostia, 'gateway to the kindly city of Rome' – as Alexander called it – from the Pope's allegiance. Alexander took the opportunity to renew his pleas to Ferdinand and Isabella to intervene in Italy, but to Charles VIII of France the revolt appeared to smooth the path of his own projected invasion. Meanwhile the existing order was breaking down elsewhere in Italy. In Naples French pretensions were further excited by new unrest among the nobility; in Florence the Medici were threatened by a financial crash, accompanied by the preaching of the revolutionary mystic, Savonarola; and in Milan, the regent, Ludovico Sforza, was attempting to wrest the despotate for himself. It was Ludovico, knowing that he was not strong enough to maintain his position unaided, who made the fatal and decisive call to the French in 1492. The rightful heir to the Duchy of Milan had married a princess of the Neapolitan house. The quarrel therefore affected the French claim to the throne of Naples, and the precise form of Ludovico's appeal – an offer to help Charles VIII vindicate that claim – threatened to plunge the whole peninsula into the crucible of war. Peter Martyr wrote to Ludovico's brother:

> What a great wickedness this is, to have raised Tisiphone from Hell till in your blindness you cannot see your own perdition approach! Ludovico may say, 'Oh, it is hard to yield a sceptre for servitude', but the wise man replies, 'No fruit of violence ever endures'. I, who suffer from the misfortunes of my homeland – of which the French were always the incarnate enemy – think it folly to place a viper or scorpion in one's own bed in the hope that it may poison one's neighbour's. Oh, immortal Gods! What madness is this? Does the serpent, well fed and fired with the heart of a lion's carcass, refrain from biting his enemy? You will all see. Charles, if he has any sense, will know how to exploit his chance.

The prediction proved fair – though Peter Martyr seems to have feared that Ferdinand and Isabella would content themselves with the bait of Roussillon and Cerdagne and not intervene in Italy to redress the upset of a French invasion. And here he underestimated his royal master and mistress. In 1493, King Ferrante of Naples died and the throne passed to Afonso, the sworn enemy of Ludovico Sforza. In January 1494, Charles VIII crossed the Alps. Darkness was falling over Italy, at the end of forty years' twilight between peace and war. The remaining events of 1494 were described eloquently and accurately in a letter of Peter Martyr to the Count of Tendilla that December:

> What Italian can take up his pen without crying, without dying, without being consumed by pain? When Ludovico heard that his nephew was dead, he returned to Milan. He usurped the Duchy. Some think his nephew died of poison. I do not share that opinion at all. He died of a fever brought on by the conjugal excesses from which he would not abstain even when ill – but in any case, Ludovico has been proclaimed Duke.
>
> King Charles continued his advance. Against the Pope's will he entered Rome in arms. Ferrante, son of King Alonso of Naples and heir (if the fates allow) to the throne, who was in Rome with some soldiers, fled precipitately when Charles arrived. Violence, sack and rapine are going on, though

Charles forbids them, just as one would expect of these French brigands. . . .

Pope Alexander lay hidden for a time in Hadrian's fort – that is, the castle of Sant' Angelo. Under assurances from Charles, he returned to his palace, where Charles went to kiss his feet. At the King's insistence, Alexander made a cardinal of Giovanni Materone, who is the King's amanuensis and a great gleaner of money. I omit other details.

On the advice of Ludovico and his brother, Cardinal Ascanio Sforza, King Afonso has abdicated, passing the reins of power to his son, Ferrante. The luckless man is fleeing to Sicily. Ludovico and Ascanio both intend to protect Ferrante because he is nephew of both of them through their sister, and are dissuading Charles from attacking Ferrante, who is now King. They say that their alliance with Charles is against their enemy, Afonso, not Ferrante, their nephew, whom they declare they will not abandon. Thus first with my King and Queen, and now with Ludovico and Ascanio, Charles in his anger burns with threats of vengeance. Raving and heedless he calls Italians and Spaniards alike disloyal. Nevertheless he has left Rome for the Kingdom, taking with him Zizimus, the Grand Turk's brother, who – you will recall – was a hostage of the Pope's. Such is the state of Italy . . .

While Pope Alexander was buffetted from flight into captivity he continued his appeals to Ferdinand and Isabella to act as a counterweight to the invading French. Now the factors which Alexander urged on their consideration were three: the injustice of the French claim to Naples, the need to restore the independence of the papacy, and the hope of reviving the concert of Christendom against the Turks. This must be remembered for the sake of comparison with the purposes that can be detected in the diplomatic correspondence of Ferdinand and Isabella. In March the Pope had been pleading with Charles in these terms:

We now write again to his Majesty, strongly commending the pious intent of his expedition against the infidel and urging the same in order that, laying aside the Neapolitan war which altogether impeded the expedition we had planned and strew the way of Italy and all her Christian neighbours with dire perils and calamities, he may embrace the way of justice which we have offered to his Highness concerning the kingdom, and prosecute the right he claims by legal ways and not by war.

In September, 1494, the Pope sustained the same theme in more desperate circumstances to Ferdinand and Isabella:

Your Majesties, in whom for your Catholic spirit we especially confide all matters of greatest honour, we seek a haven from this most turbulent storm and beseech your aid ... so that if our life, our papal dignity and the estate of our sacred Roman Church you desire to be saved from so many perils, as we doubt not you do, know that we need help and that most rapidly.

The Catholic Monarchs were anxious to answer the papal summons, but they realized that the case, though seemingly urgent, was likely to alter rapidly, and could be safely watched for a while. Above all, they wished to take possession of Rousillon and Cerdagne and to make sure of their domination over Navarre before acting in Italy. They were fortunately assisted by the disorders within Navarre: these they were able to exploit by playing off the factions and obtaining a peace treaty which virtually made Navarre their protectorate. They were in fact determined not to be sucked unwillingly into the maelstrom of the Italian war. It was, I hope to suggest, not even true to say that their hand was forced by the French invasion while their policy was otherwise purely defensive.

From the end of 1494, when they began a series of diplomatic manoeuvres and – more gradually still – of military commitments to reverse the pattern of French success in Italy, it is remarkable that in their appeals to other powers – the independent Italian states, Maximilian and Henry VII – to join them in putting pressure on the French, they exactly echoed the Pope's own reasons for opposing Charles VIII – the injustice of the French King's recourse to arms, the independence of the papacy, the concert of Christendom. Nor did they ever mention any claims of their own over Naples, but canvassed the view that the kingdom was a feudatory of the Pope. For instance, as a result of Ferdinand's and Isabella's diplomacy, all the Italian powers except France, but including Maximilian, the Pope, Ludovico Sforza (who by now regretted the introduction of the overweening French) and the Catholic Monarchs themselves, formed a Holy League 'to the attainment of peace and for the quiet of Italy and the safety of the whole Christian religion, for the preservation of the dignity and authority of the apostolic see, for the guardianship of the rights of the Holy Roman Empire and for the defence and conservation of the common statutes of the aforesaid parties in this consideration, union, bond, alliance and league'. The last Holy League in Italy had been compacted in 1455, when the stated objects were much the same; then the enemy had explicitly been the Turk. But now, although the new League was apparently intended to anticipate the reconstitution of a Christian concert, and was to endure for twenty-five years, its initial task was obviously the expulsion of the French. The parties bound themselves to combine against 'any who unharmed and unprovoked shall attack any of the aforesaid'. Charles VIII's invasion had already placed him in that category.

The same laudable frame of reference was used by Ferdinand and Isabella to justify the French war in negotiations with England and in inviting that country's Monarch to join the Holy League. Henry VII was besought 'as a Christian prince' to 'aid the apostolic seat' and 'obey the Pope'. It is worth comparing these expressions with not only the Catholic Monarchs' diplomatic correspondence with their allies in the League, but also the Pope's with prospective partners in that alliance. Alexander justified the League to the King of Portugal as 'for the common and universal benefit of the whole of Christendom'. The extension of the Holy League to include countries outside the strictly drawn orb of the Mediterranean was a triumph for Spanish diplomacy, especially as Ferdinand and Isabella never expressed openly the anti-French nature of the alliance. They were able to rely on the Pope to do that for them. Alexander acted virtually as an extension of the Spanish chancery, urging Maximilian to make open war on France, and the kings of England, Spain and Portugal to join the League. The Catholic Monarchs' diplomatic service was justly flattered by their success in persuading Maximilian and the Pope to give powers to the Spanish ambassador in London to negotiate on their behalf, as well as that of his own sovereigns, for England's entry into the League. Henry VII was duly persuaded with remarkable rapidity in little more than a year, partly coaxed by the prospect of the hand of Katharine of Aragon for the Prince of Wales, partly urged by his own enmity for France. Henry undoubtedly had no illusions concerning the professed nature of the League, but it is instructive that the King of Scots was sufficiently impressed with the altruism of Ferdinand's and Isabella's arguments to contemplate an alliance which was effectively directed against his ally, the French monarch.

It can therefore be seen that to their allies the Catholic Monarchs represented the confederation against France in entirely disinterested terms and as far as they referred to the French at all, made the defeat of that power seem merely a means to the achievement of a broader unification of Christendom in the face of the Islamic threat. To Charles VIII, however, they confessed a somewhat different and less selfless motive. In December 1494, they informed him unmistakably of their own ambitions in Italy. They desired in effect the conquest of Naples for themselves on the grounds that it was an appurtenance of the Aragonese crown, just as the conquest of Granada belonged to Castile. 'It fell to them (Ferdinand and Isabella)', read their ambassadors' instructions, 'to reconquer the kingdom of Naples and that of Granada, which were both usurped from their predecessors'. In the light of that admission two conclusions seem inescapable. In the first place, apart from their public utterances, Ferdinand and Isabella cherished ambitions of territorial aggrandisement in Italy which they revealed to the French but kept secret from their own allies. Secondly, it is therefore wrong to suggest that the Catholic Monarchs were drawn unwillingly into the Italian war or that their policy towards France was purely defensive. To return to the image of the maelstrom, they had deliberately allowed it to turn until it created a vacuum at its vortex – a power-vacuum in the Kingdom of Naples which they were ready with their own might to fill. To Charles VIII fell the task of removing the cadet branch of the Aragonese house which ruled in Naples. Subsequently, after 1495, the combination of rebellion in Naples against French rule with the action of the states whom Spanish diplomacy aroused against France enabled Ferdinand and Isabella to invade Naples and occupy the country. It must be added that expansion in Italy was a peculiarly Aragonese tradition among the kingdoms of Spain, and that this policy can fairly be supposed to have been Ferdinand's own. It was as if he wished to achieve for Aragon in Naples what he and Isabella had achieved in Granada for Castile.

The Holy League was too frail to triumph by unaided diplomacy. Just as their policy towards France during the Granada war had depended on their diplomatic service, Ferdinand and Isabella had to rely on their army to defeat the French in the Italian war. They were fortunate to lead a people which for twelve years had been truly consecrated to war and to the effort it called forth; as a consequence they possessed a well-trained soldiery. Above all, the coming campaigns would show that they had a commander of genius in Gonzalo Fernández de Córdoba, the 'Great Captain' under whom Spanish troops acquired a reputation for invincibility that lasted a hundred and fifty years. In the first phase of the war, from 1495 to 1498, Ferdinand's freedom of action was trammelled by the need to champion his dispossessed Neapolitan cousin, Ferrante, who had also subscribed to the Holy League; and when Gonzalo de Córdoba invaded Naples from Sicily in 1496 it was ostensibly on Ferrante's behalf. Shortly after landing, the Spaniards suffered their first military check at Seminara: but it was also virtually their last. With Naples in revolt and the hostile northern Italian states in their rear, the French were rapidly finding their hold on the country to be untenable. Recovering from his initial setback, Gonzalo de Córdoba split the French forces and obliged the southernmost of them to capitulate at Atella. The remainder were left with little object save flight.

The Neapolitan dynasty was thus dependent now on Spanish arms for its survival, but Ferdinand still intended to replace it altogether at a propitious moment. The death of Charles VIII in 1498 was in some ways a blow to his plans, for it tended to dissolve the Holy League and raise the threat of a new league against Spain, should Ferdinand's power appear a greater menace now in victory than the French seemed in defeat. In the new situation, Ferdinand actually connived at the re-introduction of the French into Italy in order to prevent the formation of a new combination against himself. In this cunning manoeuvre, he was greatly assisted by the continued Italian ambitions of the new French king, Louis XII, who claimed suzerainty over the Duchy of Milan. By the secret Treaty of Granada of 1500, Ferdinand agreed to support Louis' pretensions and to divide the Neapolitan kingdom equally with him. Thus the main force of the hostility of the erstwhile League powers continued to be directed against France, while Ferdinand effortlessly seized control of half the coveted inheritance. And under the command of Gonzalo de Córdoba, the Spanish troops were free to proceed with the conquest of the French-occupied portion of Naples. The next three years' campaigns, and brilliant victories by Gonzalo de Córdoba at Cerignola and the river Garigliano, delivered Naples up to a Spanish domination that would last for two and a half centuries. Though the French kings continued for fifty years to cast their considerable resources into the furnace of Italian war, the Spanish hegemony over the peninsula burned unconsumed amid the flames, with an increasing brilliance as the sixteenth century lengthened. That future had been pre-figured even before the death of Isabella the Catholic. And before his demise, Ferdinand was asserting his authority, from his Neapolitan base, in northern Italy as well.

Although Italian affairs dominated the foreign and dynastic policies of Ferdinand and Isabella from 1492 onwards, the monarchs also kept up relations with the beys of North Africa, the Sultan of Egypt, and the island communities of Rhodes and Malta, whom they aided in resistance against the Turks. They corresponded as far as Hungary and Poland on the same subject. They were much preoccupied with the maintenance of favourable mercantile relations with England and Flanders and, nearer home, with upholding their influence in Navarre. Above all, a kind of mirror-image on a larger scale of Spanish expansion in the Mediterranean could be seen at the same time in the waters of the Atlantic, where Portugal also participated; the monarchs therefore had to put considerable diplomatic effort into the partition of zones of navigation and spheres of influence with the Lusitanian kings. Making allowance for piracy and the Portuguese share of the Atlantic sea-lanes, Ferdinand and Isabella brought the Atlantic and the western Mediterranean under a single hegemony, which stimulated the interpenetration of the economies and cultures of the two areas in the next century and profoundly affected the history of the period. The Iberian peninsula wore a face of Janus that looked both east and west. We too must now turn and look through the eyes of the westward-gazing mask.

8

Expansion Overseas

(i) The Monarchs and the Settlers

In the fullness of time it has become apparent that the greatest achievement of the Catholic Monarchs' reign was the discovery and colonization of America. But this was by no means clear to contemporaries. The 'Enterprise of the Indies' was denounced by many of the monarchs' advisers as a waste of effort and resources. Yet they persevered because the conquest of the New World responded to the demands of some of their own dearest ambitions, as well as to elements of the traditions they inherited and the needs of their time.

All the Spanish kingdoms – and none more than Castile – had been created in a process of expansion, the reconquest of peninsular territory from the Moors. It was understood, however, that the struggle would be continued overseas in Africa and the Atlantic. Long before enduring conquests in mainland Africa became a practical proposition for the Christians of Spain, jurists of the crowns of Castile and Portugal began to argue over whose was the prior or superior right there. Alfonso XI had told the Pope in 1345 that 'the acquisition of the kingdoms of Africa belongs to us and our royal right' because of his predecessors' record of war against the Moors. In the next century the doctrine was developed so that Castile's title to the *tierras de allende* – the lands of beyond – rested on the supposed lordship over the further shores exercised by the old Visigothic kings, whose rights the Castilian monarchs were thought to have inherited. The same kind of argument was extended even beyond Africa proper to include the Canary Islands. These signs of Castilians' mental preparation for overseas expansion multiplied in the fifteenth century, under the influence of the example of the Portuguese, who carried the crusade against the Moors across the sea to Ceuta in 1415, settled the Azores and Madeira archipelago in the next two decades, and explored the west coast of Africa. By the time of Ferdinand and Isabella, Portuguese rivalry prompted Castilian interference in Guinea, where the monarchs licensed piracy and illicit trafficking between 1475 and 1479, and the Canaries, where they launched a pre-emptive attack on the key island of Gran Canaria in 1478, arriving on the scene just before a rival Portuguese expedition. To the cogency of legal concepts and of Portuguese emulation were added commercial and strategic reasons for expansion. It was important to Castile's economic interests to maintain contact with the sources of the gold trade and the now departed Spanish Muslim realms; the gold was brought mysteriously northwards by Arab 'middlemen' from mines of uncertain location in the West African interior. These we now know to have been in the Bure and Babuk regions of the upper Niger, and Lobi on the Upper Volta, where gold was easy to extract from the alluvial soil. The Genoese by an overland route and the Portuguese by sea had both tried and failed to penetrate the secrets of this traffic; now King Ferdinand attempted the same task. It was expressly part of his purpose in meddling in Africa and the Atlantic, according to the chronicler Palencia, to establish communications with 'the mines of Ethiopia'. Next after gold among the needed commodities was slaves; then came fish, dyestuffs, ivory and shells. Finally, expansion was impelled by the need for space – land to cultivate, not for directly demographic reasons (for it is a popular misconception that Spain was overpopulated) but in order to grow the sugar and corn with which Europe generally was insufficiently supplied. And beyond the local attractions of Africa and the eastern Atlantic lay the hope of establishing contact by sea with the spiceries of the Orient. At the time, the spice-trade was carried overland to the Levant and picked up by Italian, chiefly Venetian, traders in the eastern Mediterranean

– a route which made supply uncertain and prices high.

Lastly, Spain was stimulated to expansion by the goad of Islamic pressure in the Mediterranean. If exploration was thrust far enough along the coasts of Africa, at least a commercial advantage might be gained over the enemy – the Portuguese hoped actually to outflank the Turkish-controlled trade-routes from the Orient. Alternatively, Christian peoples might be encountered to provide allies against Islam, or converts made to help weigh the balance of war in Christendom's favour. Castilian missionaries had obtained papal authority to evangelize on the Guinea coast – the contemporary name for West Africa – as early as the 1460s, though we do not know what use they made of their privileges in that respect. The nearer parts of Africa were already in Muslim – albeit not Turkish – power, and direct blows could be struck by expansion in that direction. In the Treaty of Alcaçovas of 1479, Ferdinand and Isabella expressly reserved to Castile the conquest of the stretch of coast opposite the Canary Islands, where their subjects established a garrison at Santa Cruz de la Mar Pequeña, and continued to make raids and attempts at conquest in a sporadic and individual fashion. In 1492 the monarchs commissioned the conquistador Alonso de Lugo to organize these efforts, but the vastness of the area and the strength of resistance confined him to raiding and the maintenance of coastal footholds. The fall of Granada in 1492 released energies for assaults elsewhere on the mainland. In 1495 the Pope confirmed Castile's rights – for although these had long been assumed, pontifical clarification was useful in the face of conflicting Portuguese claims – and in 1497 a major and successful expedition, which conserved many elements of organization and personnel from the time of the Granada war, seized Melilla for the monarchs. But the same years saw the rise of the Barbary corsairs and, correspondingly, the difficulties of making more than local North African conquests increased. In that area of expansion Ferdinand and Isabella were limited to a coastal, military presence and could not establish settled colonies.

But already before the completion of the Reconquest, when Castilian expansion overseas could be launched in earnest like the ships that bore it, settlers from Andalucia had begun the colonization of the Canary Islands. The first migrants had been shipped there by Jean de Béthencourt and Gadifer de la Salle, the Norman lords who conquered part of the archipelago, acknowledging the suzerainty of the King of Castile, early in the fifteenth century. Béthencourt appealed for colonists at a low social level, who would work the soil themselves and aim at a new exploitation of the conquered lands. In some ways this was a departure from previous medieval colonizing experience, which had usually been aristocratic or mercantile in character. Where a new agronomy was introduced, as in the conquests of the Teutonic Order, the land had been worked by the existing peasantry; or else a merchant 'factory' or quarter had been settled for the purpose of trade, without any disturbance of the existing economic framework, as in the Italian and most Catalonian colonies in the eastern Mediterranean. Colonization at a low social level had not been uncommon, but in the inchoate Spanish Empire would be practised with a new intensity in combination with the transformation of the economies of the settled lands by means of new crops and methods of cultivation. In the Canaries, Béthencourt's beginnings were only tentative: even in the two islands he peopled with his Andalucian recruits, Lanzarote and Fuerteventura, economic reliance on the traditional products – dyestuffs, shells and goats – continued. In the next phase of the conquest, the isle of Gomera remained uncolonized, its Spanish conquerors merely replacing the traditional leaders of society without disturbing the rudimentary pastoral economy, or the tribal, neolithic way of life. But with increased intensity as the century drew on, colonies proliferated and the changes they brought grew more radical. The decisive phase came with the reign of Ferdianand and Isabella, who completed the conquest of the Canary Islands, encouraged their 'peopling' with colonists by means of fiscal exemptions, and imposed a policy of land-and water-sharing, which encouraged sugar production. Madeiran and Valencian personnel were deliberately introduced to run the irrigation and refining industries. Genoese capitalists were brought in with sufficient money concentrations to set up the waterways and mills, and Negro slaves imported to supplement the indigenous and colonial labour-force. As well as sugar, corn was cultivated on dry lands by poorer settlers; and other Spanish crops like grapes, quince and saffron were introduced and nurtured in a garden economy of the Andalucian type, which grew up in the hinterlands of the growing townships. Cattle, pigs and sheep were imported to supplement the goats, while Castilian co-operative pastoral methods were promoted. The indices of the rapidity and extent of change are clear. Before the monarchs' reign, sugar was unknown on Gran Canaria; but within a few years Bernáldez could call it 'a land of many canes'. A clerygyman who visited La Laguna in 1497, within a year of its foundation, found 'only two or three shanties' – but by the end of the reign it had some 6,000 inhabitants. To a great extent, the architect of the new kind of colonial economy was Alonso Fernández de Lugo, who had served in the conquest of Gran Canaria and took command for the wards in Tenerife and La Palma: he seems to have realized that because of the distribution of rainfall in the archipelago, the western islands could be adapted for sugar-farming in a way that had not been possible in the earlier conquests. He introduced the sugar-cane in 1484, as soon as the conquest of Gran Canaria was completed, and risked controversy and unpopularity during his governorship of Tenerife by favouring foreign technicians and capitalists.

It had been partly an economic factor – the demand for sugar – that caused the development of a new kind of colonial economy in the Canaries under the Catholic Monarchs. But Castile was in a sense predisposed to be a great colonizing nation by her juridical traditions – the doctrines of expansion developed during the Reconquest and particularly a principle enshrined in the thirteenth-century legal compilations, that one established title to a *res nullius* by settling it. A critical phase in the elaboration of that principle, as in the history of the Spanish monarchy generally, began in May 1486, when a Genoese adventurer named Christopher Columbus invited Ferdinand and Isabella to sponsor his plan for an exploratory transatlantic voyage, such as had never before been accomplished in recorded history.

On his first voyage under the monarchs' patronage in 1492 Columbus discovered the Antilles and immediately realized the prospect of an advantageous trade in gold from Hispaniola, cotton, mastic, a brazil wood and other commodities – not least of all in slaves. He aimed therefore at a colony not of the Canarian type – not, that is, a total exploitation of the new lands – but a mere mercantile establishment, a trading factory, such as he had known at first hand in the Genoese merchant colonies of the Mediterranean and the Portuguese factory of São Jorge da Mina. He intended that the labour resources of the colony would be supplied by the Indians. He envisaged a large floating and only a small permanent population of colonists and made little effort to ship out labourers. According to his companion, Michele de Cuneo, almost all the personnel he took on his second voyage expected to return to Spain within a few years.

He selected men with technical skills to accompany him – soldiers, sailors, artisans, functionaries, skilled miners and agriculturists. Among the three hundred representatives of different trades whom the monarchs ordered him to take on his third voyage, only fifty labourers figured, and they were accompanied by only thirty women. Ferdinand and Isabella, however, could not be satisfied with a mere trading factory. They wanted the new discoveries to be 'peopled' – that is, colonized at all social levels by their own subjects, in order to bring them firmly under the political control of Castile. As they wrote to the municipalities of their kingdoms in commendation of Columbus's third voyage: 'We have commanded Don Cristóbal Colón to return to the island of Hispaniola and the other islands and mainland which are in the said Indies and supervise the preserving and peopling of them, because thereby our Lord God is served, His Holy Faith extended and our own realms increased.' Nothing could be more explicit. The monarchs did not lose sight of the main purpose of all their provisions: the extension of their own power. They therefore reserved to themselves the metal deposits and logwood of Hispaniola, and were particularly insistent that in dividing the land, Columbus was to alienate no jurisdiction from the crown, but to preserve all the legal sources of power in the monarchs' hands. These aims can be observed in the instructions issued to Columbus before his departure on the third voyage.

Whatever persons [the monarchs wrote] wish to go to live and dwell in the said island of Hispaniola without pay can and shall go freely and shall there be frank and free and shall pay no tax whatsoever and shall have for themselves and for their own and their heirs the things [*sic* – '*cosas*' – for '*casas*' – houses] which they build and the lands which they work and inheritances which they plant in the lands and places which shall be assigned them there in the said island by the persons who through you (Columbus) have and shall have charge.

The object of Columbus's permission to divide the soil was said to be the cultivation of grain, cotton, flax, vines, trees and sugar-cane, and the erection of houses and sugar-mills.

For the monarchs particularly desired that the soil of the Indies should be divided among the colonists, and a new agronomy introduced, just as was being effected by their command at the same time in the Canary Islands. They repeated the same policy, based on land grants and fiscal exemptions, for encouraging immigration, as had been used in the Canaries. Lastly, the elements of the new agronomy were not to be cultivated to the exclusion of the pastoral sector, which the monarchs were determined to favour in their new as in their older realms. Within a few years, as in the Canaries, the labour force of the new colonies was expanded by the importation of Negroes, though the paganism and indiscipline of black slaves so perturbed the early governors, and the Portuguese monopoly of the trade was so strong, that the supply was only intermittent under the Catholic Monarchs. Isabella was personally opposed to the employment of Negroes because she was afraid that their pagan practices would impede Spanish efforts to evangelize the Indians. Even though after her death Ferdinand removed all restrictions on the trade in blacks, the labour force of the New World colonies remained far more heavily dependent on indigenous sources than did that of the Canary Islands; as Columbus insisted, 'The Indians are the wealth of Hispaniola – for they perform all labour of men and beasts'.

Ferdinand and Isabella had established Castile's first colonies and settled their economic modalities – except in the matter of black labour – for generations to come. But outside the economic field, expansion brought peculiar problems of law and government, and put existing Spanish juridical concepts and political institutions to the test, changing some and discarding others. Some difficulties arose from differences and novelties in the methods by which the new lands were conquered. In the Reconquest of Granada, for instance, the monarchs were able to keep control from an early stage, because they controlled the sources of finance – indulgences, clerical subsidies, special taxes and booty – and because the forces of the *hermandades*, municipal levies and Military Orders were under their command. Moreover, the nobility was willing to play its part in colonizing the conquests, whereas nobles were relatively reluctant to join in expansion outside the peninsula : a few invested or took part in the Melilla and Oran campaigns, but of these only the Duke of Medina Sidonia would make a contribution further afield in the Canary Islands – and like that of the Medina Celi in the New World his interest there was mainly commercial. When one thinks of the usefulness of the Portuguese Order of Christ in the early history of Portuguese expansion, the failure of the Castilian Military Orders to participate outside Spain appears significant. (But it must be acknowledged that the Orders in both countries were reluctant to associate themselves with overseas enterprises and the role even of the Portuguese Orders was nominal or at best vicarious.) Above all, the reconquered peninsular lands were governable because they were contiguous with Castile and similar in agronomy and climate.

To exacerbate the effects of their relative remoteness, the methods of finance employed in the conquests of the Canaries and the New World displayed ominous features for the future of royal government there. In the Canary Islands from 1477, the monarchs had placed the burden of financing the conquest on the royal exchequer, and indeed the first expeditions relied heavily on public finance : the methods of finance and recruiting of these early days were largely borrowed from the *Reconquista*. But as the conquest wore on and more expeditions were despatched, private sources of finance and means of recruiting tended increasingly to displace public ones. Instead of wages, the *conquistadores* would receive the promise of *repartimiento* or a share of the soil; instead of the yield from the sale of indulgences or the direct use of the royal fifth to meet the expenses of war, fifths yet uncollected were pledged as rewards to conquerers who could raise the necessary finance elsewhere. In other words, the conquest of the islands was begun with the financial arrangements of the *Reconquista*, and terminated with those of the conquest of the New World.

The monarchs retained a strong, personal interest in the conquest of Gran Canaria, shouldering a large part of the financial burden themselves, introducing their own officials with an accounting system that ensured the continual participation of the *contaduría mayor*, and wielding appointments freely at all levels of command, whereas in Tenerife and La Palma, owing to the much smaller role of public finance in the preparation of the conquests, the governor had far greater privileges and powers than his counterpart on Gran Canaria. These, it seems, he supplemented with ambitions to rule in the maximum degree of independence from peninsular control. In the earliest days of his colonial administration, Alonso de Lugo was able to retain all appointments and administrative enactments (such as the *repartimiento*) in his own hands, in spite of attempts by the monarchs to give popular institutions a role such as they had on Gran Canaria. Columbus threatened to match on Hispaniola the standards of gubernatorial independence set by Lugo on Tenerife.

Columbus's 'broad power' as he called it consisted in royal grants of two types – economic concessions and jurisdictional or administrative rights of a distincly feudal character. Where his formal powers of feudal eminence and jurisdiction are concerned, the source of Columbus's power lay in the conjunction of the offices of Admiral, Viceroy and Governor and their being made inseparable and hereditary. The effect, one could suggest, was to turn the Ocean Sea and all its lands into a feudal seigneury only a short way removed from a principality. Columbus was to have, firstly, in his own sphere, all the jurisdictional rights of the admirals of Castile, consisting of dispensing the highest form of justice and imposing the penalty of death. He also possessed the right of pardon and could judge causes arising in Castile in connexion with the Ocean trade. The nomination of subordinate officers Columbus did not enjoy in its entirety, but could only present a short-list to the monarchs – it seems doubtful, however, whether this modification applied in practice. As Viceroy and Governor, Columbus would be able to enjoy similar rights of jurisdiction and appointment and could command the obedience due to the monarchs. His dignity as Viceroy, being hereditary and inseparable from his other charges, was higher than that of the Aragonese Viceroys, on whose office his was in some respects modelled.

It seems that Columbus gave rather more thought to the

implications of the concessions than the monarchs; later, as the enormous extent of his discoveries was revealed, Ferdinand and Isabella were obliged to disregard or supplant many of his offices and powers. Theoretically, the only means open to them to restrain him was the judicial investigation of a governor's conduct, the *residencia* or *pesquisa*, to which he was submitted twice during his term. He was the only official of the Spanish crown up to that time, apart from Alonso de Lugo in Tenerife, to undergo such a process while still in office. The same means were used to keep his son and successor, Diego Colón, in check. The fact that Columbus was never able to rule his domains in surly independence was partly a consequence of the fact that he exercised his privileges not in his own right but as representative of the monarchs: the local opposition that grew in the colony was able both to complain and act. Moreover, his colony was to be so underdeveloped that Columbus had few opportunities to apply his jurisdictional powers – and he had perforce to spend much of his time in Castile. The monarchs were able to interpret the terms of their grants in a way most unfavourable to Columbus, depriving him of his privileges and breaking the exclusivity of his titles and offices. After an arduous litigation, the Columbus family finally gave up their claims to Columbus's privileges, long after their substance had been lost, in 1556. In more dramatic terms, the episode can be seen as the triumph of a centralizing monarchy over a feudal tendency at the periphery of its empire.

The insubordination of the governors was excelled by the ungovernability of the colonies, for they were compounded partly of adventurers and ne'er-do-wells: by the very nature of the colonies as frontier societies, even the best settlers were naturally men of restless and indomitable disposition. Hispaniola under Columbus had a continuous history of violence and rebellion; he repeatedly pleaded with the monarchs to send him friars for the reform of his people and lettered officials to cope with the judicial problems that were beyond his capacity. Because of the vast distances involved, and the cost of communication between the colonies and Castile, local litigation was held up and embittered by appeals to the peninsula; justice was impaired, and complaints against governors' excesses piled up in the colonies without redress. Ferdinand and Isabella quickly found a partial solution in frequent changes of governor or frequent judicial enquiries into the administrations. Under the governor or other local representative, the political life of the colonies had the municipal forms characteristic of Castile: administration was in the hands of a municipal or insular council – *cabildo* – whose members were usually elected locally and confirmed by the monarchs. The Canaries also had popular assemblies or *concejos*, which served as a check on the activities of governors and councils. In these early years, political institutions remained thin on the ground, and the growth of the colonies would soon prompt the introduction of regional, permanent, royal tribunals called *audiencias*.

Once colonies had been established, the next task was to regulate their trade. In common with medieval precedents the monarchs appear to have thought of establishing a staple for the particular products – gold and spices – which they hoped to receive from the Indies trade. They were sensible from the first of the need to control navigation there, to ensure their own participation in the unexpected profits, and as early as the capitulation of Santa Fe (granted to Columbus in 1492) they warned the explorer that he must share the organization of shipping to any lands he might discover with officials whom Ferdinand and Isabella would appoint. On Columbus's return they set Juan Rodriguez de Fonseca to that task. It was probably his idea to centralize the entire Indies trade in Seville, where goods would be stored on arrival or prior to departure, and registers kept of all ships and cargoes. Accordingly the monarchs established the House of Trade (*Casa de Contratación*) under Fonseca and Francisco Pinelo, whom they had employed in financial projects since 1478 and who had assisted Columbus. Here was concentrated the great Sevillan monopoly of the Atlantic trade, which despite fluctuating fortunes would resist other ports' attempts to break it, and form a cornerstone of Europe's economy for more than a century.

(ii) The Monarchs and the Savages

For Ferdinand and Isabella, no problem was as great as that of the treatment and regulation of the indigenous inhabitants of their conquests. Discussion of the fate of the Moors of Granada belongs elsewhere in this book, but the cases of the aboriginal

Canary Islanders and the Arawaks of the West Indies (with the Caribs who also dwelt there but present more singular features) are analogous in various ways.

It seems that the Canary Islands may originally have been inhabited by Cro-Magnon man, supplemented by later migrations of Berber and negroid types from mainland Africa. In consequence their appearance varied a great deal and contemporaries likened them to Europeans, Gipsies, Moors and American Indians. Their material culture was as perplexingly paradoxical as the evidence about their origins. Despite some technical skills like embalming and dye-stamping, they were ignorant of the baking of bread and – what is more surprising in the case of island peoples who dwelt within sight of other islands – did not know the art of navigation. They built no constructions, save dwelling huts in the eastern islands, but rather sheltered in caves. What we know of their religion is accounted for only by fertility-cult objects and their practice of embalming their dead; surviving items of their religious vocabulary are evidence of fertility-cults, but curiously extend to dog-worship, which may be a Berber feature, and have been said to show scattered traces of Mohammedan influence; it is more likely, however, that they were as untouched by Islam as by Christianity – as the Muslim polymath, Ibn Khaldoun, observed. Their political institutions again varied a great deal but were generally monarchical and tribal, shaped by the exigencies of their semi-nomadic, pastoral and cereal-raising culture in this arid region of few permanent waterways. In spite of their backward material civilization they were not without a surprising degree of political organization, which is reflected in their capacity for war, for though literally armed only with sticks and stones they repeatedly defeated European armies by stratagems.

The Arawaks have survived in some numbers to our own day and so are less of an anthropological mystery, forming part of the mainstream of Amerindian development. They were technologically more advanced than the Canarians – they built and sailed canoes and beat soft metals – but had no domestic beasts to rear for food. Their life-style was therefore more agrarian and sedentary. Like the Canarians they were peaceful until provoked – an important factor in how Europeans would understand them – but could be formidable in resistance. Their religion was atavistic and involved small cult objects, their polity tribal and monarchical without the complex hierarchy of the Canarians. The Caribs were comparable in their primitivism but their cannibalistic offences against natural law and disinclination to peace put them altogether outside the pale of the Spaniards' consideration. Their treatment never taxed the Spanish monarchs' conscience as that of the Canarians or milder Indians did.

In many ways the crucial similarity between the Canarians and Indians was that they were naked: that was the first fact Columbus noticed about the Indians and the first which Europeans had observed about the Canarians; indeed for every European observer of primitive peoples till well into the sixteenth century, clothes were the measure of difference between primitivism and civilization; conformity of dress was a sign of conformity of manners. The promotion of European *couture* was a major preoccupation of the proselytizers of the Moors and the Spanish settlers among the Indians. Beatriz de Bobadilla, heiress of the isle of Gomera and enslaver of its people, argued before Ferdinand and Isabella that the Gomerans could not be considered truly Christian on the ground that 'they go about naked'. Hieronymus Münzer at about the same time displayed the same state of mind when he wrote of the Canarians, 'They all used to go naked, but now use clothes like us'. Then he added, very characteristically of his epoch, 'Oh, what doctrine and diligence can do, that can turn beasts in human shape into civilized men!' But in terms of the two cultural traditions of which men in the late Middle Ages disposed – that of Christianity and that of classical antiquity – social nakedness had a profound significance: it evoked in the context of the first idea of primitive innocence, in that of the second, the legend of the age of gold.

Both these concepts were of great importance in the formation of European ideas about the Canary Islanders and Indians. Accounts of the Canary Islanders influenced notions of the age of gold; Peter Martyr and his correspondents thought the Indians a model of sylvan innocence. Of both peoples, it was thought that their uncorrupt state peculiarly fitted them to hear the gospel and helped to create the widespread impression that the existing and often harsh juridical norms for the treatment of pagans were unsuited to them.

But the fundamental question the savages raised in European minds concerned their nature – were they true men, possessed of rational understanding? Once accepted as such, they had to be fitted into the biblical and classical panorama of the origins of mankind. The Indians were given genealogies going back to Herodotus and the sons of Noah; the Canarians were traced back to remote incidents in Jewish or Moorish history. Even then, there were *degrees* of humanity: peoples without the civilized advantages of European-style polity and laws might suffer dire consequences, as was made clear by Fray Martín de Córdoba in a pedagogic work written for Isabella's personal edification in her youth:

> It is said that barbarians are those who live without law; the Latins those who have law; for it is the law of nations that men who live and are ruled by law shall be lords of those who have no law; wherefore without sin they can take them as slaves because they are by nature the slaves of the wise who are ruled by law.

Many contemporaries shared Fray Martin's rather rough-and-ready reading of Aristotle and Roman law; and it was only missionaries and proto-ethnographers who evinced respect for the native civilizations. Generally the nudity, sexual laxity and inferior material culture of the savages caused them to be condemned as 'bestial' in their habits and 'by nature inclined to vice'. Ovando, who succeeded Columbus as governor of Hispaniola, essayed two experiments in Indian autonomy and concluded that they were incapable of self-government.

What Europeans thought of their religion would also affect the juridical standing of the savages, since it was an old canonistic principle that offences against 'natural law' – including idolatry and blasphemy – could put pagans outside its protection. This in fact was the favourite line of attack of those who wished to kill or enslave Indians and Canarians, though Ferdinand and Isabella allowed the argument only in the case of the Caribs. They agreed with Columbus that the Arawaks' religion was innocuous – 'they have no sect', was their way of putting it – and reminded him to let the slaves he took 'be from among the idolaters'. The Canarians' religion seems to have struck contemporaries as almost equally insipid: direct observers noticed only their cult-images and occasionally suggested that they 'worship celestial phenomena', though slavers and *conquistadores*, anxious to make out a case for their own activities, imprecated the natives' idolatry. From the evidence of the Inquisition records, it seems that the Canarians were thought easy to convert, for there was never any case of apostasy or crypto-paganism among them.

Above all, two factors obscured contemporaries' understanding of the primitive peoples. Firstly, if modern anthropological science originated in the response of missionaries and jurists to the problems they encountered with primitive peoples, there was yet a long period of overlap with the time when scholarly enquiry was bridled by a prevailing taste for sensational, amazing and salacious tales. Cannibalism, supposed physical prodigies, ritual deflowering of virgins, exposure of infants and ritual suicides – these were the elements of indigenous cultures which attracted most attention at the time. Secondly, European observers imposed on the natives their own standards and terms. Everything in the indigenous polity of the Canaries, for instance, was expressed in terms of the familiar feudal hierarchy of the day until the islands seemed as densely crowded with kings, dukes, villeins, vassals and even bishops as contemporary Europe. This cultural anachronism was a serious obstacle to understanding between the savages and their conquerors. In the New World, the European grasp of the indigenous forms of government would have important consequences in legal controversy: one has only to think of Bartolomé de Las Casas's arguments that the sophistication of their political systems provoked the Indians' reasonableness and constructive capacities; or of the argument over how Cortés and Pizarro treated the heads of native monarchies. For the Canarians, the implications were as serious but more limited. Because their system was assumed to be akin to that of their conquerors, their enforced adhesion to the forms of homage was lent a significance by the Europeans which the natives themselves were ill-equipped to understand; among the justifications for the sanguinary Spanish reaction to the rebellion on Gomera in 1488, Ferdinand said that the natives had betrayed their vassallic oath to their lord. The same problem of mutual incomprehension must have affected the ceremonies of mass baptism, as well as of swearing fealty, which generally accompanied the Spanish victories. During the conquest of Gran Canaria, the natives repeatedly made peace, attended by these ceremonial acts, as seed-time approached, but returned to a life of heathendom and armed resistance as soon as their crops were sown.

The chief importance for contemporaries of all their observations of the savages lay not in their contribution to early ethnography but in their usefulness in solving the great problems of whether and how the natives could be evangelized, what rights they had, whether they possessed sovereignty, whether they could be warred on or enslaved. By Ferdinand's and Isabella's time, thanks to the efforts of Llullian missionaries, who were devoted to the cause of peaceful conversion, and the humane pontiffs who had followed Eugenius ɪᴠ, doctrines favourable to the savages had achieved currency on all these points.

In 1477, however, a new factor intervened which acted as a catalyst around which the prevailing doctrine on savages' rights was altered. In October of that year, Ferdinand and Isabella took the conquest of the three still unsubdued Canary Islands under their own wing, out of the hands of the local seigneurs and private adventurers, whose efforts had been so unproductive in the preceeding years. On the question of whether the islanders should be enslaved, the Catholic Monarchs upheld the cautious doctrines of Pope Eugenius and the missionaries. In 1477, their liberation of 'certain Canarians who are Christians and others who are on the road to conversion' on the grounds that 'it would be a source of bad example and give cause why none should wish to be converted', may be compared with the aim expressed by Eugenius forty-three years previously when he spoke of the danger of pagans being deterred from joining the faith. No doubt the monarchs' attitude was not uncoloured by the exigencies of power: enslavement would have involved a change in the natives' status from royal vassals to personal chattels, whereas the monarchs' aim was as far as possible to exclude intermediate lordship from the institutions by which they ruled their monarchy (or at least to limit it where it existed already). In this respect, their ordinances against enslavement of the Canary Islanders were motivated in a way akin to those by which they protected the Indians of the New World. Columbus's first plans for enslaving the Indians aroused the monarchs' immediate disapproval. 'What does he think he is doing with my vassals?' Isabella is traditionally said to have asked. They commissioned a 'junta of theologians' to examine the proposed enslavement, and when they pronounced unfavourably, ordered Fonseca to have the slaves liberated and their owners compensated. This was almost a re-enactment of their reaction to the enslavement of the Gomerans in 1489.

It was equally in the interests of extending their own power that the monarchs insisted on their right to make war against the savages. This was made clear by their attitude to the bulls of indulgence for the conversion of the Canarians, promulgated by Sixtus IV in 1478. The Pope, continuing the traditions of peaceful evangelization and apparently sharing the common opinion that to make war on the islanders was unlawful, designated the funds expressly for the conversion of the natives and the erection of religious houses. By an insidious abuse of language, however, the monarchs' writs on this subject described the bulls as 'for the said conversion and conquest' or with equivalent phrases. Antonio Rumeu de Armas has recently shown that this early case of 'double-think' caused a rift between the monarchs and some of their clergy, in which opponents of the use of violence actually attempted to suspend the collection of funds. At the end of the day, the success of the monarchs' policy brought their expansionist and evangelistic aims into perfect harmony: it would be but a short step now to Alexander VI's bulls on the New World, where the duty of evangelization would be seen as making the Castilian conquest just. This was an important moment in the elaboration of the canonistic doctrine of just war: conversion had never in itself been generally considered a sufficient pretext (though it had been advocated by individuals) up to that time.

In the remainder of the monarchs' reign one final development was still to come. Most clerics and religious continued to espouse exclusively peaceful methods of conversion. And Ferdinand and Isabella were not ill-disposed towards attempts along those lines, provided obedience to themselves was among the objects to which the missionaries sought to persuade their congregations: for instance, the mission of Fray Antón de Quesada, whom the monarchs despatched to Tenerife in 1485, involved a brief both to convert the natives and reduce them to royal authority. Meanwhile, peaceful conversion revived in peninsular Spain when Granada was conquered and proselytization of the new community began. The tenacity of the pacific point of view about conversion during these wars led to the separation in doctrine of a war of conversion from a war waged in order to subject the heathen and so render by peaceful means possible conversion. This was not a point contrary to existing doctrines but merely a question which earlier jurists had left in doubt. Under this new doctrinal distinction, Ferdinand and Isabella were free to make war on the Indians and Canarians as on rebel subjects, theoretically without prejudice to the question of peaceful conversion. The custom grew up of addressing to the savages what the Spaniards called 'requirements' – demands, that is, to acknowledge the monarchs' sovereignty and adopt Christianity, or else accept responsibility for the warlike consequences of refusal. This distinction had a pre-history during the Reconquest, when the Christians had copied from the Moors the practice of challenging an opponent, prior to closing in combat, to embrace the true faith or die. The overlapping paradigms between the conquests of Moors and of pagans can be seen from a comparison of the terms of capitulation, to which Moorish cities were obliged to subscribe whenever they surrendered to Ferdinand and Isabella, with a privilege apparently granted to a group of submissive Canarians in May 1481 : they were taken, like the Moors, 'beneath our protection and royal defence' and were given the same rights as Christian subjects; but the necessary preliminary to all this was that 'reduced and converted to our Holy Catholic Faith, they sent to us to give and tender their obedience and fealty and recognized us as their King and Queen and natural lords'. Here the overlap with the Moors, and the use of the terms of a 'requirement' can be clearly discerned. Other instances occurred in the Canaries throughout the 1480s, until Alonso de Lugo claimed to have put the terms of a 'requirement' formally to the people of La Palma in 1492, including the point made in the privilege of 1481 that those natives who submitted were to be treated equally with the Catholic Monarchs' Spanish subjects. Bernáldez's chronicle supports Lugo's account, saying that the natives were 'required many times'. Nicolás de Ovando reported to the monarchs in 1502 that he had put similar 'requirements' to the rebellious natives of Hispaniola.

Evidently the attitude Ferdinand and Isabella adopted towards the Indians of the New World and the question of their juridical standing were not dissimilar from those they evinced towards the Canary Islanders: the implicit doctrine that the monarchs' title to the unconquered islands gave them the right to wage war upon the inhabitants, was also present, *mutatis mutandis*, in the great Alexandrine bulls on the conquest of the New World and in the *Requerimiento* (the formalized and definitive revision of the earlier 'requirements', as it was settled in 1513 and proclaimed thereafter to most of the peoples the Spaniards encountered in the course of their conquests) The likelihood that the Spaniards' experience in the Canaries may have influenced or predisposed them in their relations with the Indians seems strongly suggested; again the islands may have helped to develop an institution of the conquests). The likelihood that the Spaniards' experience in the origins in the Reconquest, for soldiers in the Canaries would certainly have been familiar with the challenges common between Christians and Moors; yet their 'requirements' to the savages of the islands seem to go beyond those origins and tend towards the *Requerimiento*: certainly they are juridically closer to the latter for the ignorantly pagan and unaggressive islanders were not comparable in those respects to the Moors. It must be remembered, however, that during the reign of Ferdinand and Isabella, Spanish attitudes to the savages were still at a protean phase. One of the most curious documents in the history of the Spanish Empire records that in the summer of 1472 Lope de Salazar – no doubt the *conquistador* of that name whom chronicles and other records mention – 'went to Tenerife to the band of Anaga to make a treaty between the said island (that is, the Spaniards on Gran Canaria) and the said tribe of Anaga'. We are given no details of the terms he made, but they included the stipulation that the natives of other tribes could be raided by the Spaniards; immunity from such attacks was evidently the price of the Anagans' friendship. This case must be unique in the annals of the Spanish Empire, where a native tribe was treated with on equal terms, without having to start from an inferior juridical position. Elsewhere the natives were held in law to be subjects already of the Spanish crown and could only either acquiesce in the requirements of the Spaniards or be treated as rebels. Ferdinand and Isabella honoured Lope's treaty with, if anything, supererogatory zeal, for in 1493 the peacemaker, who had turned slaver, was arrested and punished 'as a breaker of treaties'.

9

Unbelief, Heresy and the Church

'Obscene, detestable, vile, execrable ... to be ostracized from all human contact.' This description of the Jews comes not from any cheap pamphlet-propaganda of the twentieth century, but was uttered by one of the most enlightened figures of the reign of Ferdinand and Isabella, the humanist scholar, Peter Martyr of Anghiera. 'My sovereigns', he concluded, 'were the wisest of men to think of exterminating that despicable and infected herd.' It is hard to understand or explain such language. In part, objections to the Jews were no doubt strictly religious. The Hebrew faith was in many cases only imperfectly understood, and its esoteric, ritualistic nature made men suspicious. The Jews kept themselves to themselves and did not proselytize, thereby stimulating the fear Christians felt for them and exacerbating the lack of comprehension. In a period when natural disasters were rife and mortality high, simple people inevitably sought out scapegoats, and a purpose which in other countries was often served by witchcraft accusations was met in Spain, where witchcraft persecutions at this time were relatively rare, by fulminations against the Jews and heretics. Among the more lurid practices popularly ascribed to the chosen race were cannibalism and infanticide. More generally admitted – and much quoted in sermons of the time – was the belief that Jews were collectively guilty of Christ's murder. Of course many high-ranking and well-educated ecclesiastics had a thorough knowledge of and respect for Judaism, formed through a history of dialogues in which they disputed the merits of their respective faiths with the rabbis; it is rare to find a text from a well-informed source in Ferdinand's and Isabella's reign which makes untrue accusations against the Jews, and most of the pressure for their persecution emanated from the prejudiced or ignorant.

The most sensational case of the period to come before the Inquisition concerned some Jews and Jewish converts to Christianity, who were accused of conjuration over a Host and of crucifying a Christian child on Good Friday; devotion to the 'Holy Infant of La Guardia', as this child came to be known, became a significant cult at the time. There seems evidently to have been an area in which the phobias excited by the Jews and popular suspicions of occult practices overlapped. Torquemada, the Grand Inquisitor, called in a memorandum to the monarchs for measures against 'Jews, blasphemers, deniers of God and the Saints and equally sorcerers and necromancers.' It was widely believed that occult practices generally were on the increase in Europe. In 1484 Innocent VIII issued the first bulls against witchcraft amid fulminations against 'incantations, spells, conjurations and other accursed charms and crafts', causing miscarriages, deaths and failure of crops. There is some evidence that increasing fears of sorcery and conjuration afflicted Spain too: in 1492 for instance, when Ferdinand and Isabella appointed Juan de Lanuza to govern Valencia, they authorized him to increase the prevailing penalties for divination or conjuring up the Devil. There may have been some genuine increase in the amount of occult activity, but most of the growing fear can safely be ascribed to social tensions, ignorance and the inadequacy of existing law to cope with society's sub-rational complaints against the elderly and eccentric. It is curious that Spain in the next century suffered far less from witchcraft denunciations than much of the rest of Europe, and it may be that the Inquisition acted as a safety-valve in this respect by providing an alternative framework of accusation and investigation for men to vent their grievances against their neighbour, in cases where traditional courts would have no jurisdiction.

Some of the prevailing hatred of the Jews was socially inspired in a peculiar sense which we shall explore in a moment, and some the product of economic jealousy. Andrés Bernáldez's attitude to the Jews displayed all the irrational fears of an expanding racial minority which are familiar in our own day. 'All their work was to multiply and increase', he complained; and he betrayed the economic jealousy which made many Christians hate them by exclaiming, 'They never wanted to take manual work, ploughing or digging or walking the fields with the herds . . . but only jobs in the towns, so as to sit around making money without doing much work'. In fact, as it was hard for the Jews to make their way in any profession, save in small numbers in the service of their own communities, and because they often had literate and numerate skills, they tended to find unpopular work as rent- and debt-collectors, tax-farmers and money-lenders. They were released for this last occupation by their exemption from the canonistic usury laws by which in theory Christians were bound. Even the Jews were restrained by the civil law from exacting usurious interest, but an usurious rate was never defined. In practice most of the market in small loans was in Jewish hands; capital risk – and therefore interest – was much higher than today: rates of thirty per cent were not thought excessive, but many lenders charged much more. It is apparent from Inquisitorial records that the fact that a man practised usury, or was a tough businessman, could be treated as *prima facie* evidence of Judaism.

The monarchs were sensitive about complaints that their predecessors and the great lords had favoured the Jews unfairly. 'The seigneurs and monarchs ever protected them', objected Bernáldez with undoubted accuracy, 'because of the great profits they got from them'. For the Jews, who 'belonged' to the kings and were under their protection without any intermediate lords, paid special taxes, provided generous subsidies in times of need and were liable for a variety of payments to the monarch by virtue of his lordship. Their dangerous position in society made them the close dependents of their protectors, and often meant that they could be of special value in service. In the words of one of Isabella's writs

'All the Jews of my kingdom are mine beneath my defence and protection and it is my part to shield and defend them and maintain them in justice'.

An ineluctable question is whether in addition to the religious and economic grounds of objection, subjects of Ferdinand and Isabella hated the Jews for racial reasons. It was certainly possible within the framework of contemporary patterns of thought to believe in long-enduring inequalities between races. It was widely discussed, for instance, whether primitive peoples or Negroes were possessed of reason or understanding, or whether, lacking these essential qualities, they were more like beasts than men. The concept of natural law could be a source of other grounds for reducing alien peoples to an inferior level, for the inability to recognize natural law was widely held to incapacitate a people for civilized life. Aristotle's doctrine of the natural inferiority of some men to others reinforced and extended these patterns of thought.

None of this was sufficient, however, to induce racial feelings in the modern sense; none of the grounds of discrimination known at the time could be considered 'biological'; the only characteristic of inferiority which might have been thought congenital or coterminous with racial differences was that of lack of rational understanding – and though doubts were expressed, for instance, in Ferdinand's and Isabella's time of the rationality of the Canary Islanders and American Indians, the overwhelming consensus among contemporaries was that they were truly men. There was somewhat more doubt about the Negroes, who certainly did not enjoy the same consideration as fair-skinned savages until the sixteenth century was well advanced. Bartolomé de las Casas, for instance, the philanthropic apostle of the New World, sought to liberate the Indians from the rigours of enforced labour by recommending the importation of Negroes to replace them; and it was not till the end of his life that he repented of the injustice of his suggestion. Nevertheless though Negroes remained at a disadvantage, the stigma of sub-rationality does not seem to have clung to them very closely; many were freed from slavery – a clear indication of faith in their rational status. In Valencia the manumitted blacks formed a confraternity which shared all the usual civic privileges. Ferdinand and Isabella thought Negroes capable of exercising offices of responsibility, and in 1475

appointed one Juan de Valladolid, a Negro in the royal household, to supervize the affairs of the free black community of
Seville and dispense justice among them, 'because you are of
noble lineage among the said Negroes'.

Contemporary Spaniards' indifference to race in the modern
sense can be illustrated from the modalities of their colonial
societies, where intermarriage was common and where men of
mixed or purely indigenous blood could and did hold offices of
importance. The leaders of indigenous society were rapidly
assimilated; evidence of descent from rulers among the savages
was accepted as evidence of noble rank by Spanish judicial
enquiries. It is probably fair to say that the subjects of
Ferdinand and Isabella were sensitive to differences rather of
status than of race.

On the other hand, it must be acknowledged that the
fifteenth and sixteenth centuries in Spain, and the reign of
Ferdinand and Isabella in particular, witnessed the rise and
multiplication of the imagery of 'pure blood' in polemical
literature and of so-called 'statutes of purity of blood' which
sought to exclude from some orders and professions men of
Jewish and in many cases Moorish descent within – usually –
four generations. The ingenious and gifted historian, Américo
Castro, has suggested that purity of blood was a characteristically Jewish preoccupation, associable with the Hebrew interest
in genealogy and abhorrence of mixed marriages, and that it
was ironically imparted to the Christians in the course of
acculturation between the two faiths. However that may be, it
seems clear that under Ferdinand and Isabella the inspiration
for the movement was not racial but religious. This is apparent
from the arguments voiced against purity statutes by such
opponents as Alonso de Cartagena, bishop of Burgos in the mid-
fifteenth century (the son of Bishop Pablo de Santa María
who had been a convert from Judaism), and Alonso de
Montalvo, the jurist of Ferdinand and Isabella: the basis of
their indictment was that purity statutes treated all converts
alike as Judaisers without distinction; in other words, the
statutes' basis of objection to the converts and their progeny
was not that they had Jewish blood but that by virtue of their
Jewish background they were prone to apostasize or commit
heresy. There are hints in contemporary sources that purity
statutes were in part a response to attempts by *conversos* to

buy or bribe their way into offices – though there is no evidence of the justice of the assertion. Ferdinand and Isabella were unsympathetic towards purity statutes; they attempted for example to dissuade the Jeronimite order from adopting one, but the order felt that its orthodoxy was in peril and after a heated controversy the advocates of 'purity' prevailed. The movement continued to gain ground thereafter. It is curious in this connexion to observe that the Spanish royal house too was remotely affected by Jewish blood, through its founder, Henry of Trastámara and his mother, Leonora de Guzmán, mistress of Alfonso XI; contemporaries of Ferdinand and Isabella, however, forgot or ignored the fact.

Moors could be the victims of prejudices as widespread, if not as vituperative. At the root of this problem was the Christian population's sense of physical threat. The Moors in Spain belonged to a powerful and hostile culture, which occupied the far shore of the Mediterranean, and which might at any time use them as the bridgehead of an invasion. The Spain of Ferdinand and Isabella was shaken by rumours of 'the coming of the Turkish dog'. An anonymous memoir warned the monarchs to disarm their Mohammedan subjects in anticipation. When the *mudéjars* of Granada rebelled in 1499, it was widely believed that their action was part of a conspiracy with 'the Moors across the sea' in North Africa, who it was feared were about to surprise the coasts. Royal officials in areas of Moorish settlement lived lives of permanent unease and distrust. Fernando of Zafra, the monarch's secretary, who was responsible for much of the administrative work of the Kingdom of Granada after its conquest, uttered representative sentiments when he repeatedly urged Ferdinand and Isabella to encourage Moorish emigration. 'I could wish all of them would leave', he said, and 'I like them better there (i.e. in Africa) than here'.

Throughout the 1480s the signs multiplied of the approaching end of the era of cultural co-existence in Spain between Christians, Moors and Jews. Religious considerations were partly responsible for the pejorative atmosphere: Ferdinand and Isabella, like almost all their contemporaries, were deeply afflicted by the genuine and conscientious fear that Christian souls would be lost for eternity by the insidious influence of the rival faiths. It was expressly for this reason that they established the Castilian Inquisition in 1479 and extended it to all their realms over the following years. At intervals during the fifteenth century and with increased intensity under Henry IV, Castilian royal counsellors had demanded an inquisition which would embrace the whole realm and owe responsibility not in the first instance to the bishops nor directly to the pope but to the king, within whose patronage its offices should fall. Henry had lacked strength to put the plan in hand, but no sooner had Ferdinand and Isabella brought the civil wars to a close than they acted to bring such an office into being.

It is hard at this remove of time to judge contemporary assertions that an inquisition was necessary because the populace was 'infected' with Jewish customs, and, as Bernáldez said, 'this was a result of the constant contact they had with the Jews'. Ferdinand and Isabella had expressly accepted this point of view when they expelled the Jews from Zaragoza in 1486.

It is at least clear that many converts from Judaism were either insincere or ill-informed about their new religion, and persevered in Mosaic customs which their enlightenment by the gospel ought to have displaced from their way of life. Jewish converts were sufficiently numerous, and sufficiently conspicuous in importance, to lend an air of widespread Judaizing to the urban society in which they generally dwelt. It is apparent from Alonso de Montalvo's expostulations and Fernán Pérez de Guzmán's defence of the *conversos* that all converts were popularly condemned, whether sincere or not, as crypto-Jews. The kind of suspicion which prevailed of the converts is best illustrated by a forged 'Reply of the Jews of Constantinople to the Jews of Spain' of the 1480s; it must be stressed that this document was utterly spurious and tells nothing of the intentions of the converts, only of the fears of the Old Christians; in this respect it might be compared with such twentieth-century propaganda forgeries as *The Protocol of the Elders of Zion*.

To what you say of how the King of Spain forces you to become Christians, you will do so for you can do no other. To what you say of how they take away your property, you will make merchants of your sons to usurp theirs. To what you say of how they take your lives, make physicians and apothecaries of your sons that you may take theirs. To what you say of how they destroy your synagogues, you will make friars and clerics of your sons to destroy their Church. To what you say of other vexations, you will place your sons in the households of the kings and lords that they may obtain office therein and avenge you on all the Christians . . . and you shall rule in their kingdoms.

The Inquisition's original brief confined its investigations to cases of heresy and apostasy, but it soon began to respond to deeper defects in society and, later on, to more malignant purposes in individual minds. The Inquisition became a forum for personal animosities, petty jealousies and social and economic rivalries to be elaborated. In the first place, its courts were far more attractive to men with grievances than the regular courts of the land, for the Inquisition could convict on suspicion and keep the names and testimonies of witnesses secret, could treat purely incidental evidence as conclusive, was swifter in condemnation than exculpation, and finally, though its punishments were usually mild, they could often be draconian. Above all, the judges of the Holy Office took every denunciation seriously; they could not afford to treat any accusation lightly, for the eternal repose of the accused's soul was assumed to be at stake, and, in almost every case, the Inquisitors were men of great probity on whom their responsibility weighed heavily. The effects of these factors electrified society: grievances too unspeakable or too vile or too vague to be aired in the courts were associated with a heresy-accusation and tried before the Inquisition; men too powerful to be accused at any other tribunal were hauled to the Holy Office; supplicants too poor to be heard elsewhere found the Inquisitors ready to lend an ear. Sometimes professional rivalry was at the bottom of the business. In one of the thousands of cases tried in these years a newly-appointed public notary was accused of Judaizing by his rival for the office; yet the offence which constituted the grounds of the accusation – the scribe's wife was alleged to have made lamb for supper on Friday – was a most palpable fabrication, for no Jew would have cooked lamb on his sabbath, any more than a Christian on a fast-day. This was only one of innumerable cases where idiosyncrasies of diet (usually abstinence from ham or bacon) were treated as *prima facie* evidence of apostasy. In some areas Inquisitors extended their interference to the realm of private morality, especially among clerics, and clerical abuses that might indicate deficiencies of faith. Heresy could be given an extended definition in the service of the state: in 1489 Ferdinand described rebellion against one's natural lord as heresy, and later in the reign, after Isabella's death, the Inquisition tried cases of treason in Navarre.

Although in the strictly religious sphere, Judaizing was the principal object of the Inquisitors' scrutiny, their competence was more extensive here too. But there was little other heresy in Spain at the time. Individual cases of purely academic heresies formulated in the course of learned argument, were endemic among theologians, but of limited importance because isolated from widespread social movement: in the next reign, however, after the Reformation had plunged consciences into the crucible all over Europe, heresies even of this type would come to he persecuted, though under Ferdinand and Isabella, by and large, they continued to escape. There were exceptions, however, particularly where the suspect was in a prominent position in the Church or an educational institution. Pedro de Osma, of the University of Salamanca, was arraigned by the Archbishop of Toledo at the Pope's behest, just before the Inquisition was set up; later, Hernando de Talavera, royal confessor and Archbishop of Granada, was investigated by the Inquisition for which he had displayed a marked lack of enthusiasm and from which he had protected the Moorish neophytes of his diocese. At a lower level of society, there may have been an heretical element in the revolutionary millenarianism of the Galician peasant rebellions, in common with similar movements elsewhere, but the Inquisition made no effort to intervene. Far more significant for contemporaries appeared the highly individualistic 'spiritual' heresies to which the mendicant friars and literate laymen were peculiarly prone. In the reign of the Catholic Monarchs it became increasingly hard to draw a firm line between – on the one hand – an enlarged and personal type of devotional life, based on direct experience of God or first-hand study of the scriptures, and on the other an heretical rejection of the mediatory Church and the traditional ideas of a 'catholic sense' in which the scriptures could be objectively interpreted. The multiplication of scriptural translations and foreign devotional works – stimulated by the spread of printing – and the enlargements and reform of the Franciscans, among whom 'spiritual' tendencies in the heterodox sense were strong, produced in the Spain of Ferdinand and Isabella the beginnings of a movement of 'illuminism' – heretical spiritual exaltation – that would feed the fires of the Inquisition for years to come. The *Vita Christi del Cartujano*, a devotional work in the new style, was translated into Spanish by Ambrosio de Montesino in 1501 and became a favourite work of Isabella's and many of her subjects. The book was not specifically unorthodox, but its influence naturally went beyond the letter of its own prescriptions; the individual piety and intimacy with God which it sought to inculcate could broadcast the seed of heresy unless used with care. The *Imitatio Christi*, the most seminal work of the genre in the rest of Europe, was diffused in various versions and editions in Spain. And in the first few years of the sixteenth century imitative Spanish works appeared. At about the same time, Cardinal Cisneros's reforms of the Franciscan order introduced unintentionally some of the personnel and ideas of Italian 'spirituals' – and it was in the same order, through mystical excesses in some Castilian friaries and the movement called *Beatismo* among the nuns, that 'the illumination which proceeds from the darkness of Satan' was first cast in the next few years. The Fransciscans had probably expanded too rapidly; and it is tempting to think that the absence of 'purity statutes' in their order led to the imperfect assimilation of dangerously large numbers of converts.

The reign of the Catholic Monarchs was the most sanguinary phase in the history of the Inquisition, no doubt because it was also the first. Thereafter, the problem of heresy was much diminished precisely as a result of the rigour with which Ferdinand and Isabella acted; not even the effects of the Protestant Reformation in the next century brought an increase in the numbers of those condemned to the stake. Even in the period when the gruesome turnover was most rapid, the Inquisition was never gratuitously bloodthirsty, but generally mild by the standards of the time. By the very nature of its task few accused escaped without any form of punishment; this was because the crime of heresy was so destructive in its effects on the heretic's soul, that it was better in case of doubt to assume guilt, and relieve the accused of the effects of his supposed sin by the imposition of confession and penance, than to give the prisoner the 'benefit of the doubt'. On the other hand, the overwhelming majority of the Inquisition's punishments were mild, ranging from simple acts of public penance to fining and imprisonment. For the first ten years of the Inquisition a contemporary's estimate of seven hundred condemned to death and five thousand penanced is probably not an unfair guide to the fate of the accused. Thereafter, the rate of condemnations slackened. Compared with confessional persecutions in other countries, and the slaughters of alleged witches in which secular courts indulged elsewhere, the record of the Spanish Inquisition is less shocking than the popular stereotype would have it. It is of course true that the Inquisitorial tribunals were ruthless in the use of torture to obtain evidence; but again, the barbarities of torture must be judged against the torments that awaited in hell a heretic who did not confess his fault. Contemporary critics of the use of torture had to take this fundamental belief into account; Juan de Lucena, who courageously attacked the Inquisition in a memorandum to the monarchs, argued that torture actually imperilled souls, since men in their anguish uttered and falsely confessed to heresies they did not really believe. Nor was torture peculiarly the tool of the Inquisition but also of civil courts in certain cases all over Europe.

The establishment and spread of the Inquisition constituted only one of many signs in the 1480s that the limits of tolerance had been reached. More than against heretics and crypto-Jews, hatred and persecution were directed at the persistent, frank unbelievers, the *mudéjars* and the Jews. Township after township imposed distinctive clothing and ghetto conditions on their Jewish communities, until under the weight of the petitions they received both in the *Cortes* and in the course of daily business, the monarchs made such practices mandatory. Pressures mounted for the total expulsion of the Jews. In part these were financial. Between 1484 and 1491 the diocesan authorities expelled the Jews from Andalucia in order to raise funds for the Granada war by forcing their property onto the market cheaply and exposing and creaming off their liquid wealth. Ironically, the persecution of *conversos* by the Inquisition had impaired the royal finances: the urban converts were a major source of fiscal revenue, but the zeal of the Inquisitors was driving increasing numbers of them to flee the country. Púlgar's complaints that the *conversos* of Seville were emigrating in fear of the Inquisition and so critically diminishing the royal dues has been verified by recent research in the taxation returns of that city. Yet the importance of financial considerations in influencing the monarchs in favour of expulsion of the Jews must not be exaggerated. They could have exacted a 'ransom' and still allowed the Jews to stay : the rabbis actually offered the sum of 300 000 ducats – roughly a third of the royal profit on the expulsion. The monarchs were much affected by strictly religious considerations and by the strength of feeling in the country. Nevertheless, the years 1489–92, the period of the final effort in the Moorish war, were a time of acute financial stringency, when the prospect of a large inflow from the Jews must have exerted a powerful attraction.

On 30 March 1492, amid general acclaim from their Christian subjects, Ferdinand and Isabella ordered the Jews to depart. A contemporary Jewish account is evocative because of its intentionally biblical language :

> There went out a decree from the kings with the force of law like a law of the Medes and Persians and the herald cried with a loud voice, 'It is proclaimed unto you, all families of the kingdom of Israel, that if you accept baptism and bow down and adore the God of the Christians, you shall eat of the fat of the land as I do, you shall dwell in the land and do trade therein. And if you refuse and disobey and do not acknowledge the name of God and do not serve my master, then go forth, leave my country, the soil of the Spains and Sicily and Mallorca and Cerdagne, which are beneath my rule, and let there not remain in my kingdom within three months a single one of all who bear the name of Israel'.

Among some – perhaps most – of the Jews the severity of the royal policy provoked despair and apostasy; but those who remained true to their old faith found their fervour kindled by the anticipation of a new exodus. When Abraham Seneor accepted baptism, his successor, Isaac Abrabanel, did much to uplift the morale of his co-religionists. Christians regarded the sufferings of the Jews as divine punishment, just as the Jews saw it as a divine trial of faith; but although as Bernáldez said, 'no man was unmoved by pity for them', all agreed in condemning the obduracy of those expelled and in approving the royal policy. Columbus was among many who cited the expulsion as proof of the monarchs' religious zeal.

There is no way of assessing the numbers expelled. They are unlikely to have been as many as 100,000. The effects of the exodus on the Spain the Jews left behind are equally difficult to gauge. There were clearly short-term financial effects for the crown and economic consequences to the country of the sudden release of large amounts of property and money. In the longer term, Ferdinand and Isabella have been much criticized for depriving Spain of a useful and constructive community. On the other hand, some action to resolve the crisis of tolerance between the Christian and Jewish populations was the only statesmanlike course in the circumstances. Moreover, the monarchs' action completed a longstanding movement of assimilation of the two races: when Jews were converted, they became free to intermarry with Christians and to use their talents in the mainstream of Spanish culture, forming a single people, much enhanced by the fusion of two bloods. Many of the great figures of Spanish art and literature in the 'golden century' which followed the expulsion were of *converso* descent. Yet had the Jews not been induced to convert, they would have remained an isolated and endogamous community with a culture of their own, to the great impoverishment of Spain. The Catholic Monarchs' action did bring many conversions in its wake, led by that of the chief Rabbi, Abraham Seneor, himself; Ferdinand and Isabella found sufficient justification in that happy result.

The Catholic Monarchs had to bring diplomatic pressure to bear on Portugal to induce King Manuel to expel the Jews, including many fugitive Castilian and Aragonese Jews, from there in 1497. Yet curiously, with respect to the question of expelling the Moors as well, the positions of Castile and Portugal were reversed. The Portuguese Moors were driven out in 1497 and actually applied with success for permission to settle in Castile. Although Ferdinand had conceived the ambition – as we saw – of expelling the Moors from the whole peninsula early in the Granada war, he seems to have realized that so radical a solution was impractical. The *mudéjars* were far too numerous and economically far too useful. In parts of the Crown of Aragon the running of agricultural estates depended on their labour. From the concessions granted to the Portuguese Moors, from the guarantees given in the Granada Capitulations and from the monarchs' generally benevolent policy towards the Moors in the years immediately following the collapse of their last strongholds, we can safely judge that for most of the 1490s no expulsion was contemplated. Between 1499 and 1501, however, the turbulence and rebellion which broke out among the Moors, and their unwillingness to submit to the persuasions of the missionaries sent by the monarchs to convert them, caused royal policy to change. The issue over which violence broke out concerned the fate of the *elches* – that is, converts from Christianity to Islam or Muslims of Christian descent. The Moors generally had been exempted from investigation by the Inquisition for a period of forty years, should they embrace Christianity. Hernando de Talavera, Archbishiop of Granada, had procured this concession for them not only because he was doubtful of the merits of the Inquisition but also because he realized that converted Moors would need time to assimilate their new faith. The case of Muslims who had once been Christians, however, was somewhat different. The evidence of the apostasy could not be explained away so easily. Moreover, not only was there a case for unleashing the Inquisitors upon the *elches*, but sadness at the loss of their souls was a source of great personal grief to the monarchs. It was probably expressly to deal with the problem of the *elches* that Ferdinand and Isabella sent Cardinal Cisneros, Primate of Spain, to Granada in 1499.

The *elches* had explicitly been included in the guarantee of confessional liberty which the monarchs gave to Granada on capturing the city; the Christians were limited to peaceful methods of evangelization. Cisneros hoped to restore the *elches* to the fold not by discarding this framework but rather – where previously Talavera and the Governor of Granada, the Count of Tendilla, had tried to make baptism attractive by rewards and positive inducements – by exerting pressure to persuade them to return to Christianity. This was not forcible conversion in the strict theological and canonical sense, for the *elches* could still choose their own response to the new situation. The Moorish community felt, however, that this new conversion was effectively forcible and hence in breach of their terms of surrender. Following the erosion of their culture by emigration and conversion, this turn of events alarmed them. The rebellions which ensued between 1499 and 1501 – a kind of encore of the Reconquest – decided the monarchs in favour of harsh action to rid themselves of the menace of the Moors. Following an increasingly rigid series of limitations of their freedom of movement the Moors were expelled from Castile, including Granada, though not from Aragon, in 1502.

The methods of evangelization promoted by Ferdinand and Isabella were in some ways the same for Moslems as for the more primitive pagans for whom they acquired responsibility in the Atlantic archipelagoes. In the first place, the monarchs insisted, following the consensus among canonists and theologians, that baptism should not be forced. In the Spanish tradition, forcible conversion meant presenting the unwilling catechumen with no alternative but death. The options allowed to the Jews in 1492 or the Moors of Granada in 1502, who were faced with a choice between baptism and expulsion, were believed to fulfil the requirements of voluntary conversion. Juan de Lucena pointed out to Ferdinand and Isabella that this was no better than forced baptism and therefore – he argued – ineffective; his conclusion was that former Jews should be exempt from the jurisdiction of the Inquisition, but, not suprisingly, his views found no sympathizers. As we have seen, the Canary Islanders and American Indians were 'required' to embrace the faith or accept the consequences, which would include war and bloodshed; but though there were isolated protests from independent thinkers like Las Casas, neither the monarchs nor their advisers saw this as incompatible with the aims of conversion by persuasion. Secondly, Spanish evangelization was characterized by the effort to impose on the neophyte the whole of the proselytizers' culture – not just his creed but his way of life, his laws, tongue, political society, manners and dress. In the Canaries, Alonso de Bolaños, who was in charge of the Franciscan mission to the islands and mainland Africa, sought to teach the natives 'a fuller observance of the faith, mechanical arts and our other ways of life'. Columbus was convinced that to teach the Indians the rudiments of Christian belief would be an easy matter; thereafter it would only remain to teach the Indians to work productively, build, dress after the European fashion, speak Spanish and 'learn our customs'. The same criteria were fundamental in the conversion of the Moors. Hernando de Talavera, to whom the monarchs entrusted the Archbishopric of Granada and the task of evangelization, made that absolutely clear in his pastoral instructions to Moorish converts:

> That your way of life may not be a source of scandal to those who are Christians by birth, and lest they think you still bear the sect of Mohammed in your hearts, it is needful that you should conform in all things and for all things to the good and honourable way of life of good and honourable Christian men and women in your dress, the style of your shoes, the custom of shaving, in eating and keeping table and preparing meat the way it is commonly prepared, and especially and more than especially in your speech, forgetting as far as you can the Arabic tongue, and making yourselves forget it, and never letting it be spoken in your homes.

The Spaniards consistently underestimated the difficulties of evangelization. The hardening of policy towards the Moors was caused in part by the excessive optimism of the 1490s. In the New World they were disabused of their early belief that the gospel would be easily spread and made the fatal error, which missionaries of succeeding generations would lament, of failing to investigate the pre-conquest religions and destroy all records of them, so that the natives persevered in pagan practices undetected. Although the monarchs' avowed principal desire was to convert the savages, they in fact did little to accomplish this. The measures they took were largely precautionary – prohibiting enslavement and ill-treatment – or else consisted in exhorting the lay colonists on the spot to have 'conversation' (that is, contact) with the natives and teach them the faith. But the need for professed missionaries was lamentably neglected. This may have been partly because the Franciscan friars who traditionally played this role, despite their effectiveness in proselytizing, had shown themselves incapable, in controversies of the 1470s and 1480s, of preserving good relations with the lay arm or secular clergy; their missionary privileges had been renewed and revoked at intervals, and their own internal discipline much impaired, until by the 1490s their mission was eclipsed even in the Canaries and Africa. It was an unpropitious time to introduce them into the New World. Columbus asked the monarchs and the Pope alike to send missionaries, and Ferdinand and Isabella made what were perhaps tentative efforts to interest other orders in the job. Fray Bernardo Buil, whom they sent with Columbus on his second voyage, made an inauspicious start. (He had been a monk and hermit of Montserrat who was allowed to leave his community on papal and royal business, not a member of a mendicant order). He developed an instant antipathy towards the Indians and returned quickly home. The Jeronimites proved unwilling to fill the gap; and eventually it was to the Franciscans and Dominicans and finally, much later, the Jesuits, that the apostolate of the New World chiefly fell. The Franciscan missionary impulse carried some members of the order across the Atlantic but it is impossible to determine how many during Isabella's reign. Cardinal Cisneros obtained privileges from Rome, and about two dozen friars in all received commands or permissions from the monarchs, though probably only a proportion of such commands were actually fulfilled. Despite Isabella's piety and professed concern in the conversion of the Indians, the contribution of her own reign was negligible.

The monarchs did not, however, neglect the apostolate of Castile. Their religious understanding of the duties of kingship – the aim Ferdinand formulated during the Granada war of 'constituting Spain to the service of God' – made their pursuit of power over the Church not a simple extension of secular control, but a purifying and revitalization. Their aims were threefold: reform of the religious orders in particular and the clergy generally; the subordination of the bishops to the crown; and the displacement by the monarchs themselves of the Roman Curia in some of its functions with respect to the Castilian Church. Reform genuinely depended on the increase of royal power, because it was precisely the lax and indulgent nature of ecclesiastical discipline that encouraged abuses by letting them go lightly punished; and the monarchs saw their first task in this connexion as that of challenging the independence of ecclesiastical courts and arrogating to themselves greater jurisdiction over the clergy. There was, moreover, some basis in canon law for the monarchs' view that clerics guilty of temporal crimes should not have the benefit of trial before the Church courts, or, at least, should be turned over to the secular arm for sentence if found guilty. For a cleric condemned by ecclesiastical judges could purge his offence simply by reciting the penitential psalm, *Miserere mei domine*. Even quite heinous crimes could thus go effectively unpunished. It was in this area of controversy that the monarchs were most successful in enforcing reform. Ferdinand and Isabella provoked acrimonious disputes with bishops and abbots jealous of their own jurisdictions by sending lay jurists to assist ecclesiastical seigneurs in the administration of justice. In the 1490s for instance, the Archbishop of Santiago refused to comply with this policy in Galicia and defied the royal representatives, Dr Espinar and the Licentiate Rojas. In 1500 the monarchs retaliated by ordering all the Church courts of Galicia either to employ lay judges or to refrain from imposing merely spiritual penalties for temporal offences. Two years later this legislation was extended to the whole of Castile.

Except where there was a clash of episcopal jurisdiction with their own, Ferdinand and Isabella favoured the bishops and promoted their power. Their object here was to limit the excesses which the Roman Curia had fallen into the habit of committing on judicial and fiscal matters. The opinion of the latest and most authoritative investigator of the monarchs' ecclesiastical policy is that the King and Queen were seeking only to return to the rule of canon law where the pope's jurisdiction over bishops and appropriations of church revenue to Rome were concerned; the monarchs largely succeeded in limiting the popes' dispensations and suspension of recognized canons by refusing to admit them or to allow the clergy to act on papal commands in such cases. Further, Ferdinand and Isabella succeeded in having many appeals cut off before they went to Rome to be tried in the Curia, and having them dealt with instead by the Spanish bishops. The combined opposition of monarchs and bishops to curial excesses was made possible by the degree of control the monarchs exercised over episcopal provisions and, indeed, ecclesiastical appointments generally. It was traditional that ecclesiastical patronage should be in the ruler's gift, instead of the pope's, in any territory reconquered from the Moors: such privileges had been conceded by earlier popes in order to encourage the Reconquest. In their reign, Ferdinand and Isabella had this expressly confirmed in Granada and extended to the Canary Islands and New World, while securing for themselves a much increased role in all their kingdoms. They did not hesitate to use underhand methods:

G

they omitted all the exceptions and qualifying clauses, for instance, in the version they published of Innocent VIII's bull of 1486, granting them patronage in Granada and the Canaries. To have ecclesiastical offices in their gift, of course, was an important source of power for the monarchs, not only to do good for the Church, but also to reward their supporters. But the strong religious element in their policy secured them the support of good Churchmen, and the appointments they made were almost uniformly successful. Men like Talavera, Cisneros and Diego Deza, with their ardour for reform, made the Spanish Church outstanding in its day and helped to dispel anti-clericalism and forestall the Reformation. Some bishops – Juan de Fonseca, the organizer of expansion in the New World, is the most noteworthy example, or Juan de Ortega, bishop of Almeria, who helped organize the *Hermandad* – were more conspicuous in the royal administration than in their spiritual functions, but Church and State were so intimately linked that both spheres of activity could benefit from the overlap and from the exchange of influence : the control of the monarchs assisted reform; the spirituality of their ecclesiastical supporters and advisers enhanced their government.

Above all in the context of their reform of the religious orders can the sincerely religious motivation of the monarchs be perceived, as can the closeness of this cause with that of the pursuit of their own power. The religious communities of the kingdom were not uniformly corrupt, but many, as Cisneros said, were 'given to dissolution and very profaned'. Monasteries and nunneries were degenerate with the penetration of secular habits, pecuniary corrosion, moral laxity and the abuse of the seigneurial power of which many houses were possessed. Of the friaries, many had resisted the 'Observance' movements and continued to live remote from their own rules and ideals of poverty and service; above all, it was the monarchs' intention to purge the 'claustral' friaries which had abandoned the tradition of pastoral and missionary work outside the house, and lived more on the lines of monastic communities. The 1480s were marked by important if tentative efforts at reform, but it was in 1494, when the monarchs confided Cisneros with the task among his own Franciscan order, that the spiritual war began in earnest. The popes initially supported the reform, but it did mean that royal jurisdiction was wielded as never before within the religious orders, and Cisneros's intrusions in houses which resisted him were often unceremonious and devastatingly uncompromising. Threatened houses resisted by appealing to Rome, and Alexander VI wavered in his attitude. Nevertheless, Cisneros put his reliance on royal support and ignored papal commands to moderate his ardour to exempt houses from his work. The result was to make Spain the nation par excellence of religious reform and to go some way towards realizing Ferdinand's ambition of a country 'constituted to the service of God'.

Epilogue:
Ferdinand after Isabella

Isabella's health declined throughout 1503, as she nursed the ailing Juana. At times she could not see to write, at others, was too weak to walk. She withdrew from the labours of government gradually as the strength drained from her, and the use of her name dwindled from the superscriptions of royal documents. No one dared foretell her death but everyone knew it was impending. The tension and alarm always current at a king's demise began to grip Castile at the approach of this queen's. For Ferdinand ruled only by virtue of his marriage to Isabella. The heiress, Juana, was evidently incapacitated for government by her illness, and her husband, Philip the Fair of Flanders, was a foreigner with little understanding of Castile.

When the Queen finally succumbed in Medina del Campo on 26 November 1504, each man's *obiter dicta* reflected his own character and interests as much as hers. Most men remembered the dissolution of justice at her reign's beginning and how internal peace had been restored; Columbus felt consoled for her death by her escape from the harshness of a wearisome world; Cardinal Cisneros recalled how she had befriended the Church. Isabella's own reflections, betrayed in her will, were divided between pride in her achievements and guilt for the vows broken in gaining the throne and the laws transgressed to keep it. She also feared for the grim future of the monarchy under Juana's frail rule. Ferdinand's thoughts returned to the anguished time of Prince John's death. He now mourned Isabella in similar terms (referring, as the custom was, to the bowels rather than the heart as the seat of the emotions):

Although her death is for me the greatest hardship that could come to me in this life and on the one hand the grief of it – for what I have lost in losing her and what these kingdoms have lost – pierces my entrails – yet on the other, seeing that her death was as holy and Catholic as her life, there is therefore hope that our Lord has her in His glory, which for her is a better and more lasting realm than those she ruled here.

Ferdinand sustained throughout the rest of his life the cult of Isabella's memory which he began on that day. And it is remarkable that he never omitted in his communications with the *Cortes* of Castile to recall the Queen in terms of this sort. He was especially careful to deck her memory with splendour in the most politically sensitive of all the documents he had to address to Castile – the notice of his second marriage.

For Isabella's death interrupted the era of co-operation between Castile and Aragon. Philip the Fair would not permit a regency under Ferdinand in his lifetime; Ferdinand would not lightly surrender all power in Castile; nor would the magnates, who had now enjoyed a sufficient term of peace and retrenchment, suffer strong government from any quarter. Baulked by Philip, Ferdinand threatened to sunder the destinies of Castile and Aragon. He married Germaine de Foix, of the House of Navarre, and though the son he had by her did not survive, the new marriage raised the prospect of a future division of the inheritance of Ferdinand and Isabella.

Isabella's death had been 'the greatest hardship' for Ferdinand in a political sense. But the demise of Philip the Fair in 1506 provided the King of Aragon with an occasion for pleasure. According to a story Macchiavelli relates, on hearing the news, Ferdinand donned white ermine and a scarlet doublet, rather than conventional mourning. For now the clause of Isabella's will came into operation whereby he was to be regent after her death in the expected event of Juana's incapacity. At the behest of Cardinal Cisneros, who assumed the regency temporarily when Philip died, the Catholic King returned to rule in Castile.

Even after the bitter experience of 1504–6, it is curious that Ferdinand did not now abuse his power in Castile for narrowly Aragonese ends. Though he remained chiefly occupied with the defence and extension of his gains in Italy, he upheld and defended the Castilian monopoly of the Indies and when he conquered southern Navarre annexed that to the Castilian crown too. But he appears to have been convinced that the continued juncture of the two realms would be a burden to both. His plans to hand on the Crown of Castile to the elder of his grandsons and that of Aragon to the younger were only narrowly frustrated at the time of his death – amid decrepitude of conscience, fear of renewed French success in Italy, and the dangers of revolt in Castile under the continuing strain of war – in the village of Madrilejo on 25 January 1516.

Despite the differences of character, taste and matrimonial interest which separated them during the lifetime of both, Ferdinand and Isabella had sustained a remarkable political partnership. We have suggested that the working of joint rule was a result of necessity, imposed by the emergency conditions of their reign and elaborated in extemporizations. The pursuit of a common foreign policy was based on a new community of interest, which Aragon and Castile had not previously enjoyed. But it is more noteworthy that though the theme of joint rule recurred in Spanish history after Isabella's death, it never again functioned as it had done under the Catholic Monarchs. Though the prospect of princedom, and the long struggle to win the crown against Juana, 'la Excelente Señora' dominated the early years of their married life and united their interests, much personal adjustment was necessary before the couple could rule successfully. In the course of their reign they both showed political sagacity, but Ferdinand was superior in that connexion, and outlived his wife, because Isabella never adequately subordinated her preoccupations as a wife and mother to the demands of monarchy. Their statecraft was dominated by a religious concept of monarchy; though they could be ruthless and unscrupulous in the secular pursuit of power, they justified those excesses in divine terms, in a way that is hard, perhaps impossible, to grasp today. The element in the political circumstances of their reign which best helps us understand their statecraft is the fact that their secular enemies – the Moors and Turks – were also confessional foes. Therefore they could hope at one and the same time for 'the increase of our realms' and to 'constitute Spain in the service of God'. In its political implications, as well as in the private history of their marriage and family, theirs had been an unique matrimonial experience, which for over a quarter of a century dominated the history of Spain, and for much longer thereafter profoundly affected the history of the world.

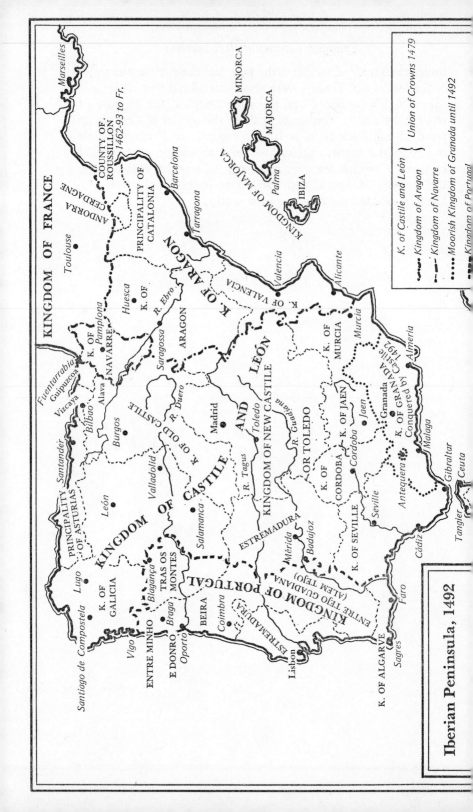

Iberian Peninsula, 1492

KEY   K. – Kingdom; Rep. – Republic; D. – Duchy; M., Mar. – Marquisate;
      Pr. – Principality

Bibliographical Guide

Primary sources are listed in alphabetical order, secondary works cited in glosses on the chapters of this book.

CONTEMPORARY CHRONICLES, TREATISES, ETC.

A. Bernáldez, *Memorias del reinado de los Reyes Católicos*, ed. M. Gómez-Morenzo and J. de M. Carriazo (Madrid, 1962)

Cancionero del siglo XV, ed. R. Foulché-Delbosc (Madrid, 1912-15)

Fray Martín Alonso de Córdoba, *Jardín de nobles doncellas* (Madrid, 1953)

Crónica incompleta de los Reyes Católicos, ed. J. Puyol (Madrid, 1934)

Cronicón de Valladolid, ed. P. Sainz de Baranda (Madrid, 1848) (Colección de Documentos ineditos para la historia de España XIII)

D. Enríquez del Castillo, 'Historia del quarto rey Don Enrique', in J. M. de Flores, ed., *Colección de crónicas de los Reyes de Castilla* (Biblioteca de Autores Españoles, lxx, Madrid, 1878)

Epistolario español, i, ed. M. Ochoa (Bibl. de Autores Españoles, lxii, Madrid, 1870)

G. Fernández de Oviedo, *Libro de cámara del Príncipe Don Juan* (Madrid, 1870)

L. Galíndez de Carvajal, *Anales breves* (Bibl. de Autores Españoles, lxx, Madrid, 1878)

D. de Gois, *Crónica do felicissimo rei D. Manoel*, ed. J. de Sousa Cardoso (Coimbra, 1949-56)

F. Guicciardini, *Diario del viaggio in Spagna* (Florence, 1932)

Fernán Pérez de Guzmán, *Generaciones y semblanzas* (Madrid, 1924)

N. Macchiavelli, *Il Principe* (Turin, 1963 [many earlier editions])

Lucius Marineus Siculus, *De Hispaniae Laudibus* (Basle, 1497); *De Rebus Hispaniae Memorabilibus* (Alcala 1530); *Vida y hechos de los Reyes Católicos* (Madrid, 1943)

Memorias de Don Enrique IV (Madrid, 1913)

Alonso Diaz de Montalvo, *Leyes* (1484); *Códigos Españoles*, i (Madrid, 1848)

Ambrosio de Montesino, Prologue to *Vita Xti del Cartujano* (1502)

Hieronymus Münzer, 'Itinerarium Hispanicum', ed. L. Pfandl, *Revue Hispanique*, xlviii (1920)

Alonso Ortiz, *Tratados* (Seville, 1493)

Alonso de Palencia, *Alphonsi Palentini Gesta Hispaniensia* (Madrid, 1834); *Dos Tratados* (Madrid, 1870); *Crónica de Enrique IV* and *Guerra de Granada*, trans. A. Paz y Melia (Madrid, 1904-9); *La Cuarta década de Alonso de Palencia*, ed. J. López de Toro (Madrid, 1970)

Bachiller Palma, *Divina retribución* (Madrid, 1879)

Petrus Martyr Anglerius, *Opus Epistolarum* (Alcalá, 1530); *Epistolario*, i, ed. J. López de Toro (Documentos inéditos para la historia de España, ix, Madrid, 1953); L. García y García, ed., *Una embajada de los Reyes Católicos a Egipto* (Valladolid, 1947)

F. Pinel y Monroy, *Retrato del buen vasallo* (Madrid, 1677)

Hernán (Fernando) de(l) Pulgar. *Libro de los Claros Varones* (Seville, 1500), *Crónica de los Reyes Católicos*, ed. J. de M. Carriazo (Madrid, 1943)

Hernando de Talavera, *Católica impugnacíon* (Barcelona, 1961)

Diego de Valera, *Epístolas y varios tratados* (Madrid, 1878); *Crónica de los Reyes Católicos*, ed. J. de M. Carriazo (Madrid, 1927); *Memorial de diversas hazañas*, ed. J. de M. Carriazo (Madrid, 1941); *Espejo de verdadera nobleza*, ed. M. Penna (Bibl. de Autores Españoles, cxvi, Madrid, 1959)

RECORDS

Archivo General de Simancas, Catalogo XIII, Registro del Sello (Valladolid, 1950 – in progress)

F. Arribas Arranz, *Documentos de los Reyes Católicos relacionados con Valladolid* (Valladolid, 1953)

F. Bejarano, *Documentos del reinado de los Reyes Católicos en el Archivo Municipal de Malaga* (Madrid, 1961)

Bulario pontifiácio de la Inquisición Española, ed. B. Llorca (Rome 1949)

Bullarium Franciscanum, n.s., iii, ed. J. Pou y Marti (Rome, 1929)

Calendar of State Papers relating to Spain, i, ed. G. Bergenroth

R. Carande and J. de M. Carriazo, *El tumbo de los Reyes Católicos del Concejo de Sevilla* (Seville, 1958 – in progress)

D. Clemencín, 'Ilustraciones sobre varios asuntos', *Memorias de la Real Academia de la Historia*, vi (1821)

Colección de Cortes de los reinos de León y Castilla, iv

Colección de documentos inéditos del Archivo de Indias [those relating to the Catholic Monarchs can be found with the aid of the calendar and index by E. Schaefer, (Madrid, 1947)]

Colección de documentos inéditos para la historia de España [viii, Juana's wedding armada; xi, xiv, correspondence with Zafra and matters pertaining to Granada; xiii Ferdinand's account of the battle of Toro – another version in *Tumbo del concejo de Sevilla*, i; xviii, *Anales* and *Adiciones genealogicas* of Galíndez de Carvajal; xxi, pact of 1473 with Medina Sidonia; lxxxi, 'Información de loque Pero Sarmiento dÿo'.]

M. Danvila, 'Tres documentos inéditos', *Boletín de la Real Academia de la Historia*, xxxix (1901)

J. Fernández Alonso, 'Instrucción de Alejandro VI a Fray Boil', *Cuadernos de historia de España* (1960)

M. de Foronda y Aguilera, 'Honras por Enrique IV y proclamación de Isabel en Avila', *Boletín de la Academia de Historia*, lxiii (1913)

M. Garrido Atienza, *Las capitulaciones de Granada* (Granada, 1910)

E. Ibarra y Rodriguez, *Documentos de asunto económico* (Madrid, 1917)

R. Konetzke, *Documentos para la formación social y económica de América*, i (1953)

M. A. Ladero Quesada, *Los mudéjares de Castilla en tiempos de Isabel I* (Valladolid, 1969)

A. Paz y Melia, *El cronista Alonso de Palencia* (Madrid, 1914)

L. Suárez Fernández, *Documentos acerca de la expulsión de los judiós* (Valladolid, 1964); *La política internacional de Isabel la Católica* (Valladolid, 1965 – in progress)

A. de la Torre, *Documentos sobre relaciones internacionales de los Reyes Católicos* (Madrid, 1950); *La casa de Isabel la Católica* (1954)

A. de la Torre and L. Suárez Fernández, *Documentos referentes a . . . Portugal durante el reinado de los Reyes Católicos* (Valladolid, 1958-63)

A. and E. A. de la Torre, *Cuentas de Gonzalo de Baeza* (Madrid, 1955)

The monarchs' wills are appended to D. J. Dormer, *Discursos varios de historia* (Zaragoza, 1683) and that of Isabella variously reprinted, for instance in a separate edition by F. Arribas (Valladolid, 1944) and M. Ballesteros Gaibrois, *La obra de Isabel la Católica* (Segovia, 1953)

Secondary Works

GENERAL

The *Índice Histórico Español* provides a comprehensive three-monthly bibliography of Spanish history; the period before the commencement of the *Índice* is treated in B. Sánchez Alonso, *Fuentes de la historia española e hispanoamericana* (3 vv., Madrid, 1952) and D. Gomez Molleda, *Bibliografía española, 1950-1954* (Madrid, 1955). Of the nineteenth-century general histories of Ferdinand and Isabella only J. H. Mariéjol, *L'Espagne sous Ferdinand et Isabelle* (Paris, 1892) can fairly be described as useful still. More recently, there are: A. Ballesteros y Beretta, ed., *Historia de España*, iii (Barcelona, 1922), translated by B. Keen, and R. Menéndez Pidal, ed., *Historia de España*, xvii (2 parts, Madrid, 1969), which is of fundamental importance. Among general histories, those which present a helpful or original perspective for the study of this reign are A. Castro, *La realidad histórica de España* (Mexico, 1962), C. Sánchez Albornoz, *España: un enigma histórico* (Madrid, 1959), J. Vicéns Vives, *Historia económica de España* (Madrid, 1964), J. Vicéns Vives, ed., *Historia social y económica de España y America* (Barcelona, 1957), J. H. Elliott, *Imperial Spain* (London and New York [St Martin's Press], 1963) and P. E. Russell, *Spain – a Companion to Spanish Studies* (London, 1973). Various important essays are usefully translated in J. R. L. Highfield, ed., *Spain in the Fifteenth Century* (London 1975). There is no bibliography of Ferdinand of any value, though J. Vicéns Vives, *Fernando II de Aragón* (Zaragoza, 1962), the first volume of an uncompleted life, deals with the subject brilliantly down to *c.* 1481. Of the scores of biographies of Isabella, only T. de Azcona, *Isabel la Católica* (Madrid, 1964) really passes muster; despite its antiquity and frankly eulogistic nature, I have found D. Clemencín, *Elogio de Isabel la Católica* (Madrid, 1820) still useful especially in my third chapter.

CHAPTER I

On Gothicism, R. Menéndez Pidal's introduction to *Historia de España*, xvii, and his 'Los godos y la epopeya española', in *España y su historia*, i (Madrid, 1957). On polyglot culture, A. E. Beau, 'Sobre el bilingüismo en Gil Vicente', *Studia philologica: homenage a Dámaso Alonso*, i (Madrid, 1960) and R. Menéndez Pidal, 'La lengua de Cristóbal Colon', *Bulletin Hispanique*, xlii (1940).

On Carrillo, the laudatory biography by F. Esteve Barba (Barcelona, 1946) gives basic facts but is untrustworthy in its judgements. I am indebted to E. Benito Ruano, 'Los "Hechos del Arzobispo de Toledo" por Guillén de Segovia', *Anuario de Estudios Medievales*, v (1968). There are biographies of Cardinal Mendoza by A. Huarte y Echenique (1912), R. Lacadena y Brualla (Zaragoza, 1939) and A. Merino (Barcelona, 1942): all help with the facts, but none is critically executed. L. Serrano, *Historia de Guadalajara y sus Mendozas* (4 vv., Madrid, 1942) is a much better book, indispensable on the history of that clan. J. Torres Fontes, 'La conquista del Marquesado de Villena', *Hispania*, xiii (1953), gives an appreciative assessment of the Marquess and, despite its inexplicable error in locating Henry IV's demise in Segovia, is invaluable for the study of the war of succession, as is the same author's *Don Pedro Fajardo* (Madrid, 1953). For the war and its background in Galicia, at the other end of the country from Fajardo's operations, A. López Ferreiro, *Galicia en el último tercio del siglo XV* (Santiago, 1883) remains unsurpassed. I have also used the last two works named in chapter 4. López's *Historia de la Santa Iglesia de Santiago*, vii (Santiago, 1905) is also important.

On Afonso's coinage Batalha Reis, *Monedas de Touro* (1935), and on his contacts with France and England and French attacks on Castile, A. J. Dias Dinis, 'Dois embaixadores de Afonso V', *Itinerarium*, i (1955); I. Zumalde, 'La muerte de Juan de Lazcano', *Ensayos de historia local vasoa* (San Sebastian, 1964) and M. Sarasola, *Vizcaya y los Reyes Católicos* (Madrid, 1950).

On the Battle of Toro, the exchange between S. Viterbo, 'A batalha de Touro', *Revista Militar* (1900) and C. Fernández Duro, 'La batalla de Touro', *Boletín de la (Real) Academia de (la) Historia*, xxxviii (1901).

CHAPTER 2

On Ferdinand's early life, Vicéns Vives, *Fernando II* and *Fernando el Católico, Rey de Sicilia*. M. Gual Camarena, 'Servidores del Infante Don Fernando' *Estudios de Edad Media de la Corona de Aragon*, vi (1956), is illuminating. There are biographies of Juana Enríquez by N. Coll Julia and C. Muñoz y Roca Tallada, Condesa de Yepes.

On Juana's legitimacy, the monarch's marriage and the succession, O. Ferrara, *Un pleito sucesorio* (Madrid, 1945); J. B. Sitges, *Enrique IV y la Excelente Señora* (Madrid, 1911); G. Marañon, *Ensayo biológico de Enrique IV* (Madrid, 1954), which should be compared with his *Diagnóstico Etiológico* (Madrid, 1943), p.838; L. Suárez Fernández and V. Rodríguez Valencia, *Matrimonio y derecho sucesorio de Isabel la Católica* (Valladolid, 1960); and J. Meseguer

Bibliographical Guide

Fernández, 'La dispensa del impedimento de consanguineidad', *Archivo Ibero-Americano*, xxvi (1967). The last two works have not affected my assessment, which owes more to Vicens Vives and Azcona.

On Guisando, Vicéns Vives's interpretation remains sound, despite replies by L. Suárez Fernández, 'En torno al pacto de Guisando', *Hispania*, xxiii (1963) and J. Torres Fontes, 'La contratación de Guisando', *Anuario de Estudios Medievales*, ii (1965). B. Cuartero y Huerta, *El pacto de los Toros de Guisando* (Madrid, 1952) is of small worth.

For the extant portraits of the monarchs, J. de D. de la Rada y Delgado, 'Retratos de Isabel la Católica', *Boletín de la (Real) Academia de (la) Historia*, vii (1883); A. M. de García Pavón, 'Retratos de Isabel I', *Revista de Archivos, Bibliotecas y Museos*, Ist s., xvii (1907); *Retratos de Isabel la Católica procedentes de la cartuja de Miraflores* (Madrid, 1907); D. Angulo Iñiguez, 'Un nuevo retrato de Isabel la Católica', *Boletín de la (Real) Academia de (la) Historia*, cxxvii (1950), 'El retrato de Isabel de la colección Bromfield Davenport', *Archivo Español de Arte*, xxvii (1954), 'Un nuevo retrato de Don Fernando', *ibid.*, xxiv (1951); S. Rivera Manescau, 'Unos nuevos retratos de los Reyes Católicos', *Revista de Bibliotecas. Archivos y Museos*, lvii (1951); E. Pardo Canalís, *Iconografía de Fernando el Católico* (Zaragoza, 1963); M. Sandoz 'Note sur le portrait de Ferdinand d'Aragon du Musée des Beaux-Arts de Poitiers', *Cahiers de Bordeaux – Journées Internationales d'Etudes d'Art* (1954).

CHAPTER 3
The section on kingship depends chiefly on my own research. On the intellectual background, J. A. Maravall, *Estudios históricos del pensamiento español* (Madrid, 1967) and J. Cepeda Adán, *El concepto del estado en tiempos de los Reyes Católicos* (1956).

On the court, A. Prieto Cantero, *Casa y descargos de los Reyes Católicos* (Valladolid, 1969); M. Solana Villamor, *Cargos de la casa y corte de los Reyes Católicos* (Valladolid, 1962); J. de M. Carriazo, 'Retratos literarios de la corte de los Reyes Católicos', *Archivo Hispalense*, xxiv (1956), 'Amor y moralidad bajo los Reyes Católicos', *Revista de Archivos, Bibliotecas y Museos*, lx (1954), which I have also used in chapter 2. Prince John's court in Fernández de Oviedo's *Libro de cámara;* concerning Ortiz's treatise on his education, G. M. Bertini, 'Un diálogo humanístico sobre la educación del Príncipe Don Juan', *V Congreso (de Historia de la Corona de Aragón)*, v (1961). On humanism and Italian influence generally, R. B. Tate, *Ensayos sobre la histografia peninsular siglo XV* (Madrid, 1970) and especially on the culture of noblemen

P. E. Russell, 'Arms versus Letters: towards a definition of XVth century Spanish Humanism', *Aspects of the Renaissance*, ed. A. Lewis (Texas, 1972). See also A. Farinelli, *La Bibliotheca del Santillana e l'umanesimo italiano-ispanico* (Turin, 1929); A. de la Torre, 'Beatriz de Galindo "La Latina" ', *Hispania*, xvii (1957); C. Real de la Riva, 'Un mentor del siglo XV', *Revista de Literatura*, xx (1961) [about Valera].

CHAPTER 4

On opposition to the monarchs, M. A. Ladero Quesada, 'Las coplas de Hernando de Vera', *Anuario de Estudios Atlanticos*, xiv (1968). On the economic burden of war, J. Torres Fontes, 'Las tribulaciones del concejo murciano en octubre y noviembre de 1489', *Anales de la Universidad de Murcia*, xiv (1956); F. Sevillano Colom, 'Las empresas nacionales de los Reyes Católicos y la aportación de Valencia', *Hispania*, xiv (1954); M. A. Ladero Quesada, *Castilla y la conquista del reino de Granada* (Valladolid, 1967 – part II; though outdated, S. M. Soto, 'Organización militar de España por los Reyes Católicos', *Boletín de la Sociedad Castellana de Excursiones* (1904) is helpful. On the population, V. Navarro González, 'La población de España en tiempos de los Reyes Católicos', *V Congreso*, iv (1962). On the economy generally, R. Carande, *Carlos V y sus banqueros*, i (1965); 'Economía y expansión bajo los Reyes Católicos', *Boletín de la Academia de Historia*, cxxx (1952). The grain shortage is almost definitively dealt with by E. Ibarra y Rodriguez, *El problema cerealista en España durante el reinado de los Reyes Católicos* (1944); also J. A. García de Cortazar y Ruiz de Aguirre, 'El aprovisionamiento de trigo a Vizcaya a fines del siglo XV', *Homenaje al professor Alarcos García*, ii (1967). On the Mesta, J. Klein, *The Mesta* (Cambridge, Mass., 1920). On the Spanish merchants, M. Mollat, 'Le rôle international des marchands espagnoles dans les ports occidentaux à l'époque des Rois Catholiques', *V Congreso*, iv (1962), and on the Genoese H. Sancho de Sopranis, *Los Genoveses en Cadiz* (Jerez, 1939) and C. Verlinden, 'Les influences italiennes dans l'économie et dans la colonisation espagnoles à l'époque de Ferdinand le Catholique', *V Congreso*, iii (1954). On Riberol, A. Rumeu de Armas, *Alonso de Lugo en la corte de los Reyes Católicos* (Madrid, 1954) and L. de la Rosa Oliveira, 'Francisco de Riberol y la colonia genovesa en Canarias', *Anuario de Estudios Atlánticos*, xviii (1972). On communications, C. Alcázar, 'Comunicaciones en la época de los Reyes Católicos', *Curso de conferencias sobre la política africana de los Reyes Católicos*, v (1953), E. A. de la Torre, 'Viajes y transportes', *Hispania*, xiv (1954).

On joint government, A. de la Torre. 'Isabel la Católica, corregente en Aragón', *Anuario de historia de derecho Español*, xiii (1953).

On the legists and bureaucrats, J. A. Maravall, 'Formación de la conciencia estamental de los letrados', *Revista de Estudios Políticos*, xlviii (1953); R. de Ureña, 'Los incunables jurídicos de España', *Boletín de la Academia de Historia*, xcv (1929); V. Beneyto Pérez, 'Ciencia del derecho en la España de los Reyes Católicos', *Revista General de Legislación y Jurisprudencia*, cxciv (1953); R. Fuertes Arias, *Alfonso de Quintanilla* (1909 – an impassioned and rudimentary biography which could now be improved on); J. Sarmiento Lasuen, 'Alfonso de Quintanilla', *Boletín del Instituto Fernán González* (1951), D. Zaforteza y Musoles, 'Algunas notas sobre los Sánchez', *Archivos de Genealogía y Heráldica*, ii (1953), J. Reglá Campistol, 'Un pleito entre Juan de Coloma y los canónigos de Tarazona', *V Congreso*, ii (1956).

On the chancery, M. S. Martín Postigo, *La cancillería castellana de los Reyes Católicos* (Valladolid, 1959); F. Arribas Arranz, 'Los registros de cancillería de Castilla', *Boletín de la Academia de Historia*, clxiii (1968). On the *hacienda*, M. A. Ladero Quesada, *La hacienda real castellana entre 1480 y 1492* (Valladolid, 1967); 'La hacienda castellana de los Reyes Católicos', *Moneda y crédito*, no. 103 (1967); *La hacienda real de Castilla en el siglo* xv (La Laguna 1973)

On the nobility L. Suárez Fernández, *Nobleza y monarquía en la Castilla del siglo XV* (Madrid, 1963) and his contribution to *Historia de España*, xvi and xvii; J. R. L. Highfield, 'The Catholic Kings and the Titled Nobility of Castile', in J. R. Hale, J. R. L. Highfield and Beryl Smalley, eds., *Europe in the Late Middle Ages* (London and Evanston [Northwestern University Press], 1965); M. Tascón, *Declaratorias de los Reyes Católicos sobre reducción de juros y otras mercedes* (1952) [on the Cortes of Toledo]; J. Manzano Manzano, 'La adquisición de las Indias', *Anuario de Historia de derecho Español*, xii (1952) [for its important remarks on the use of crown lands in patronage]; J. L. Cano de Gardoqui and A. de Bethencourt, 'Incorporación de Gibraltar a la Corona de Castilla', *Hispania*, xxvi (1966); M. Grau, 'Un pleito secular de la comunidad y tierra de Segovia', *Estudios Segovianos*, (1954). On the Military Orders, A. L. Javierre Mur, 'Fernando el Católico y las Ordenes Militares', *V Congreso*, i (1955), L. P. Wright, 'The Military Orders in XVIth Century Castillian Society', *Past and Present*, no. 5 (1970).

Valuable general histories of the *corregidor* are those of F. Albi (Madrid, 1943) and B. Gonzalez Alonso (Madrid, 1970), but on the towns particular examples must be consulted: L. Serrano y Serrano, *Los Reyes Católicos y Burgos* (Madrid, 1943); E. Benito Ruano,

Toledo en el siglo XV (Madrid, 1961); M. Ballesteros Gaibrois, 'Un hecho poco conocido de Isabel la Católica', *Anales de la asociación española para el progreso de las ciencias*, vi (1941); and *Valencia y los Reyes Católicos* (Valencia, 1943). An important document not mentioned above is 'Jura de los Reyes Católicos en Jérez', *Revista de Archivos, Bibliotecas y Museos*. 1st s., ii (1872). Ferdinand's attempts at municipal reform outside Castile can be followed for comparison's sake in the works of Vicéns Vives and J. Mercader in *V Congreso*, i (1955), but also see A. Canellas López, 'Fernando el Católico y la reforma municipal de Zaragoza', *Cuadernos de Historia* (supplements to *Hispania*), viii-ix (1955-6), and G. Sorgia, 'El consejo municipal de Cagliara y la reforma de Fernando el Católico', *Revista del Instituto de Ciencias Sociales*, vii (1966). The *Fuero de Baza* has been edited by J. Moreno Casado (Granada, 1963) and, with the other *fueros* conceded by the monarchs, has been helpfully studied by J. Lalinde Abadia.

On the background to institutional history and the terminology involved, M. Colmeiro, *Historia de la economía política en España* (2 vv., Madrid, 1965) [a brilliant product of nineteenth-century historiography, re-edited]); J. M. Font Rius, *Instituciones medievales españolas* (Madrid, 1946); L. G. de Valdeavellano, *Historia de las instituciones españolas* (Madrid, 1970); and A. García Gallo, *Curso de historia del derecho espagñol*, (Madrid, 1945).

On the restoration of internal order, R. Prieto Bancés, 'El orden público en Asturias en la época de los Reyes Católicos', *V Congreso*, i (1955) and J. Lluis y Navas Brusi, *Cuestiones legales sobre la amonedación española bajo los Reyes Católicos*, i (Madrid, 1960). R. Bosque Canceller, *Murcia y los Reyes Católicos* (Murcia, 1953) is also interesting for the details it gives of the Fajardo and Chacón families, and the marriage which united those families respectively of nobles and *letrados*, though the author's interpretation is rather stilted. Aragon was never reduced to order as effectively as Castile, no doubt because Aragonese kingship was weaker and because the emergency conditions prevailing in Castile were not to be found in Aragon. See. F. Solano Costa, 'El reino de Aragón durante el gobierno de Fernando el Católico', *Cuadernos de Historia* xvi-xviii (1963-65), and M. Dualde Serrano, 'Misión moralizadoa de Juan de Lanuza', *Estudios de Edad Media de la Corona de Aragón*, v (1952).

On the Hermandad, L. Súarez Fernández, 'Evolución de las hermandades', *Cuadernos de Historia de España*, xvi (1951); C. Haebler, Die Castilischen Hermandades', *Historische Zeitschrift*, n.s., xv, and M. Lunenfeld, *The Council of the Santa Hermandad* (Miami, 1970).

On the 'modernity' of the monarch's state, A. Ferrari Nuñez, *Fernando el Católico en Baltasar Gracián* (Madrid, 1945); the contributions of Vicéns Vives and Maravall to *V Congreso*, i (1955) and ii (1956); A. de la Torre, 'El concepto de España', *Revista del Archivo, Biblioteca y Museo del Ayuntamiento de Madrid*, xxiii (1954); J. A. Maravall, *El concepto de España en la Edad Media* (Madrid, 1954) and 'The Origins of the Modern State', *Cahiers d'histoire mondiale*, vi (1961).

CHAPTER 5

On the Granada war generally, A. de la Torre, *Los Reyes Católicos y Granada* (Madrid, 1952); M. A. Ladero Quesada, *Castilla y la conquista del reino de Granada* (Valladolid, 1967); J. M. Carriazo, *En la frontera de Granada* (Seville, 1971) and contribution to *Historia de España* xvii (part I). Those works give a virtually complete bibliographical guide, but one cannot forbear to mention: on the origins of the war, M. Ladero Quesada, 'Dos temas de la Granada Nazari', *Cuadernos de Historia*, iii (1969) and J. Torres Fontes, 'Las relaciones castellano-granadinas desde 1475 a 1478', *Hispania*, xxii (1962). On the capitulations, the analysis by Garrido, listed above among the sources and Carriazo's 'Asiento de las cosas de Ronda'. On finance and recruitment, M. Ladero Quesada, *Milicia y economía en la guerra de Granada* (Valladolid, 1964); E. Benito Ruano, 'Aportaciones de Toledo a la guerra de Granada', *Al-Andalus*. xxv (1960); and F. Sevillano Colom, 'Las empresas nacionales de los Reyes Católicos y la aportación de Valencia', *Hispania*, xiv (1954). On the papal contribution, J. Goñi Gaztambide, 'La Santa Sede y la reconquista del reino de Granada', *Hispania Sacra*, iv (1951). On the fall, M. Pescador del Hoyo, 'Como fue de verdad la toma de Granada', *Al-Andalus*, xx (1955). On the Moors, the documents published by Ladero (listed above) and J. T. Monroe, 'A Curious Morisco Appeal to the Ottoman Empire', *Congresso luso-espanhol de estudos medievais* (Oporto, 1968). On the colonization, M. A. Ladero Quesada, 'Mercedes reales en Granada anteriores a 1500', *Hispania*, xix (1969) and 'La reproblación de Granada', *Hispania*, xxviii (1968). A guide to an interesting pictorial source concerning the war is J. de M. Carriazo, 'Los relieves de la guerra de Granada', *Archivo Español de Arte y Arqueología*, iii (1927).

CHAPTER 6

I have followed indications from F. de Llanos y Torriglia, *En el hogar de los Reyes Católicos* (Madrid, 1943). On Isabella and the courtly poets I rely on R. O. Jones, 'Isabel la Católica y el amor cortes', *Revista de Literatura*, xxi (1962) and A. D. Deyermond, *A Literary History of Spain, the Middle Ages* (London, 1971); these poets are illuminated by F. Marquez Villanueva, 'Investigaciones sobre Juan Alvarez Gato', *Anales de la Universidad Hispalense*.

xvii (1956) and F. González Ollé, 'Noticias de la corte de los Reyes Católicos', *Revista de Archivos, Bibliotecas y Museos*, lxix (1961).

On Hernán Peraza and Beatriz de Bobadilla, A. Rumeu de Armas, 'La reivindicación del derecho de conquista sobre las Canarias mayores', *Hidalguiá*, vii (1959) and 'Beatriz de Bobadilla y Cristobal Colón', *Anuario de Estudios Atlánticos*, xvi (1970).

On the panegyrists, R. del Arco y Garay, 'Un panegírico de Fernando el Católico por el humanista Juan Sobrarias', *Boletín de la Real Academia Española*, xxxii (1952) and the recent facsimile edition (Madrid, 1951) of D. Guillén de Avila, *Panegírico a la Reina doña Isabel* (Valladolid, 1509). On Nebrija, J. Senior, 'Dos notas sobre Nebrija', *Nueva revista de filología española*, xiii (1959) and R. B. Tate, 'Nebrija the historian', *Bulletin of Hispanic Studies*, xxxiv (1957).

On painting generally, C. R. Post, *A History of Spanish Paintings*, ix, (New York, 1938 [Kraus Reprint Corporation]) remains the standard work. On the Flemings, F. J. Sánchez Cantón, 'El retablo de la Reina Católica', *Archivo español de arte y arqueología*, vi (1930); J. Gómez Moreno, 'La capilla real de Granada', *ibid.*, i (1925); J. Rousseau, 'Peintures flamands en Espagne', *Bulletin des commissions royales d'art.* vi (1867); E. Bermejo, *Juan de Flandés* (Madrid, 1962); N. Reynaud, ' "Le Couronnement de la Vierge" de Michel Sittow', *Revue de Louvre*, xvii (1967); A. E. de la Torre. 'Michel Sittou', *Hispania*, xviii (1958). On the hispano-Flemish school, J. V. L. Brans, *Isabel y el arte hispano-flamenco*; J. A. Gaya Nuño, *Fernando Gallego* (Madrid, 1958); J. Guidol, 'Las pinturas de Fernando Gallego', *Goya*, iii (1956). On sculpture, R. H. Randall, 'Flemish influences on Sculpture in Spain', *Bulletin of the Metropolitan Museum of Art*, xiv (1956); M. Martínez Burgos, 'En torno a la catedral de Burgos' and other articles in *Boletín del Instituto Fernán González*, xii (1957). Isabella's tapestries show similar features to her paintings, on which, and on her books, F. J. Sánchez Cantón, *Libros, tapices y cuadros de Isabel la Católica* (Madrid, 1950). On music, H. Anglés, *La música en la corte de los Reyes Católicos* (Barcelona, 1951). On clothes, D. Angulo Iñiguez, *Isabel la Católica - sus retratos, vestidos y joyas* (Santander, 1951). On Ferdinand's taste, J. Camón Aznar, 'Fernando el Católico y el arte de su tiempo', *V Congreso*, iii (1961); L. Torres Balbas, 'El ambiente mudéjar', *Conferencias sobre politica africana*, ii (1951); 'Los Reyes Católicos en La Alhambra', *Archivo Ibero-Americano*, xi (1951). On the children, A. de la Torre, 'Maestros de los hijos de los Reyes Católicos', *Hispania*, xvi (1956); G. Mattingly, *Catherine of Aragon* (London and New York [Random House], 1963) [this can be compared with the entertaining but less circumspect account by Salvador de Madariaga in *Mujeres Españolas* (Madrid, 1972)]; M. Prawdin,

Juana la Loca (Barcelona, 1953) [the author's scepticism about Juana's madness makes an attractive but questionable thesis]; J. M. Cordeiro Sousa, 'Notas acerca de la boda de Isabel de Castilla con el príncipe Alfonso', *Revista de Archivos, Bibliotecas y Museos*, lx (1954); A. de la Torre, 'Don Manuel de Portugal y las tercerías de Moura', *Revista Portuguesa de Historia*, v (1951); H. D. Hulst, *Le mariage de Philippe le Beau avec Jeanne de Castille* (Antwerp, 1958); M. Gómez Imaz, *Noticias al fallecimiento del Príncipe Don Juan* (Seville, 1890).

My account of the assassination attempt is based on the contemporary relation appended to the *Libro de cámara del Príncipe* and the version of Pero Carbonell, printed in *Historia y vida*, i (1968). On Carbonell, J. E. Martínez Ferrando, 'Aportación acerca del Archivo Real de Barcelona', *V Congreso*, iii (1961). On the repurcussions Montalvo's treatise (listed above) and L. Batlle y Prats, 'El atentado contra Fernando el Católico y el municipio gerundense', *Cuadernos de Historia*, xix-xx (1966-7).

CHAPTER 7

Still fundamental after three hundred years is the 'Historia del Rey Don Hernando', the last part of Zurita's *Anales de Aragón*. More recently, J. Calmette, *La question des Pyrenées et la marche d'Espagne au Moyen Age* (Dijon, 1947). J. M. Doussinague, *La política internacional de Fernando el Católico* (Madrid, 1944) concentrates on the period after Isabella's death. On the origins of the Italian war, Vicens Vives, *Fernando el Católico, Rey de Sicilia* and Calmette, 'Une ambassade espagnole à la cour de Bourgogne en 1477', *Bulletin Hispanique*, vii (1905); 'La politique espagnole dans le guerre de Ferrare', *Revue Historique*, xcii (1906); 'La politique espagnole dans l'affaire des barons napolitains', *ibid.*, cxvii (1914); 'La politique espagnole dans la crise bretonne', *ibid.*, cx (1912); and N. Rubinstein, 'Firenze e il problema della politica imperiale in Italia al tempo di Massimiliano I', *Archivio Storico Italiano*, cxvi (1958). On Gonzalo de Córdoba, L. M. de Lojendio, *Gonzalo de Córdoba* (Madrid, 1942) but on military aspects P. Pieri, *Il Rinascimiento e la crise militaire italiana* (Turin, 1952). On the diplomatic service, G. Mattingly, *Renaissance Diplomacy* (London, 1955 and Baltimore, 1963 [Penguin Books]) and 'The Reputation of Dr de la Puebla', *English Historical Review*, lv (1940); A. de la Torre y del Cerro. 'Don Juan Margarit', *Conferencias de la Escuela Diplomática de Madrid* (1948); M. Batllori, 'Bernardino Carvajal en Anagni', *Miscellanaea Historiae Pontificiae* xxi (1959). In rebutting Machiavelli's interpretation of Spanish policy, R. Menéndez Pidal, *Los Reyes Católicos segun Maquivelo y Castiglione* (Madrid, 1952) goes to the other extreme. On Rhodes, A. de la Torre,

'Fernando el Católico y los caballeros de Rodas', *Hidalguia*, i (1953).

The collections of documents by de la Torre and Suárez Fernández, listed above, are studied by Suárez in his introductions to *Política internacional de Isabel la Católica* and it is chiefly his interpretation that I have challenged.

CHAPTER 8

On Africa, A. Rumeu de Armas, *España en el Africa Atlántica* (2 vv, Madrid, 1956), 'La torre africana de Santa Cruz', *Anuario de Estudios Atlánticos*, i (1955). On Béthencourt, M. Mollat 'La place de la conquête normande des Canaries dans l'histoire coloniale française' *ibid.*, iv (1958) and E. Serra Ráfols and A. Cioranescu, eds., 'Le Canarien', *Fontes Rerum Canariarum*, viii and xi. Though not particularly helpful on the colonization, A. Pérez Voituriez, *Problemas jurídicos internacionales de la conquista de Canarias* (La Laguna, 1969) is important on Béthencourt. On Lugo, E. Serra Ráfols, *Alonso Fernández de Lugo* (Santa Cruz, 1973), his edition with L. de la Rosa Oliveira of 'El adelantado Don Alonso de Lugo y su residencia' *Fontes Rerum*, iii, and 'Reformación del repartimiento', *ibid.*, vi.

On Columbus's feudal privileges, C. Verlinden, *Cristóbal Colón* (Madrid, 1957), ch. V. On Columbus generally, S. E. Morison *Admiral of the Ocean Sea* (Boston, 1942) supplemented by various works of A. Rumeu de Armas, especially *La Rábida y el descubrimiento de América* (Madrid, 1963) and *Hernando Colón* (Madrid, 1973). I give a short, up-to-date account in F. Fernández-Armesto, *Columbus* (London, 1974). On Ovando, Ursula Lamb, *Frey Nicolás de Ovando* (Madrid, 1956).

On the finance see F. F. R. Fernández-Armesto, 'Finance and Administration of the Conquest of the Canary Islands', forthcoming in *Anuario de Estudios Atlánticos*. On colonization, the documents collected by Konetzke and listed above and the article by Carande, listed under chapter IV. C. Bermúdez Plata, ed., *Catálogo de pasageros a Indias*, i (Seville, 1941) commences in 1509. See also R. Konetzke, 'El estado español y la emigración a Indias', *Saitabi*, iii (1945). On foreign participation in expansion, R. Pike, *Enterprise and Adventure: The Genoese in Seville and the Opening of the New World* (New York, 1966 [Cornell University Press]); M. Marrero Rodríguez, 'Los genoveses en la colonización de Tenerife', *Revista de Historia (Canaria)*, xvi (1950); C. Verlinden, 'Gli italiani nell' economia delle Canarie', *Economia e Storia*, viii (1960); 'Le rôle des Portugais', *Homenaje a E. Serra Ráfols*, iii (La Laguna, 1970); 'Les influences italiennes', etc., *V Congreso*, iii (1954).

On the Casa de Contratación, E. Schaefer, *El Consejo real y supremo de Indias*, i (Seville, 1935); E. Ibarra y Rodríguez,

'Precedentes de la Casa', *Revista de Indias* (1941). On the New World trade generally one must mention P. Chaunu et al., *Séville et l'Atlantique*, viii (3 pts, Paris, 1955).

The section on savages relies largely on my own research. But see A. Rumeu de Armas, 'Contacto de razas', *Cuadernos de historia*, i (1963) and *La política indigenista de Isabel la Católica* (Valladolid, 1969); J. H. Elliott, *The Old World and the New, 1492-1650* (Cambridge, 1970) and L. Hanke, *Aristotle and the American Indians: A study in Race Prejudice* (London, 1959 and Bloomington, 1970 [Indiana University Press]). On the general influence of Aristotle see A. R. Pagden, 'The Diffusion of Aristotle's Moral Philosophy in Spain c1400-c1600', forthcoming in *Traditio*. On slavery the general works of Verlinden and A. Domínguez Ortiz and D. J. Wölfel, 'La curia romana y la corona de España', *Anthropos*, xxv (1930). Also V. Cortés, *La esclavitud en Valencia durante el reinado de los Reyes Católicos* (Valencia, 1964).

CHAPTER 9

Among innumerable books on the Jews, A. Neuman, *The Jews in Spain* (2vv, Philadelphia, 1944); J. Caro Baroja, *Los Judíos en la España Moderna*; Y. Baer, *History of the Jews in Christian Spain* (2vv, Philadelphia, 1963 [Jewish Publications Society]); J. Amador de los Ríos, *Historia social de los judíos en España*, iii (Madrid, 1876).

On 'purity', A. Castro, *La realidad histórica de España* (Mexico, 1962); A. Sicroff, *Les controverses des statut de 'pureté de sang'* (Paris, 1960).

On the *Santo Niño*, I. Loeb, 'Le Saint Enfant de la Guardia', *Revue d'Etudes Juives*, xv (1887) contrasted with F. Fita, 'El martirio del Santo Niño', *Boletín de la Academia de Historia*, xi (1887). The most interesting historical aspects are indicated in B. Llorca's contribution on the subject to *V Congreso de historia de la Corona de Aragón* ii (1956).

On the Inquisition, E. van der Vekene, *Bibliographie der Inquisition* (Hildesheim, 1963); N. López Martínez, *Los judaizantes y la Inquisición* (Burgos, 1954); J. de M. Carriazo, 'La Inquisición y las rentas de Sevilla', *Homenaje a Carande*, ii (1963). On heresy and illuminism, M. Menéndez Pelayo, *Historia de los heterodoxos españoles* (Madrid, 1880-2) and M. Bataillon, *Erasmo y España* (Mexico, 1966).

On the Moors, M. A. Ladero Quesada, 'Notas sobre la política confesional de los Reyes Católicos', *Homenaje al profesor Alarcos García*, ii (1967) and the collection of sources cited above. On Talavera, no biography is adequate; see J. Domínguez Bordona, 'Algunas precisiones sobre Fray Fernando de Talavera', *Boletín de la Academia de la Historia*, cxlv (1959). Azcona's pages on Cisneros and Talavera are of great importance.

On the church, all Azcona's work is useful. On the episcopate and patronage, T. de Azcona, *La elección y reforma del episcopado* (Madrid, 1960); A. de la Hera, 'El regio patronato de Granada y las Canarias', *Anuario de Historia de derecho espanol*, xxvii – viii (1957-8); J. Peraza de Ayala, 'El real patronato de Canarias', *ibid.*, xxx (1960). On the religious and missions, J. García Oro, *La reforma de los religiosos* (Valladolid, 1969; and the summary of his unpublished thesis in *Revista de la Universidad de Madrid*, xiv, 1965); Azcona's observations in *Isabel la Católica* and 'Nuevos documentos sobre la reforma', *Estudios Franciscanos*, lxvii (1966); N. Rodriguez Pazos, 'Los franciscanos españoles en el pontificado de Sixto IV', *Archivo Ibero-Americano*. x (1950) and P. Catala y Roca, 'Los monjes que acompañaron a Colón', *Studi Colombiani*, ii.

Index

DATE DUE

AP 2 '79			
NO 12 79			
MAR 15 '84			
AP 10 '84			
NOV 1 1 '86			